Praise for

A COLD PEACE

"*A Cold Peace* is a highly valuable contribution to the debate over foreign policy, domestic policy, and, most important, the connection between the two. All who are concerned with America's well-being at home and abroad would benefit greatly from reading this book."

—Cyrus R. Vance, former Secretary of State

"A bracing new book. . . . Garten makes his case with exceptional clarity and balance, born of [the assumption that] relations between America, Germany, and Japan pose the 'critical question determining the shape of the world as we head for a new century.' . . . Garten can handle the economics, security issues, and politics of all three countries; it is above all the broadness of *A Cold Peace* that makes the book so useful. Garten is always detailed, never provincial."

—Jonathan Rauch, *The Washington Monthly*

"Jeffrey E. Garten feels strongly and writes convincingly about the challenges facing American leadership today. No reader will be left in doubt about how much needs to be done at home and how much still rests on the United States internationally."

—Paul A. Volcker, former chairman of the Federal Reserve

"There is much in this book to chew on. . . . Jeffrey E. Garten's *A Cold Peace* is a fair, informed and clear account that explains how we got where we are and why we need, in Garten's words, 'a revolution in our thinking about where the world is headed and how we had better change our own priorities.' . . . Garten discerns and describes with skill the cultural and social matrices that have produced the three different and competing forms of capitalism now practiced in America, Germany and Japan."

—Jim Hoagland, *The Washington Post Book World*

"Garten goes much deeper in exploring the historical roots of today's economic and political conflicts than other recent analysts. . . . [His] book can perhaps best be understood as a reflection of the profound shift in thinking under way within the traditional U.S. foreign policy elite. . . . Although the American establishment sees foreign and domestic policy as inextricably intertwined, Garten says the first priority today is to attend to the home front."

—Tom Redburn, *International Herald Tribune*

"The range of Mr. Garten's book is clear testimony of the breadth of his experience."

—Paul Krugman, *The New York Times Book Review*

"[Garten is] astute in perceiving the differences among the U.S.'s 'liberal market economy,' Japan's 'developmental economy' and Germany's 'social market economy' and the differing degrees of openness these engender."

—Charles Wolf, Jr., *The Wall Street Journal*

"Timely and provocative . . . Garten foresees a grand power triangle made up of the U.S., Germany, and Japan, within which alliances will shift depending on the issues at stake."

—William J. Holstein, *Business Week*

"Simply written and forcefully argued, A *Cold Peace* should be read by the widest possible audience."

—Peter G. Peterson, former Secretary of Commerce

"Insightful and challenging . . . Garten's prescriptions for change deserve careful consideration."

—James Schlesinger, former Secretary of Defense

"A sharp analysis . . . [Garten's] diagnosis of the U.S. predicament is telling and provocative, and shows that Americans have the intellectual tools to deal with their problems, if not the political will."

—Richard Ryan, *The Christian Science Monitor*

"Garten brings a wealth of knowledge to his subject. . . . A *Cold Peace* is a popular history of our times and a warning to heed history's lessons."
—Bill Montague, *USA Today*

"A *Cold Peace* is a cold shower. It will make Americans both uncomfortable and invigorated with its penetrating analysis and passionate summons for action."
—Winston Lord, Assistant Secretary of State for East Asian and Pacific Affairs

"When a quick and well-informed mind challenges conventional assumptions, some troubling questions are bound to arise about the present and future state of the world. Drawing on his experience in government and business, Jeffrey Garten shows quite eloquently how easily serious frictions can arise among Germany, Japan, and the United States, and how difficult it is likely to be for them to cooperate with their different kinds of capitalism and their diverse histories. . . . This is a challenging, helpful book."
—*Foreign Affairs*

"An important, clear-eyed book for anyone struggling to come to grips with the changing world order."
—*Publishers Weekly* (starred review)

"A thoughtful and often excellent analysis."
—*Kirkus*

"A superb study of the global economic divisions in the 1990s and beyond."
—Governor Mario Cuomo

"A thoughtful and often excellent analysis."
—*Kirkus*

"A superb study of the global economic divisions in the 1990s and beyond."
—Governor Mario Cuomo

A COLD PEACE

A
COLD
PEACE

America, Japan, Germany, and the
Struggle for Supremacy

JEFFREY E. GARTEN

A Twentieth Century Fund Book

TIMES BOOKS

RANDOM HOUSE

Library of Congress Cataloging-in-Publication Data

Garten, Jeffrey E.
    A cold peace: America, Japan, Germany, and the struggle for supremacy/Jeffrey E. Garten.—1st ed.
        p.   cm.
    "A Twentieth Century Fund book."
    Includes bibliographical references and index.
    ISBN 0-8129-2205-0
    1. United States—Relations—Japan.   2. Japan—Relations—United States.   3. United States—Relations—Germany.   4. Germany—Relations—United States.   5. United States—Foreign relations—1989–   6. World politics—1985–1995.   I. Title.
E183.8.J3G37   1992
303.48'273052—dc20   91-58013

First Paperback Edition

To my father and mother,
Colonel, U.S.A. (Ret.), and Mrs. Melvin Garten

PREFACE TO THE
PAPERBACK EDITION

When I put the finishing touches on the hardcover edition of A *Cold Peace*, in April 1992, I knew that the world was changing with stunning speed and that events would quickly test my three basic conclusions. The first of these was that the most important framework for thinking about America's role after the Cold War was its relationships with Japan and Germany. The United States would face challenges not merely in the realm of trade and finance, I argued, but also in the sharing of burdens for peacekeeping with its allies. My second conclusion was that ties among Washington, Tokyo, and Berlin were coming under enormous strain, especially with the demise of a common military enemy. If current policies continued, I said, we could expect increasing divisiveness and conflict. Finally, I indicated that America must take the lead in working with Japan and Germany to forge a revitalized alliance. This would take more than skillful diplomacy; it would require major changes within the United States to restructure the domestic economy and to address many deep-seated social problems. I argued that this kind of domestic rebuilding would be essential in order to enhance America's competitiveness in the global marketplace, thereby ensuring that the country will remain prosperous, confident, and outward looking. A lot has indeed happened since this book was first published, but I believe that my basic thesis is as valid today as it was then.

The centrality of Japan and Germany to American interests was demonstrated during the long presidential campaign of 1992. Bill Clinton was elected in large part because of his emphasis on economic revival. He focused on the "new realities of the global marketplace" and the need to preserve and create high-wage jobs. The competition that he worried about, at the high end of the job spectrum, certainly wasn't coming from Mexico, China, or Russia. When Clinton called our attention to those nations where the public sector, private business, and labor practice a more cooperative kind of capitalism than exists in America, his examples were not Italy, Norway, or India. His foreign policy pronouncements highlighted the need for more multilateral cooperation, as opposed to America's acting alone. The nations from which he expected more commitment were obviously neither Great Britain nor France, both of which had steadfastly stood by the United States in the Gulf War. Nor was he referring to regional powers like Saudi Arabia or Taiwan, whose help could only be limited. No, in all these cases the implicit and often explicit objects of his remarks were Japan and Germany, next to America the two powerhouses of the post–Cold War era.

Through the course of 1992, events moved in the direction of diminishing cooperation among America, Japan, and Germany. Early that summer the Big Three, as I call them, took different policy stances over environmental protection at the Earth Summit in Rio de Janeiro. The differences were especially telling, since each nation had spent years preparing for the conference and the environment represented one of the defining issues of foreign policy after the Cold War. A month later, at the annual economic summit in Munich, the Big Three were unable to reach agreement on how to arrest the global recession. For the third consecutive year, the pattern of disagreement and inability to act on crucial issues continued. Nineteen ninety-two also saw the Big Three stand by passively as the crucial Uruguay Round of trade negotiations languished. One hopes that the negotiations will finally end in 1993, but the six-year marathon, characterized by disagreements about the rules of the trading system itself, will have reflected how tenuous global economic cooperation has become. Finally, Washington, Tokyo, and Berlin did nothing to halt the mass slaughter of men, women, and children in the former Yugoslavia. Such inaction made a mockery of NATO, other Western European security organizations, and peacekeeping through the United Nations—collective security alliances that the Big Three should have been shoring up.

Beyond the sorry diplomatic record, domestic politics in each of the three countries revealed further reasons for concern about the future. The United States held a presidential election in which the balance between domestic and international issues was unrealistically and dangerously focused inward. Bill Clinton rightly recognized how much had to be done at home, but he often gave the impression that domestic policies would be his top priority. In Japan, widespread scandals enveloped the cabinet and the ruling Liberal Democratic Party, all but eliminating any outward-looking policy from Tokyo for years to come. Germany's close-to-home focus was no less intense. The huge influx of refugees from Eastern Europe became a total preoccupation, escalating into widespread neo-Nazi violence in some cities in the fall. At the same time, the rising costs of unification led the Bundesbank to raise interest rates to sky-high levels, without regard to the consequences abroad. The action of the German central bank brought about the collapse of European monetary cooperation in early October, raising questions about the very feasibility of European economic and political cooperation—questions epitomized by the failure of the European Community to gain ratification of the Maastricht Treaty by the end of 1992 as planned.

As 1993 began, three international crises seemed certain to bring the roles of Tokyo and Berlin into new conflict with Washington. America embarked on a massive humanitarian mission to feed millions of people in Somalia. Washington and its coalition partners were again confronting Saddam Hussein. And some kind of increased allied intervention in the former Yugoslavia seemed possible. In all these cases America was—or would be—acting out the role of the sole remaining superpower, with Japan and Germany almost nowhere to be seen. It was only a matter of time before the same questions that arose during the Gulf War in 1991 were raised again: Why aren't Japan and Germany carrying more of the load, not just by writing checks but by sending troops exposed to physical risk? To be sure, each nation was moving further in the direction of participating in international peacekeeping operations, with Japan having sent some soldiers to Cambodia and Germany having dispatched some to Somalia. But given their importance in the world community, these measures were extremely modest, and it is a sure bet that both nations will come under continual pressure from the United States to do much more.

For America the issue of military burdensharing goes beyond not wanting to bear the cost of being the world's policeman. Americans have become less willing to devote so much time, money, and effort to foreign problems while the nation's two most important trade competitors are left to concentrate on their economies, free of global political and security burdens. My view all along has been that American anguish over this skewed division of responsibilities will grow with each occasion that the United States is forced to use its troops abroad. Moreover, frustration with this unequal distribution of military burdens could easily spill over to the economic realm and lead the United States to take a much more nationalistic approach to global economic competition than would otherwise occur.

Such an outcome would be unfortunate, for the economic picture at the beginning of 1993 was already bad enough. The American economy looked as if it were turning up, but even a return to modest growth would not solve the long-term structural problems of savings, investment, education, health care, poverty, and crime that I discuss at length in this book. I believe America's domestic restructuring will take a decade at best, even if the right policies are put in place early in the Clinton years. Meanwhile, Japan and Germany were each moving toward a serious recession as the year began. Here, too, there could be no quick fixes, not with Japan's banks holding so many bad loans, nor with Germany's requirement to pour close to $100 billion into its eastern states for each of the next few years at least.

The cumulative economic tensions of the Big Three will create new pressures in the global economy. As has been the pattern throughout most of the last fifteen years, Washington is bound once again to try to press its two allies to take whatever measures are necessary to grow faster. This time, however, America is sure to become more strident in its demands, because it is now so much more dependent on exports—and hence on foreign business conditions—for its own economic growth. There will be severe trade pressures particularly if, as expected, the Clinton administration pursues an aggressive industrial policy to promote and defend selected American industries. Currency instability is rising, too, but so far there has been no effective effort at Big Three coordination on the monetary front. The chances for progress are slim, given the turbulence surrounding the European currencies and the need for the European Community to patch up its own problems before a global pact is even a possibility. In the past, the Cold War military alliance put a limit on the political fallout from failed collaboration in trade and finance. Those days are gone.

None of these problems is insurmountable, but taken together they represent an awesome challenge. Indeed, the single biggest cause for concern is that there is no strategy in Washington, Tokyo, or Berlin—let alone in the Big Three as a whole—to come to grips with the divisive and leaderless situation that is evolving. It is an environment in which every nation must fend for itself, much like that of the 1930s. The problem is not that the three governments do not see the hazards ahead; it is not that they are oblivious of the potential consequences of their head-in-the-sand approach; and it is certainly not that they are pleased with the way their policies have been evolving. The problem is that they are overwhelmed with their own domestic concerns and don't know what to do to contain the broader international problems that are emerging.

In this environment, only America can lead the Big Three out of its collective rut. For reasons described in this book, it is unrealistic to expect Japan and Germany to be world leaders. As far as I can tell, America still has the will and the capability so long as it can revive its economic prospects and others provide a fair, helping hand. Those "ifs" are, of course, big ones.

When *A Cold Peace* was first published, it was widely commented upon in the press. I had the opportunity to crisscross the nation twice, speaking to diverse audiences and participating in at least twenty radio and television programs in which listeners and viewers called in questions. I also received a broad range of comments from Japanese and German citizens about my views.

Perhaps the most repeated comment I received was that in looking at the world through the lens of the Big Three, my focus might be too narrow. What about China—would it not be a superpower soon? What about the rest of Europe—was not Germany inextricably tied to the European Community? Where did Mexico, Brazil, Indonesia, and India fit in? These are fair comments, to be sure; the world is of course much bigger than America, Japan, and Germany. However, the focus of *A Cold Peace* is only the decade of the 1990s, and within this time frame China will not be a superpower, the European Community will not strengthen its grip on Germany (quite the opposite, in my view), and no other nations will loom so important in so many ways to America as do Japan and Germany. Certainly none will be so crucial with regard to the two major international challenges of our time: management of the world economy and collective security. And no other nations will reach so deeply into America's domestic economy by having so large an impact on trade, finance, and the rules of global competition. Nor will any others be in a similar position to serve as models for vocational training or business-labor relations, to take but two examples. My argument is not that Japan and Germany are the only countries that matter to the United States, nor that the Big Three are the only ones that really count in the world; rather, it is that the degree of cooperation among these nations is crucial to virtually every international issue.

A second question that was frequently posed was, Had I not exaggerated the strength of Japan and Germany while underestimating America's position? Recessions in Japan and Germany were just beginning as *A Cold Peace* went to press in the spring of 1992, and over the succeeding months a good deal of new evidence suggested that America's competitive position was beginning to turn around—the result of extensive restructuring in the corporate sector, higher levels of worker productivity, and the export-stimulating effect of a weaker dollar over the preceding several years.

My response was that it is important not to confuse transient developments with long-term structural trends. In this book I go back well over a hundred years to look at what has made each of these societies tick. It is with this historical perspective—a perspective that takes account of the way Japan bounced back from natural disasters, wartime destruction, and oil, trade, and currency shocks—that I fully expect Japan to recover from its current problems, and reasonably soon. As for Germany, history also reveals amazing resilience, and in time the Federal Republic is sure to restructure its eastern provinces in such a way that they become a new force for economic dynamism within a unified nation—with the most advanced technology and the most highly trained work force. It may simply take a little longer than most people had anticipated.

When it comes to the United States, I hope that the optimists are right and that American industry is reviving. Even so, big problems remain, as the recent troubles at IBM, General Motors, and American Express show. A high level of unemployment is likely to continue as Fortune 500 firms continue to slim down and as the military-industrial sector continues to contract. Moreover, America still has the lowest rate of savings and investment in the industrialized world, the poorest system of worker training, and severe social problems—including drugs, child poverty, and urban blight—that need sustained attention if they are not to undercut the performance of the American economy for a long time to come.

Some readers pointed out that I had not discussed the potential for conflict over the former Soviet Union at sufficient length. In fact, I was hesitant to deal at length with Russia and the other republics because events were moving so fast. One day Mikhail Gorbachev was the darling of the West, the next day he was toppled in a coup, and within days after he returned, Boris Yeltsin assumed power. I agree that we have seen only the beginning of turmoil in this region, and I believe that, true to the pattern of the past few years, America, Japan, and Germany will not easily coordinate approaches to such problems as the amounts of economic aid, the manner and timing of intervention in regional and ethnic wars, the response to the dangers of nuclear reactor breakdown, and the efforts to stop sales of Russian weapons to other nations.

As the events of the last several months have unfolded—the failed endeavors at economic cooperation, the growing military tensions in so many parts of the world, the tendency of the Big Three leadership to hunker down and look inward, the election of Bill Clinton—the agenda for America, Japan, and Germany in the years ahead is clearer than ever. President George Bush was ridiculed for announcing a New World Order before one existed, but he was correct in this respect: there is a crying need for the Big Three to rethink the entire set of economic and military arrangements that will govern the post–Cold War world. Three years after the collapse of the Berlin Wall, it is amazing how little has been done in this regard. But in fashioning a new system for coordinated economic management and collective security, it will not be enough for the lone superpower to put its ideas on the table. One way or another, Japan and Germany will have to agree; they will have to be convinced that the new order is in their interests and be willing to expend great effort to support it vigorously. Given the deep-seated differences in the historical, economic, and geopolitical perspectives of the Big Three, a real meeting of the minds will be an immense challenge. It is, in my view, the single highest priority for American foreign policy. As a new

American president takes over, I hope that he is not so swamped by domestic legislation and regional foreign policy crises to focus on the new architecture that must be built for world order and prosperity.

With the election of Bill Clinton, America is in the hands of a new group of men and women dedicated to rejuvenating the American economy and thereby enhancing American strength and influence. They represent a new generation of leadership, whose memory of the days when Japan and Germany were aggressive military rivals to the United States is dim at best. This is a double-edged sword. On the one hand, the American administration has the freedom to deal with Tokyo and Berlin without a good deal of the psychological baggage of the past. But on the other hand, ignoring history does not erase it. Like every president since Theodore Roosevelt, Bill Clinton is going to find that America is inextricably linked to Japan and Germany, sometimes for good, sometimes not. He will discover that these two nations will present a broad challenge to America for industrial supremacy and political influence. He will see that to deal effectively with Japan and Germany, more than with any other nations, will require a fusing of domestic and foreign policy, as well as careful coordination between economic and security policy. If Clinton succeeds, he will have taken a critical step to address the problems at home and to position the United States to lead abroad.

Dealing with these challenges will test the new administration's energies and its talents. And, as has been true for over a century, Japan and Germany will reveal America's most latent fears and raise its most fervent hopes.

March 1993

ACKNOWLEDGMENTS

Many people helped me with this book, and there is no way I can adequately thank them. Richard Moose, Peter Wolf, Vincent Mai, Anthony Lake, Kent Harrington, Henry Boettinger, Steve Nagourney, and Roger Altman waded through the earliest drafts. Steven Blank, Sherle Schwenninger, and Hans Decker gave me invaluable advice at later stages of the project. Edward Tivnan helped me throughout the process. So did Allan Garten, who provided the kind of criticism and moral support that only a close brother can. I am grateful also to the directors of the Asia Society, the Carnegie Council on Ethics and International Affairs, the Foreign Policy Association, the European Community Chamber of Commerce, and Princeton University's Woodrow Wilson School of Public and International Affairs for providing speaking forums for me to test my ideas. Richard Leone, president of the Twentieth Century Fund, was a good friend and advisor throughout the project, as was Beverly Goldberg, director of the Fund's publications. Carol Strauss of the Fund and Paul Golob of Times Books/Random House were invaluable editors. Gordon Goldstein, Tony Kaye, and Vincent Wagner helped with background information, and I am especially indebted to Kyle Brandon for research and fact checking. Pauline Smith oversaw the production of the manuscript from the first day to the last. And, most important of all, my wife, Ina, gave me the kind of enthusiastic encouragement without which I never would have started this book, let alone finished it.

FOREWORD

Economic progress is a central theme of the American experience. In the past decade, in fact, it often has seemed that the core of our common beliefs could be summarized even more narrowly as the freedom to pursue private wealth without the interference of governments—our own or those of other nations.

Until very recently, there was a consensus that one final common task remained for our national government, the defeat of communism. But this struggle, particularly in its final phases, turned out to be, as much as anything, more an economic than a military contest. There were shooting wars against the outriders of the collectivist ideology, and there was the creation of an immense capacity for global destruction. But the sharp edge of our exertions was designed not to destroy the enemy, but rather to discourage him from combat and to outstrip his capacity to compete militarily. In this sense, we succeeded better than we knew, for the material collapse of the former Soviet Union has exceeded our most optimistic view of the probable outcome of that contest.

In the aftermath of this triumph, many Americans have a nagging sense that they somehow missed the victory party. Indeed shouldn't we, who had run so many risks and borne so many burdens, have been the guests of honor? But a bit like Britain after the Second World War and France after the First, it turns out that are there many questions about our place in the new world.

Where do we stand and who are our rivals? We are, after all, a competitive people (some would say arrogant), certain for most of this century of our unique economic power and thus of our place in the world. These certainties elude us now. And to some it seems we have come full circle, confronting anew our old adversaries and sometime allies, the Germans and the Japanese. This confrontation is not among nations in arms, or even, as it was with the Soviet Union, about competing ideologies. It is quite simply about economic preeminence and, some argue, about American economic independence.

It is a subject that preoccupies our political and business leaders, and even the average citizen. It is the stuff of popular novels and the mainstay of the financial press. Indeed, in what is still the world's largest economy, there is alarm and even anger over "unfair" international competition, especially from Japan. Wholesale changes in our lifestyle, schools, and work places are advocated on the basis of their promised positive effect on our competitive position.

In the pages that follow, Jeffrey E. Garten, an investment banker and former government official who has written widely on these issues, takes this great current national debate as his starting point. And he moves far beyond the conventional arguments to explore the realities of the emerging new relationships and differing commercial strategies among the United States, Germany, and Japan. He provides information and insight that will contribute significantly to our ability to shape new policies for a new world.

Today's headlines belong to those who describe these economies in simplistic terms and who advocate simple remedies. Warlike metaphors abound, turning our economic competitors into threatening rivals. The trumpet sounds for nothing less than domestic mobilization. Garten acknowledges the drama, but focuses more usefully on the necessity to understand what is in fact happening in the world of actual business, day-to-day transactions, and multinational corporations. All too often, these "variables," ignored in the economists' model, turn out to be the crucial determinants of economic history. There is more complexity in Garten's approach, but also more realism. It is an analysis that will prove extremely valuable to those who seek an understanding of the practical challenges facing us.

Richard C. Leone, President
The Twentieth Century Fund
April 1, 1992

CONTENTS

A COLD PEACE

INTRODUCTION

If you want to know what the coming world order will be like, you will not find the answer in Moscow or Warsaw, nor in the Arab-Israeli conflict, nor in the global trade negotiations. Instead, you will have to look at the relationship among the three most influential nations today—America, Japan, and Germany. You will have to sort out how real power among them has changed during the Cold War, and how it is shifting again in the 1990s. You will have to wrestle with over one hundred and twenty years of history among the United States and its two key allies—military and economic rivalries, the Japanese and German challenge of dictatorship and fascism, the long and bloody Second World War, the holocaust in Europe and the Japanese brutalities in Asia, the American military Occupations, the Cold War alliances, and the current economic tensions and security uncertainties.

Thinking about the very different historical legacies of the three countries as well as their distinctive personalities today, you will be able to gauge the prospects for cooperation and conflict regarding some of tomorrow's big issues—protectionism, burdensharing in defense and economics, the movement of refugees, safeguarding the environment, the rise of new regional trading blocs, tensions in global organizations. Today's domestic preoccupations in all three countries will suggest how each nation is likely to act on the international stage in the future. You might see Japan and Germany and their startling upward trajectories these past forty-five years in direct contrast to the downward spiral that threatens America. You might well say that their prospects are much better than our own, and wonder whether they will be our friends, our enemies, or both. You might envy them or resent them but you'll see these two nations as a mirror in which we can see our own weaknesses and strengths, but mostly the weaknesses. And you might conclude, as I have, that the foremost requirement for the United States is not just a change in one or two policies, not just a new set of politicians or campaign slogans, but a revolution in our thinking about where the world is headed and how we had better change our own priorities. That is what this book is about.

It was in 1988 that my ideas began to take shape. I had been invited to participate in a small conference at the Aspen Institute in Berlin on "The Role and Responsibilities of Japan and Germany in the World Economy," and, on very short notice, I was asked to prepare a paper. I had two immediate problems. There was a tremendous amount to say about these two up-and-coming economic superpowers, but I had no time to do any research. In addition, it was clear to me that the issues surrounding Japan and Germany should not be discussed in a sterile, matter-of-fact style; at least I, having lived and worked in both countries, did not want to do it that way. And so I came up with a novel device for academic-type meetings—I wrote a one act play in which the top officials of an American presidential administration had gone off to Camp David to discuss what to do about the challenge from Japan and Germany. It was an approach that let me deal with both facts and emotion. In the play, the American leaders were able to express their views, including their personal hopes and fears, in the frank and casual way they might actually do on a Saturday afternoon away from the office. The strong undertone of the make-believe strategy session was that Japan and Germany were quickly becoming America's major foreign policy problems, posing threats to U.S. economic and security interests, and that Washington was in very poor shape to deal with these challenges. According to the script, America's major handicap was caused by growing economic and social strains at home, which were undermining the foundations of its real clout. My characters were expressing ideas that I thought they held, but, of course, there was a lot of me in them, too.

The reaction to my paper was as emotional as the play itself. At the conference, the American participants were anxious to explain what

Japan and Germany really meant to the United States, especially the sense that these two countries were challenging America on a broad range of issues, that they were taking more from this country than they were giving back, and that a crisis was brewing. The Japanese and German participants had a different set of concerns. They felt that America yearned in vain for a return to the "good old days" when Uncle Sam was calling all the shots, and that Washington was now poised to lash out at its allies for its own domestic shortcomings. The Japanese and Germans kept referring to what life was like in the late 1940s and the efforts and sacrifices that had been made since, and the Americans kept harkening back to the generosity of the Marshall Plan and the burdens and costs of the Cold War. Fingers were being pointed, and faces were red. It was the liveliest debate I had ever seen in this type of conference.

The play found its way to the editors of the quarterly magazine *Foreign Affairs*, who encouraged me to turn it into a more conventional article. I was delighted to do it, and "Japan and Germany: American Concerns" appeared in the winter of 1989, just before the Berlin Wall was torn down. Once again I described the problems that lay ahead for America, Tokyo, and Bonn—in finance, trade, technological competition, as well as in Europe and East Asia—but I was also discussing some of the underlying drives that made Japan and Germany similar kinds of threats to the United States. I had always assumed that *Foreign Affairs* was a coffee table journal, nice to display but rarely read, but in this case I was taken aback by letters and phone calls concerning my article. These came less from foreign policy experts than from people in other fields—businessmen, doctors, retired military, students. I also received quite a few comments from abroad.

Two kinds of reactions were particularly striking. To begin with, despite the waning of the Cold War and the general optimism that the tensions of the last forty-five years were finally ending, not one person disputed the thesis that America would encounter severe problems with its two most important allies. No one challenged either the type of problems I was identifying or the idea that most of them were rooted in history or in the different ways each society was organized. In fact, whereas I felt I had been quite blunt, most critics thought I had been too diplomatic in assessing the future.

Second, I was struck by the views from outside the country. The Germans felt I was being disingenuous by including them with the Japanese; what, they asked, do the two countries have in common? The Japanese had exactly the same reaction; they did not understand why I had lumped them together with the Germans. A British friend said I was stuck in a World War II time warp in which the allies faced the axis powers. His views were supported by someone from France and someone from Singapore, both of whom wanted to underline how enormously different Japan and Germany were in terms of their culture, their economic structures, and their current policy objectives. Since not one American even raised the issue of why I was discussing Japan and Germany in the same breath, and since it seemed natural enough to me, I began to think that there may be something about these two countries in the American mind, something that goes much deeper than the last world war, and something worth trying to describe in a more extensive look at America's interaction with Japan and Germany.

In the summer of 1990, The Twentieth Century Fund agreed to support my efforts to write a book about America, Japan, and Germany after the Cold War. From the beginning my biggest problem was keeping pace with events. After I began writing, Germany became unified, the global trade negotiations broke down, the Gulf War erupted, civil war broke out in Yugoslavia, the European Community agreed to form a union for monetary policy and foreign policy, the Soviet Union was dissolved, Germany moved from a lender to the world to a borrower, and Japan went from breakneck growth to slump. Arms reductions, undreamed of just a few months prior, were being proposed, and in America, new visions of military spending cuts revived the prospect of a peace dividend. New security concerns were arising, including ethnic and regional warfare and the prospect of nuclear weapons proliferation caused by the disintegration of Moscow's central control. The economic optimism of the 1980s was replaced by deep gloom, as America entered a prolonged recession, Japan's pace of growth slowed, and German interest rates hit their highest level since the 1940s. All the while there were countless summit meetings, foreign policy reassessments by presidents and prime ministers, and an extraordinary flood of expert commentary in the media asserting that everything was changing. Time and again I was forced to reexamine the emerging world order and the role of America, Japan, and Germany in it.

With each reappraisal, however, I came back to the same starting point: what happens among America, Japan, and Germany—what I call the "Big Three"—is still the critical question determining the shape of the world as we head for a new century. It is understandable that we are mesmerized by startling developments in Europe, the Middle East, the former Soviet Union, and our economy. No doubt there are many more surprises ahead. But many of the basics are enduring, including the historical legacies of the Big Three, the nature of power in an interdependent world economy, and the hopes, fears, and drives of people in each of the three nations.

Over the last year I have given several speeches about America, Japan, and Germany to foreign policy forums, business groups, government officials, and universities. I have found that the subject encompasses so many issues and so many feelings that in any discussion it is critical to specify my starting points and my perspective. This is no less so now.

At the outset it is important to understand what this book does *not* attempt to do.

Despite my five-year stint in the State Department on the policy planning staffs of Secretary Henry Kissinger and Secretary Cyrus Vance, I have not tried to write a traditional foreign policy book. I have not attempted to provide a blueprint for what America should do overseas, to describe all the challenges it faces, nor to offer a profound theory about international politics at the turn of the century. Of course, Japan and Germany test the United States abroad in many ways, and I have touched on a host of issues. But entire books can be written about America's defense policy, about its trade strategies, about the nature of statecraft in the year 2000, and I make no pretense of delving into these subjects in any depth except to illustrate larger points about the global challenges America faces.

This is not a book about the world economy, either. As someone who has been working on Wall Street these past twelve years, I have written many articles on this subject, and Japan and Germany certainly conjure up a host of challenges in finance, trade, and technology. But while I have referred to many such issues, I have used them only as examples of the playing fields on which the Big Three will be competing.

Still less have I tried to write a definitive treatise on each of the three countries themselves. Needless to say, for each nation there exist many works on history, politics, economics, and culture. There are some excellent comparative treatments, too, especially on contemporary issues such as business management or economic policy, and I have not tried to compete with these, either.

What then have I done? I have examined America's role in the world not from the standpoint of foreign policy or domestic policy, but from both perspectives, and I have used Japan and Germany to represent the challenges we face on every level—economic, security, psychological. There have been times, such as the late 1800s, when America was preoccupied with its internal development and wanted to stay aloof from the world. There have been other times, such as the 1950s and 1960s, when we were strong at home and abroad and did not have to think much about the connection between domestic and foreign policies. But we are now entering an era when the need for an active international policy is crucial but the basis on which it will rest at home is terribly weak. It is a time, moreover, when our ability to handle our own problems requires policies with strong international dimensions and the cooperation of other countries. We have not yet come to grips with the full meaning of the end of the Cold War, either with the implications for our lives at home or for its consequences outside our borders; most important, we have not made the connection between the two. The challenges of Japan and Germany to America force us to think about this link.

There are several other reasons why I have chosen to focus on Japan and Germany. First, next to the United States they are now the two most powerful nations, having risen from wartime collapse with unprecedented speed and force. The United States is, of course, the largest of the three by far. In terms of territory, it is twenty-six times larger than either Japan or Germany. Its population is two times greater than that of Japan, three times greater than that of Germany. The dollar is the most important currency, used for the overwhelming amount of world trade and investment across borders, and accounting for nearly 70 percent of the financial reserves held by governments around the world. American investments abroad outstrip those of any other nation. Both Canada and much of Latin America are inextricably linked to the U.S. economy, creating an emerging trading, investment, and currency bloc with awesome potential.

America's softer assets are powerful, too. No other nation has a freedom-loving ideology that is so universally appealing. No other has the capacity to assimilate and deal with so many divergent cultures, thereby making it a natural mediator in international disputes. No other has as much experience as a global leader in Europe, Asia, and Latin America. And, of course, the United States has something the others do not have at all—it is the world's only military superpower, maintaining a massive nuclear arsenal and capable of sending troops almost anywhere to defend its interests, and those of its allies.

Japan, whose economy is about the combined size of West Germany, Britain, and France, has become the world's primary banker, the source of most new lending and investing across borders. It is home to most of the world's ten largest banks. After the dollar and the mark, the yen is the world's third most important currency. Between 1950 and 1990, Japan's share of the world's G.N.P. grew from 5 percent to 16 percent, one of the largest such shifts ever accomplished by any nation in a similar period of time. During the 1980s, Japan's trade and investment performance led to cumulative surpluses of $462 billion, in contrast to America, which had a cumulative deficit of $807 billion during the same period. In the early 1980s, Japan's net investments abroad in bonds, stocks, factories, and real estate averaged $10 billion a year; by the end of the decade the figure was $192 billion. Between July 1988 and July 1990 alone, Japan's economy expanded incrementally by as much as the size of Canada's entire G.N.P. In recent years it has outpaced all other industrial countries in its economic growth, savings rate, and volume of new investment. From automobiles to flat panel computer screens, Japanese companies are moving to dominate a number of the world's most important technologically intensive industries. Not only are Japanese firms becoming models for other multinational companies' production strategy and managerial style, but they are the central driving force behind a borderless, technology-driven world economy. Moreover, Tokyo is the dominant economic power in the most dynamic region of the world —the corridor from Seoul to Sydney, encompassing Hong Kong, Singapore, Taiwan, Thailand, Malaysia, and Indonesia.

Germany has long been the economic powerhouse of Western Europe, and it has now become the most important political power, too. Although much smaller than the United States, it vies with it for being the world's biggest exporter. Whereas Japan's export achievements are concentrated in a few major industries and sold by a concentrated number of large firms such as the Sony Corporation or the Mitsubishi family of companies, Germany's exports cut across a much wider range of industries and are attributable not only to firms like Daimler-Benz and Bayer but also to thousands of small businesses across the nation who have exploited high-tech niches ranging from high-performance chemicals to environmental equipment. German firms dominate several of Western Europe's major industries, including steel, machine tools, and chemicals. Next to the U.S. dollar, the Deutsche mark is by far the currency most used in trade and finance, the preference of investors when they seek to diversify their portfolios.

I am often asked why I have so much to say about Germany and not the European Community. The major reason is that in the E.C., the importance of Germany is overwhelming. Despite all the talk about a reoriented NATO or a more integrated European Community, Germany is too powerful to disappear into the wider European framework. It has the largest economy and the largest population of any nation on the European landmass. In recent years, West Germany accounted for about a third of all manufacturing in the European Community, and a united Germany began its existence with 28 percent of the Community's G.N.P. In 1992 Germany's share of the E.C. budget was over $10 billion, three times the contribution of Great Britain and twice the amount of Britain and France combined. England, France, Italy, Spain, and the Benelux nations have linked the value of their currencies to the German mark. When Germany's central bank raises or lowers interest rates, its counterparts in Europe follow suit in hours, if not minutes. Germany is using its economic clout to demand fundamental reforms in E.C. politics, such as an enhanced role for a European parliament with more representation from Germany. Now Germany is spreading its wings eastward as well, reaching out to Poland, Hungary, Czechoslovakia, the Baltics, Ukraine, Russia, and other independent states of the former Soviet Union. Indeed, Germany is now the nerve center between London and Moscow, the country without which no major economic decision affecting the Continent can be made, the nation whose domestic and foreign policies most affect all the others for thousands of miles in each direction.

While there is no dispute about the growth of German power, there is still uncertainty about the shape of the Continent. For the last few years, the European Community has concluded agreements about economic integration, but it will take several years before we know how well they work. There are still many outstanding issues concerning the operation of a European Central Bank and a common currency, including which countries will participate fully. Coordination on foreign policy and defense is a long way off, assuming it ever occurs. There can be no strong European union without strong German support, yet polls in early 1992 showed a distinct lack of enthusiasm among German citizens. And as the E.C. is likely to take in a variety of new members, including some from Eastern Europe, the process of assimilating so many different political systems and economies is sure to weaken its cohesion for years to come. Already, for example, Sweden, Austria, Cyprus, Malta, and Turkey have asked for E.C. membership, and Poland, Czechoslovakia, and Hungary are on the verge of applying. So, for the next decade at least, Germany will still stand out, its energy, its drives, its character substantially undiluted.

Another reason why Japan and Germany are so important to America is the fact that they are not only powerful today, but they are gaining strength. Indeed, a static picture of the Big Three is misleading. In the 1990s, for example, America is going to be struggling to reverse the impact of unrestrained financial speculation, borrowing, consumption, and underinvestment in such critical areas as schools and physical infrastructure. Its national debt is climbing toward $4.5 trillion by mid-decade, compared to $1 trillion in 1980. Its social problems—from crime to health care—are increasingly debilitating. Whatever happens over the next several years—even allowing for a major reversal of trends—the nation will be extremely fortunate if, by the end of the 1990s, it can catch up to where it was twenty years earlier.

Japan is another matter. There, too, the booming 1980s saw the development of a loose-money culture, with lending and consumption excesses. But the nation kept investing—exceeding America's investment (in absolute dollars) by 30 percent in the late 1980s, even though its G.N.P. was much smaller. As the 1990s progress, Japan's economic prowess is sure to increase as the fruits of its enormous investments in new products and new processes come on line. Japan is also embarking on a multi*trillion* dollar infrastructure program, leading to better communications, better transportation, and better education. Yes, Japan's growth is now slowing, and even recession is possible. But relative to America and Germany, it is still ahead, and on more than one occasion in recent years—the 1973 and 1979 energy crises, for example, or the doubling of the value of the yen in 1986—Tokyo has shown its remarkable resiliency and ability to bounce back faster and stronger than nearly everyone anticipated. By the year 2000 Japan's economy could still be nearly the same size as America's.

As for Germany, the enormous expense of making unification work may well cause a pause in the nation's development as a major power, not only because of economic pressures but also because of the preoccupation with domestic issues. But within several years, Germany is likely to emerge much stronger than it would otherwise have been—with a larger territory, a source of eager workers anxious to make up for lost time, and a new spirited nationalism born of being a whole nation again. Germany's grip on Europe will also become stronger as it increasingly dominates the E.C., as it plays a unique role as bridge between East and West, as its special blend of free markets and social welfare becomes an influential model from Lisbon to Vladivostok, and as it wields ever more clout in the E.C., which itself will become an increasingly important organizer of foreign aid programs, technical assistance, and dispenser of trade concessions to Eastern Europe and the new republics of the former Soviet Union.

But there is much more to the picture. America, Japan, and Germany represent the three pillars on which the structure of global politics and economics will rest. Whatever kind of world order emerges, the Big Three will have the most to say about how it is managed. If they work closely together, the odds for a peaceful and prosperous world will be greatly enhanced, for virtually all the major problems of the day require substantial international collaboration. If their interests clash, the prospects will be dim. It is the Big Three, acting in concert or in disarray, who will determine whether the world economy grows or stagnates, whether trade and investment are managed in a more or less free-market framework or whether the world breaks up into protectionist blocs. These three nations will determine whether currencies are stable and whether world inflation is under control. It is they whose actions will have an enormous impact on whether the mounting political frustrations outside the major industrial democracies—in Eastern Europe, the former Soviet Union, and much of the Third World—can be contained and channelled into peaceful economic development. It is they who hold the key to whether global institutions function effectively, whether collective security is more than an empty phrase, whether the great problems of the environment, or immigration, or nuclear nonproliferation can be effectively tackled.

In the 1990s, moreover, America's fate will be closely linked to decisions made in Tokyo and Berlin. More than any other countries, Japan and Germany will exert an enormous influence on the American economy, directly through lending, investment, trade, interest rate, and currency policies. By virtue of their willingness to follow American leadership in the security area, or their inclination *not* to follow—whichever path they choose—Tokyo and Berlin will eventually have more of an impact than anyone else on how we see the world and what responsibilities and burdens we are willing to shoulder.

Japan and Germany represent a challenge to America that is not strictly foreign policy but domestic policy as well. Traditional statecraft, such as the balancing of power, the deployment of troops, or the negotiation of economic treaties, is but one part of the Big Three's critical agenda. Beyond that there is the need to mesh strategies concerning economic growth. There is the rivalry in laboratories, in stock exchanges, in schools; there is the race to attract investment and skilled workers, which itself is a competition over who has created the best transportation systems, health care programs, safe streets.

As foreign and domestic policies merge, moreover, what goes on among nations will be shaped more heavily than ever by what happens *within* them. Ironically, the smaller the world gets, and the more international coordination that is required, the more relevant will be the expression "all politics is local." In thinking about the post–Cold War world, therefore, it is especially important to examine domestic developments in the major nations—how they see themselves, their problems, their interests. In this regard, no three nations represent better case studies than America, Japan, and Germany, for all are beseiged with changing self-identities, a host of new preoccupations, and a broad set of newly perceived constraints on their behavior.

All three nations are reeling from major changes in the global environment. The end of the U.S.–Soviet rivalry that defined international politics for forty-five years has left an enormous vacuum in the framework for thinking and acting on the world stage. The massive movement of money across borders, together with instant communications, the power of computers, and the spread of technology have created a third industrial revolution that is changing the lives of everyone in ways still barely understood. Washington, Tokyo, and Berlin are each being pressed not just to share power with one another, but to simultaneously transfer political decision making down to more local arenas and up to international organizations. The result of all this is disorientation about the ends and means of national policy—a sure fire recipe for unpredictable policies at home and abroad, and hence for more difficulty among the Big Three in working together.

Aside from these general pressures, each of the Big Three is being overwhelmed by developments and uncertainties unique to them. In America, for example, the relative self-containment of a huge continental market is being replaced by a nation dependent on financial and industrial links to Europe, Asia, and Latin America. A country whose economy was propelled in large part by defense spending and research is now dismantling its military-industrial complex with no idea of long-term implications or economic substitutes. The neighborhoods of Ozzie and Harriet are long gone, increasingly replaced by single-parent homes with security alarms on the doors and windows. The refugees from Europe have given way to influxes from Latin America and Asia, and the nation hovers between being a melting pot and a boiling pot. Our extraordinary graduate schools, and our unsurpassed technology in fields such as medicine or outer space cause us to see ourselves as the world's most advanced society, but our foreign debts, our need for a cheaper currency, our emphasis on agricultural and other commodity exports, and our dismal position when it comes to secondary schooling and infant mortality puts us in the Third World category, too.

Japan is also undergoing profound change. Its enormous wealth arose so quickly that its people still consider themselves to be poor and vulnerable, an attitude reflected in the nation's cautious and defensive foreign policy. A society that prides itself on lack of class distinctions is increasingly angry with the emergence of land-rich billionaires. The population is graying faster than almost any other industrialized society, placing severe strains on labor and social services. A heretofore tightly controlled economy is being confronted by American and European demands— loud and strong demands—to open up, and to dramatically liberalize the most basic regulatory laws and customs that characterized Japan for many decades. Meanwhile, as Tokyo debates its role in the post–Cold War era —whether, for example, to play a more active military role, or to change its industrial structure to better accommodate foreign trade demands—its self-image is caught in a tug-of-war between generations with different memories and different fears. The political system, which still contains elements from Meiji times, is acknowledged at home and abroad to be too weak and too scandal ridden to make any meaningful progress, but no one expects deep-seated reform in the foreseeable future.

Germany is undergoing no less a transformation. Incorporating its former eastern region creates not only a host of problems ranging from massive tax increases to class strife, but it causes the nation to reexamine its fundamental political and cultural moorings as it reclaims its identity as both a western and eastern nation. Just as Germany regained its own sovereignty in 1990, the pressures for closer integration with the European Community are causing it to ask whether that sovereignty has much meaning when it comes to national defense, finance, labor policy, immigration, environment; indeed, in no other nation is the conflict so clear between the passionate desire for autonomy at the state and local levels and the reality of increasing supranational coordination in its backyard. Pressures from Eastern Europe and the former Soviet Union are drawing Germany into a caldron of civil strife, ethnic rivalries, and economic chaos that disturb Germany's obsession with order and stability. Yet every time Berlin moves to inject some control, it is roundly condemned for being too arrogant and assertive, with barely concealed allusions to its dark past.

By focussing on America, Japan, and Germany, we see the world as it really is. So often, we hear policy prescriptions as if all outcomes were rational and the objective good were easily attainable. How many times have we heard that protectionism is bad, that nations should share the burden of collective defense against aggression, that currency management or economic growth should be coordinated among key countries? In looking at how Washington, Tokyo, and Berlin approach such issues and in trying to understand their differing interests, their political constraints, their individual preoccupations, textbook-type coordination seems more remote and we have a much better idea of the genuine constraints on each nation.

A spotlight on the Big Three embodies another bit of reality, too. Time and again we hear about one U.S. problem after another—the demise of the U.S. automobile industry, the erosion of America's lead in semiconductor production, the growing dependence on foreign capital. There is always a strong temptation to identify problems separately and attribute them to autonomous market forces, or to unique factors within an industry. In sophisticated business and economic circles, it is often not fashionable to talk about competition between countries or national systems —better to refer to competition among firms. I do not buy that line of reasoning, and among the arguments I will make is that Japan and Germany have—and have always had—types of capitalism that are different from the American version (and different from one another, too). These distinctions, which involve the relationship between government and business, between finance and industry, between domestic and foreign policy, will be the basis of many of the problems all three nations face in the years ahead. They will be the source of increasingly fierce disputes over trade and investment, to be sure, but the different economic and social systems will become rivals for the allegiance of other nations in Latin America, Eastern Europe, and Southeast Asia, and they will produce conflicting policies in the United Nations, the International Monetary Fund (IMF), and the world trade body called the General Agreement on Tariffs and Trade, otherwise known as the GATT.

Finally, in talking about Japan and Germany, we are really talking about us. There is no clearer lens through which to see where America has been and where it is going, no better way to analyze the challenges ahead for both our policies and, more important, our way of thinking about ourselves. There are no two countries that have been a better reflection of our hopes and our fears, our finest hours and our future nightmares. During the height of American power—to take one example —nothing so defined America as the helping hand we extended to our two defeated enemies, or as the overseas presence of our proud young troops, or the insatiable demand for American dollars, American music, or American blue jeans. But in our darkest moments it is not French education or British productivity or Chinese economic clout that we fear —it is the schools, the factories, and the banks of Japan and Germany. And so when Americans look ahead, and when they want to measure what they will be up against and what they must do to preserve their way of life and standard of living, the yardsticks will not be just *our* standards but those set in Tokyo and Berlin.

＊　　　＊　　　＊

By grouping Japan and Germany together I do not mean to imply that they are identical countries or even directly comparable. It should go without saying that their culture, language, geography, and resource endowments are different, as are their physical size, G.N.P., and population. The two nations have different political systems, different ways of organizing their economies, different ways of managing their firms. The Japanese economy is far more closed to imports or to foreign investment than is Germany's. Japan is not part of NATO and the European Community as is Germany, nor is it a member of any comparable regional arrangements. From an American perspective, moreover, Germany is seen as part of the western tradition; it is a much more familiar society to us than is Japan. Tensions between America and the two nations are not the same, either. When it comes to trade policy, for example, no one is screaming about imports of BMWs or accusing Siemens of dumping electronic products at unfair prices. Few if any identify Germany as a security threat because of its economic penetration of America.

The reason for looking at these two nations together is not that they are so similar, but that at another level—at the level of how we should think about America and what it will become in the world—Japan and Germany do have a lot in common. In contrast to the United States, for example, Japan and Germany are societies of exceptionally high savers and investors. Both have had a single-minded preoccupation with economic competitiveness spanning more than a century, and both have fused foreign policy and economic interests accordingly, and in a way that now pays huge dividends. Both have given the highest priority to commercial, nonmilitary research, and both have excelled in training and education. Both have fashioned tightly woven economies where business, government, and workers are pushing in similar directions; indeed, here are two countries that, each in its own way, have found highly successful means to pursue national economic and social strategies.

As the twentieth century ends, moreover, our world is being defined by new technologies, new methods of production and distribution, new demands for education, and new requirements for massive investments in private and public infrastructure. Japan and Germany may be widely different nations but they share this distinction: among the advanced industrial countries they have worked the hardest to take advantage of this new world, and they have been the most successful at mastering it. In terms of their mindset they also have had a lot in common. Compared to America, Great Britain, and France, both Japan and Germany were late to industrialize in the nineteenth century. This led to a sense of insecurity and inferiority, a desperation to catch up, and a view about the responsibilities of the public sector in the economy, which continues to pervade their thinking even today. In addition, neither had anything approaching a true democratic revolution in which the principles of traditional liberal political thought, including a strong emphasis on individual rights and individual choice, emerged from the demands of the public, thereby making group action relatively easy to organize.

Japan and Germany often viewed the world in similar terms, too. Time and again they saw themselves as constrained and victimized by the major powers. For decades they felt the need to expand their political control beyond their borders in order to find more space for their growing populations, and to secure raw materials and captive markets. And in the process of expanding their empires, they invaded neighboring nations and committed unspeakable crimes.

The two countries have been highly influential in the way we Americans have viewed the world and played a role in it, perhaps more influential than any other two countries. For over a hundred years we have had strong interests across the Atlantic and the Pacific, and starting at the beginning of this century, Japan and Germany were our most worrisome challengers on the world scene, sometimes militarily, sometimes economically. We worried about their rapid rise to power, we opposed their totalitarian philosophies, we recoiled at their capability for brutality. From Munich we learned the meaning of appeasement. From Pearl Harbor we learned the lesson of preparedness. From Auschwitz we rediscovered the meaning of genocide; from Nanking and Bataan we also saw the darkest side of human nature. From the total defeat of Tokyo and Berlin we took on the burdens of occupation, reconstruction, and leader of the free world. From Japan and Germany's regeneration we acquired good friends, close allies, important economic partners, and now, fierce competitors.

Today these two nations are nonmilitary economic powers—pacifist trading states. For many years this was exactly what America wanted them to be. But for the future, this situation will create some of America's toughest dilemmas as we agonize over the costs and sacrifices of being the world's policeman, yet worry that if others, especially Japan and Germany, do undertake real defense missions, they will diminish our position in the world.

For most Americans, Japan is seen as a much more significant rival than Germany. Not only has it made far greater inroads into the U.S. economy, not only is it far more impenetrable to U.S. exports and investment, but in terms of future economic momentum it appears far more unstoppable. Polls now show that large numbers of Americans believe Japan is economically superior to the United States and the decline of American confidence is closely related to concerns about Japan's ascendance as an economic superpower. But with regard to America's overall concerns, weighing Japan and Germany against one another is not as simple as current preoccupations and polls, many influenced by the U.S. recession, imply. Germany is emerging as a far more well-rounded country, less of an economic giant than Japan perhaps, but also less of a political dwarf. Germany has been more willing than Japan to take dramatic political initiatives, more willing to express its political demands, more willing to tell other nations, clearly and forcefully, that it will not go along. In worrying about Japan, moreover, America faces one nation. But in confronting Germany, we are increasingly talking about taking on all of Europe. America's problems with Tokyo and Berlin may not be the same, but each presents a daunting challenge.

Tokyo and Berlin constitute another profound problem: they are becoming neither pure partners nor pure rivals but a combination of both. Traditionally, Americans have classified other nations as friend or foe. We had little trouble doing this in two world wars or during the Cold War. But Japan and Germany in the 1990s will be different. We can no longer divide our world into good and evil. It's a crucial ambiguity we will have to learn to live with.

Finally, Japan and Germany represent the poles toward which world power is shifting. This is not a prediction of American decline—it is simply an acknowledgement that the overwhelming predominance of the United States in the 1950s and 1960s could not last. But throughout history, big problems have arisen whenever power shifted. Existing assumptions about who gets what, who pays, and who decides have had to be rethought. As we shall see, such reassessments will be continuous in the years ahead, with related struggles, frustrating tensions, and conflicts.

If all this occurs in the absence of strong leadership from any one country, serious struggles are inevitable as everyone jockeys for position amid a crumbling framework for order.

I have looked at all these issues from a purely American perspective. I have, therefore, not spent a lot of time dealing with relations between Japan and Germany, although it is a subject that arises in several places. Suffice it to say here, Japanese-German interaction, historically and today, has had far less intensity and far less substance than U.S. relations with each country separately.

When Japan emerged from centuries of isolation in the 1850s and 1860s, it looked to Germany for the foundations of modern law, science, medicine, education, political theory, and military organization. However, by the turn of the century and through the 1920s, Tokyo and Berlin had become antagonists in Asia, with Germany teaming up with other Western powers, Russia, and China to limit Japan's expansion, and with Japan siding against Germany in World War I and confiscating the latter's colonial possessions in the Pacific. In the 1920s and 1930s the pendulum began to swing back toward a reconciliation of convenience, but not much more than that. Berlin and Tokyo concluded a wartime alliance in 1940, but it was a weak one, characterized by poor and halfhearted coordination. Germany, for example, gave Japan no warning before it invaded Russia. Tokyo surprised Berlin when it bombed Pearl Harbor. After 1945, the two nations had few direct dealings of great importance to either; both were obsessed with economic recovery and their relations with Washington. In addition, Japan was busy with Asia, Germany with Western Europe and East Germany, and neither had much time or energy to develop ties with one another. Whatever contact they had took place mostly in international economic organizations.

Nevertheless, Japanese-German relations are now particularly important in two arenas. Trade tensions between the two, heretofore a minor issue because of the small volume, are sure to grow as Japanese penetration of Europe increases. In addition, any assessment of the global leadership potential of either country must take account of the lack of influence that either one is apt to have over the other.

I have focussed on the remainder of the 1990s as my time frame. This has several implications. It rules out attention to important issues such as long-term demographic trends, concerted threats from parts of the Third World, and environmental problems that change the face of international politics. It removes factors such as the potential rise of major new powers, including China, the Russian Republic, and a reunified Korea. And perhaps most significantly, it has given me a particularly skeptical view about the implications of growing economic interdependence for global politics.

There can be no denying, for example, that the world is getting smaller and that nations are becoming more intertwined. Global communications, transportation, travel, trade, investment all have mushroomed; countless mergers among companies of different nationalities have occurred; production and distribution systems have become global; and consumer tastes have become more similar. In time, there may be effective international organizations to regulate trade and investment or to protect the environment. By the second decade of the next century, the European Community might behave like one nation, and the regional trading blocs now forming around the world might have dissolved into a seamless world economy. Eastern Europe might be on its feet, as may many of the former Soviet republics. In the 1990s, however, none of this is likely to happen.

In fact, I believe that the *transition* to an integrated global economy, assuming one does emerge, will create more rather than less political tension as nations resist giving up sovereignty, trade penetration jeopardizes jobs, and politicians resent their inability to control events outside their reach. In addition, I see an inevitable tendency to deal with rapid change by reasserting and reaffirming national symbols and identities, as well as cultural roots. We can see this happening in America as politicians campaign on the basis of flag, family, and the restoration of the American Dream. The fact is that policymakers don't know what to do amid so many simultaneous changes—deregulation, which gives governments less control; international mergers, which create gigantic corporations that can shift trade and juggle taxes across national boundaries; computer programs that destabilize currencies and stockmarkets within seconds. Governments often don't know whether to intervene or how; they know they have to be accountable to the constituencies that elected them, but given the global nature of the forces buffeting people's lives, politicians are impotent to do anything but argue for narrow, nationalist measures, which is the only thing that *seems* to work in the short run. It is no coincidence that the momentum for trade liberalization has slowed dramatically, and that protectionism is on the rise.

This brings us back to America, and the purpose of this book. Our nation is facing its most severe challenge since 1941, and today we are less prepared to respond than we were then. We are in danger of becoming a hobbled power, and, based on current trends, a second-rate country in the areas that will count most in the coming world order. More significantly, we risk the prospect of a declining standard of living, with attendant social strife and increasing dependence on other nations for critical capital and technology. With nearly 10 percent of the population on food stamps; with one in three children expected to be receiving some form of public assistance before they are seventeen; with 35 million people without health insurance; with one person being murdered every twenty-five minutes; with the federal deficits mushrooming; with schools losing ground to foreign competition; with a crumbling physical infrastructure; with the accelerating erosion of our manufacturing and technological base; with our banks in turmoil; with national governance characterized by political polarization, cynicism, and empty slogans—with all that and more, is there any wonder why we should be thinking about Japan and Germany and all they represent in terms of the competition we face, the cooperation we need, and, most of all, the urgency of getting a grip on ourselves at home?

CHAPTER I

Challenging Old Assumptions

Looking back, historians in the early twenty-first century are unlikely to have settled on any one explanation of how conflict among America, Japan, and Germany caused the New World Order of the mid-to-late 1990s to become a nightmare. "Economic warfare" will not precisely describe what happened, because even though protectionism increased, there was also a steady growth in business dealings, flows of money, and volumes of trade among the major nations. "Military clashes" will not be accurate because Washington, Berlin, and Tokyo will certainly not have taken up arms against one another. Something else will have come about between the Big Three, not willfully, not spitefully. It will have happened simply because these powerful nations, driven by the force of their differing histories, institutions, and cultural preferences, weighed down by new sets of responsibilities and constraints, and exhausted by having had to respond to one crisis after another simply couldn't find a way to overcome their narrowly defined interests. While the breakdown of order will have had no precise starting date, it might have evolved like this:

It is January 20, 1997. A newly elected U.S. president is delivering his inaugural speech. He points to all the failed promises of the previous administration to improve schools, to deal with drugs and crime, to rebuild America's crumbling road and rail networks, and to strengthen its tottering banking system. He calls for a crash program of internal rebuilding—a domestic Marshall Plan. He pledges his administration's total efforts to find the money to do these things, including, for the first time, truly radical cuts in the defense budget and drastic reductions in financial contributions to the U.N., the World Bank, and other international organizations. He threatens other nations whose markets are not fully open to American exports with substantial trade retaliation, and to show that he means business, he announces a tripling of tariffs on imports of Japanese telecommunications gear and German machine tools, and he promises a wide-ranging investigation by the Justice Department of potential antitrust violations by Japanese and European firms—many of the latter now dominated by German interests—whose U.S.-based facilities are part of a concentrated global network. Referring to the large military establishment that America has maintained for over half a century, and to the American blood that was shed to protect the West and Japan, and vowing that enough is enough, the president announces the withdrawal of all America's remaining forces from abroad. As the applause builds, he says he will use the North American trade bloc, consisting of the new common market of the U.S., Canada, and Mexico, as a big stick against those who don't play fair.

The events in Washington have little impact on Europe. Gathering in Potsdam, Germany, in the winter of 1997, the European heads of state have other problems to worry about. Their decision to create a European bloc of nations, stretching from Lisbon to Moscow, had been taken years before, and has created enough political and administrative headaches to preoccupy them for the next quarter of a century. Europe was dismayed, for example, when the dream of a European Community of co-equal nations faded as Germany began to dominate the new European Central Bank, the new political institutions, and the new European defense organization. More aggravation came when Berlin demanded the incorporation of several Eastern European countries into the E.C., and then proceeded to create a Teutonic coalition composed of Croatia, Hungary, and the Baltics within the enlarged E.C. Next, one crisis has cascaded over another, taking up the time and attention of German leaders more than any of the whining from Washington. There was, for example, persistent rioting in the eastern portion of Germany as widespread inequalities mounted and market reforms produced intolerable strains. Then came large-scale debt defaults of the Eastern European countries, Russia, Ukraine, and other newly independent republics, followed by waves of refugees, which stretched Germany's public finances and social tolerance to the breaking point. There was no single event, no single meeting in which it was said, "We've got to look after ourselves, above all; the Americans are no longer very relevant." They never said it exactly that way, but somehow it happened.

None of these events come as a great surprise to Japanese officials. For them, the omens were clear for a long time. They had long ago discounted the U.S. security umbrella. They knew that the long recession in the United States, which began in 1990 and lingered for years, would force them to lay off workers in their American-based factories and were prepared for the congressional outcry. As General Motors gave pink slips to over 70,000 employees, they expected increased harassment not just of Toyota, Nissan, and other auto companies, but also of Hitachi, Matsushita, and other Japanese firms operating in America, by the I.R.S., the Department of Labor, the Civil Rights Commission, the White House Office of Equal Economic Opportunity, the Environmental Protection Agency, and countless congressional committees. They knew their decision to draw closer to China in economics and politics would upset Washington, whose policy was increasingly antagonistic toward Beijing. They were not surprised that the United States resented Japan's accelerated efforts to build a tighter East Asian community with Japan at the center. But there is no panic in the Japanese cabinet. The era of the Cold War, Tokyo reminds itself, is over. The Asian nation has its own problems to worry about, including its aging population, chronic labor shortages, and its growing class divisions. Washington's new economic aggressiveness, however, has annoyed the Japanese, who have become tired of being the whipping boy for America's homegrown deficiencies. Two can play America's game, they conclude, and Tokyo's Ministry of Finance instructs Japanese lenders to slow up loans to America; its Defense Agency quietly blocks the technology transfers that the Pentagon had been expecting; Japan's space agency gives orders to accelerate "Project Independence" for its aerospace industry, one of the few sectors in which the United States was still supreme; and U.S. investors with operations from Osaka to Sapporo find out how uncomfortable life can become under the refocussed glare of Japan's regulators.

Both Berlin and Tokyo are unimpressed with the American president's lament that the United States has shouldered disproportionate military burdens. What about the German-dominated European intervention force stretching from Poland to Russia, trying to maintain some semblance of order as one nation after another has eyed its neighbors' borders and as economic and ethnic tensions have brought widespread civil disorder in their wake? What about the Japanese naval fleet, now patrolling some of Asia's contested territorial borders? What's America's beef?

Tokyo and Berlin have also stopped listening to American harangues about free market economics. Yes, they say, we all love Adam Smith, but life has become more complicated than that. The new industrial order requires big firms, big banks, harmonious labor relations, a proactive government, they say. The instability and fragility of the former communist nations require extensive support by governmental intervention. America should worry a little more about its own competitiveness than about ideology, more about its saving and investment, or its schools, than about our antitrust policies or our financial regulations. Washington wants to threaten us with its protectionist club? Let it try. No one wants a trade war, but if there has to be one, we are in a stronger position than America is to fight one.

By the late 1990s, moreover, Washington, Berlin, and Tokyo have had their fill of crisis management. The initial anxieties over the collapse of the old order in Eastern Europe, followed by worries about whether a unified Germany would again upset international politics, followed by the Gulf War, followed by civil war in Russia, followed by a dramatic economic slowdown in the industrial world—all this in the first half of the 1990s—was simply too much for political leaders to deal with. But this was not all. The Big Three were also constantly bickering over which factions and leaders in the unstable former Soviet republics to support and how. When millions of refugees started to pour into western Europe from both the East and from North Africa, another clash took place over how to respond. When political instability began to rock the Asian mainland, including turmoil in China as the old leadership died off, each of the Big Three defined a different set of primary interests. When monetary instability and protectionism increased, all hopes for close cooperation among the Big Three were dashed.

And so after the round of congratulations following the collapse of the Berlin Wall, the Cold War evolved into a Cold Peace. In its post-inaugural editorial *The New York Times* wrote, "Looking back these past few years, no one should have been surprised by the sharp erosion of relationships between America, Japan, and Germany. Most of our resentments are problems of our own making, but we needed an enemy to replace the old Soviet Union and we turned quickly on our former allies. There is more than enough blame to go around, however, for both Tokyo and Berlin seem to have fallen into their pre–World War II pattern of dominating their immediate neighborhoods and thinking very little about the welfare of the world outside their narrow concerns. The growth of global trade and investment—the borderless economy, as some call it— has been a great disappointment from the standpoint of world politics. We thought that when communism collapsed the great political and ideological rivalries of the twentieth century were over. We thought that the main challenge was to consolidate the movement for freely elected governments which embraced American-style capitalism. As we enter the twenty-first century, life looks more like the turbulent 1920s and 1930s—when order broke down and there was no nation to take the lead —than like the era of peace we spent the last half century fighting for. It is not clear how we will extricate ourselves from this mess."

A wild fantasy? Hardly. In fact, it is almost impossible to make a completely crazy projection of events these days. Whether or not you believe we're headed for trouble does not depend too much on assumptions about the kinds of problems that will arise, because the nature of those problems is pretty clear. We can expect more ethnic and regional strife outside the United States, Western Europe, and Japan. We can expect economic convulsions as national economies interact with one another with ever more competitive ferocity. We can expect that the pressure for the major industrial democracies to work as a team will be reduced in the absence of a military threat from a monolithic enemy. The really contentious issue is not whether all this will happen but whether it is within the capability of the key countries to deal with these problems in an effective way—whether the Big Three are up to the unprecedented degree of sustained cooperation that will be required. The issue is not what is the most *desirable* outcome, but what is the *likely* one. Forget the lofty speeches of today's leaders, filled as they are with references to New World Orders and the like. The critical questions are all variations on a single theme: *where are we really heading?*

CRITICAL CONSIDERATIONS

There are some big questions that need to be asked:
How will America deal with a changing domestic and international

setting? The United States is no longer in the kingpin position it once was. Whether or not we are in decline can be debated, but no one can deny that America's relative power vis-à-vis Germany and Japan has slipped. Moreover, the United States faces at least two challenges that it has not faced in half a century. Never before has it been so plagued by domestic economic and social problems, requiring new programs and massive resources at every turn. And not since much earlier in its history has it so needed the assistance of other nations to achieve its goals at home and abroad.

The American Dream is of a constant and steady improvement in lifestyle, an upward and unending spiral of individual satisfaction. But what if the dream is no longer real? Will the United States turn inward in an attempt to deal with its internal challenges, and if so, will its stance toward the outside world become increasingly distant and protectionist, mixing military withdrawal with an overly aggressive trade policy? Or will it adopt a more internationalist stance, regaining its confidence by attending to its home-grown problems and trying to create new sets of global arrangements within which it will exercise a new kind of influence, based not on single-handed domination but on more traditional diplomatic give-and-take?

What kinds of countries will Germany and Japan become? During the Cold War, these two countries were living in unique circumstances. They may have been sovereign in a legal sense, but in fact they were half-nations, riddled with inhibitions and restrictions stemming from their defeat in World War II. Partly it was because their neighbors still viewed their actions with suspicion, especially when either appeared to be too assertive. Partly it was because they derived substantial advantages from being able to concentrate on building their economies while America took responsibility for their defense.

In the mid-1990s the environment for Germany and Japan will be changing. Each nation will be less constrained in telling the world what it wants, and in pursuing its national interests; consequently, each will be acting more independently of America than it did for the last forty-five years. Americans will need to pose the most fundamental questions regarding these two countries. Before 1945 they were unstable mavericks, resisting integration into the global community except on their own terms. Are all such drives behind them now? Will they remain close allies of the United States despite the withering of a common security threat, and the passing of the generation that remembered World War II and its aftermath? Can German energy and ambition be channelled in such a way so as not to alarm and dominate its neighbors? Will Japan continue its unprecedented climb up the global economic ladder without doing more to accommodate the interests and concerns of other nations? Will either nation continue to be an economic powerhouse without projecting a military capability beyond its borders, or will the two types of power inevitably come together?

How will military and economic burdens be distributed among the Big Three? From 1945 to the mid-1960s, America shouldered most of the military and economic burdens for the free world—from fighting wars to maintaining open markets. In the ensuing decades, German and Japanese contributions increased—from helping to offset the costs of U.S. troops to providing large loans to the U.S. government. But the issues of burdensharing among the Big Three have not yet been resolved. After the Gulf War, America's growing dilemma was starkly revealed: Washington can be the world's policeman as long as others help pay the way. Few Americans find this role appealing, but what are the alternatives? How to share military leadership, and how to divide up economic responsibilities—these are the first questions. But a hard-nosed American view will have to take into account not just spreading the costs but also the degree to which the United States is willing for others to have an equal voice in the actual decisionmaking. In other words, how much power does America *really* want Japan and Germany to have?

REEXAMINING OLD ASSUMPTIONS

There are no definitive answers to these questions, but we must begin to think about them and form some general judgements. A starting point is a second look at the assumptions Americans generally make about the world.

We thought that after the Cold War, America, Japan, and Germany would be close partners in all endeavors.

Shortly after taking office, President Bush talked effusively about Japan and Germany as full partners with America. His first overseas trip was to Japan, where he promoted the idea of a "global partnership." He did not camouflage his desire to make Germany—and not Britain—the most important U.S. ally in Europe, inviting Bonn to join the United States as a "partner in leadership." Others outside the administration agreed. C. Fred Bergsten, head of the Institute for International Economics in Washington and formerly a high ranking policy maker in the Nixon and Carter administrations, wrote about the U.S.–Germany–Japan triangle in these terms: "Initiatives by the Big Three to reform and dramatically improve the international and trade regimes . . . as well as to make substantial changes in their internal economic structures, would clearly mark the beginning of a new era in collective leadership," he said. "It would show that each could adopt a new mind set: for America, a willingness to share powers with the others; for Japan, an acceptance of international responsibility; for Europe, a willingness to act jointly on global economic and monetary, as well as trade, policy." [1]

It was indeed no great leap of faith to believe that the Big Three would be drawing closer together. Ever since 1945, all the trends pointed in this direction. Under American tutelage, Japan and Germany had become democracies and market-oriented economies. Washington, Tokyo, and Bonn* had weathered many crises together—the Berlin blockade, the Korean War, trade disputes, currency crises, arguments over nuclear strategy. Indeed, the intimacy of the relationships between Washington and Tokyo, and between Washington and Bonn, was all-encompassing, a combination of parent-to-child, mentor-to-pupil, friend-to-friend on everything from political development to military protection. It was natural to conclude that the three nations shared similar values, held similar views of the world, believed in similar kinds of political and economic institutions.

But events since the end of the Cold War tell a different story. A first crack in the facade of unity was seen in the process of German unification. The division of Germany had come to symbolize what the Cold War was all about. It was, after all, on the border between two Germanys that the United States and the Soviet Union stared each other down, and it was here that the Iron Curtain went up. When this situation changed so rapidly, it might have been expected that West Germany's Chancellor Helmut Kohl would have moved in close step with his American and

---

* I have referred to Bonn as the capital of the former West Germany, using it only when discussing Germany between the aftermath of World War II and unification. Before the Cold War, Berlin was the capital of a unified Germany and since mid-1990 it has regained that status.

European allies. Instead, he displayed a startling independence, annoying the leaders of Great Britain, France, and the United States. When the chancellor travelled to the Soviet Union in July 1990 to secure the approval of Soviet President Mikhail S. Gorbachev for his unification plan, everyone else was left on the sidelines. The international issue had been transformed to a German-Soviet bilateral affair.

Turn now to the summit meeting in Houston, Texas, also in July 1990. The leaders of the industrial nations—led by President Bush, Chancellor Kohl, and Japanese Prime Minister Toshiki Kaifu—had come together for one of their annual gatherings. It was billed as a celebration to mark the end of the Cold War. After all, Germany was on the verge of unification, the Soviet Union was clamoring to join the western club, and a major relaxation of tensions beckoned. There was a high level of anticipation about how these countries would now work closely together on the issues that really counted—jobs, economic security, the environment. But things did not go according to schedule.

The first big issue at the summit was whether to give massive aid to the Soviet Union. Washington urged restraint until there was a clearer picture of what was happening there and what the actual needs were. "Thanks but no thanks," said Chancellor Kohl in so many words, indicating that Washington could do what it liked, but Germany had already made its plans quite independently. The second big issue was China. The Tienanmen Square massacre had occurred one year before. In the ensuing twelve months, there was no let-up in Chinese repression. America had cut its aid to Beijing and other nations agreed to follow suit. Now Washington wanted to hold the same line for a while longer. This time it was Prime Minister Kaifu who demurred, saying, in essence, that Japan intended to go back into China with or without the United States.

Skip ahead to Geneva, five months later. Delegates of the major trading nations were gathered to conclude four years of negotiations—the so-called Uruguay Round of the General Agreement on Tariffs and Trade (GATT)—to free up world commerce. It was the most far-reaching trade pact ever attempted, covering not just wheat, textiles, and machinery but banking, patents, and foreign investment. In the months preceding the Geneva meeting, President Bush had made it clear that the precondition for an American signature on the new treaty was liberalization of trade in agriculture. Without agreement in this area, he warned repeatedly, the United States would end its participation in the negotiations. Two participants—Europe and Japan—had to make major concessions. In Europe, the French had always been notoriously protectionist, but alone they could not carry the day. They were not alone. Germany threw its full weight behind the French in opposing the U.S. desire for freer trade in farm products. Japan, which all but bans the import of rice, did not offer anything by way of liberalization. Despite being perhaps the single most powerful force influencing the global trading system, Tokyo's voice was so low as to be inaudible. And so the talks collapsed. The American delegates went home, as they promised they would.

A fourth event was the breakdown of financial cooperation. In early 1991, finance ministers and the top central bankers of the seven major industrial nations gathered in New York. It was a particularly sensitive time. The U.S. recession was deepening. Japan was nervous about its declining stock market and the possibility of a collapse in real estate prices. Germany was facing mounting pressures to fund the costs of unification, not to mention other problems on its doorstep in Eastern Europe and the U.S.S.R. There were also the uncertainties surrounding the Gulf War. As everyone had hoped, these seven nations, led by the Big Three—the countries with all the financial clout, not to mention the three key currencies—made a big deal out of their solidarity. To the world they promised "to maintain stability in international financial markets."

Several days later, with no warning, the German Bundesbank hiked interest rates, a move prompted entirely by domestic considerations. Unconnected to that action, the Federal Reserve then lowered U.S. rates, again, solely in response to conditions at home. The huge difference between the higher interest rates in Germany and those in America put enormous downward pressure on the dollar, forcing central banks to buy up dollars in massive amounts to keep the greenback from falling too fast and too far. Because the economies in Europe had become so tightly linked, the German action put pressure on other European countries to raise their interest rates too, thereby slowing economic growth throughout Europe.

In subsequent days, Washington sent mixed signals saying that interest rates should be lower, but also intervening to support the dollar. German officials stated that it was not so important to stabilize currencies. Japan was having a domestic debate about its own policies, seemingly divorced from everyone else. There are many explanations for such chaos. But who would argue that what happened showed even a small amount of financial cooperation? And who would deny that there is something more fundamental here—an incompatibility of national goals, as recession-plagued America cried out for more growth, Germany applied the brakes, and Japan retreated into its shell? And who would dispute that this series of events showed a failure on the part of the Big Three to grasp the notion that individual nations, which do not take account of the spillover effects of their policies on one another, will not be able to achieve their goals for long?

Next came the Gulf War. On this issue of cardinal importance to America, on a question of principle about the way foreign aggression should be confronted, on an issue of war and peace—on all these matters, Japan and Germany chose to opt out to the maximum extent they could. It's true that they eventually sent a few planes to shuttle refugees, that Germany provided logistical support, installed antiaircraft missiles in Turkey, and provided Israel with Patriot missiles and other equipment, and that Japan eventually sent several minesweepers to the Gulf. It's also the case that Japan and Germany each contributed well over $10 billion to the effort, large sums by any standards. But all of this was done hesitantly, begrudgingly, and only after the most intense pressure from Washington. Everyone recognized the agonizing dilemmas in Tokyo and Berlin—the historical scars, the political constraints of using their armies abroad after forty-five years of being lectured about never doing so again. Many acknowledged their right to question whether America was going too far—whether, for example, either the supply of oil or the freedom of Kuwait was worth dying for. The issue, however, is not whether Japan and Germany were right or wrong. It is that they thought so differently from America. It is that their notion of a New World Order and the price they were willing to pay for it was at odds with Washington's most deeply held views.

Not long after the Gulf War, top American economic officials began to press Japan and Germany to lower their interest rates. The official line in Washington was that global growth was slowing, investment in Eastern Europe was not proceeding well, and that the prescription was for Tokyo and Berlin to stimulate their economies with lower cost credit. U.S. Treasury Secretary Nicholas Brady mounted a very public campaign to twist the arms of Japan and Germany. But his effort ran into a brick wall.

In the first place, both the Kaifu and Kohl governments accused Washington of mounting a thinly veiled campaign for Japan and Germany to help America get out of its recession by boosting overseas markets for U.S. exports. Secondly, both Tokyo and Berlin were more worried about inflation than growth and were in no mood to take risks by easing money. Third, they disagreed with the basic American prescription for fostering new investment in Eastern Europe or elsewhere: lower interest rates, they argued, were not as important in these nations as sound overall economic policies. Again, the pros and cons of each country's arguments could have been debated. But what was not at issue were the very different approaches they brought to the most fundamental economic questions facing the world.

Yet another division arose over the handling of Third World and Eastern European foreign debt. In the spring of 1991, the Bush administration had moved on its own to forgive virtually the entire debt owed to the United States by Egypt and Poland. Japan and Germany were furious. Not only had the United States not coordinated its policy with them, but Washington ignored their deeply held views that such wholesale forgiveness was a wrong-headed policy. Each of the Big Three had a different set of interests. America was anxious to gain quick political points with Poland and it wanted to reward Egypt for its support in the Gulf War. But Germany was Poland's largest creditor by far and was outraged that Washington had presumed to set the precedent for a debt write-off. Japan, the largest global lender, was equally concerned about setting such a precedent.

The pattern of pursuing independent objectives continued at the London Summit in July 1991. The heads of state made virtually no progress in reviving the stalled Uruguay Round of trade negotiations, despite their assertion that this was the single highest priority for the international economy. They gave an outward appearance of unity regarding aid to the U.S.S.R.—their joint position being to "wait and see," and to provide "technical assistance" in the meantime—but it was common knowledge that Germany wanted to help much more aggressively and that Japan was taking a much stingier line than the United States. Even on the issue of environmental protection, Germany was unsuccessful in getting agreement on concrete action regarding the protection of the rain forests in Brazil or new programs to protect the earth's ozone layer.

In December 1991, more cracks in the facade of Big Three harmony appeared. In Europe, the civil war in Yugoslavia continued to rage, with neither the E.C. nor the U.N. able to bring about a cease-fire. Germany grabbed the mantle and announced it would recognize the two break-away republics, Croatia and Slovenia. In Europe, Great Britain and France objected. Across the Atlantic, the United States objected. The secretary general of the U.N. asked Germany not to go ahead with recognition in such an uncoordinated and selective manner, and in the absence of a more comprehensive settlement. Said a spokesman for the German government, "We will move ahead whether any, all, or none of the European states join us."[2]

President Bush started 1992 on an equally inauspicious note. On a whirlwind visit to Japan, he set unrealistic expectations for breakthroughs on the trade front, then with great fanfare pushed the sales of one of America's least competitive products—automobiles. In the process he inadvertently kicked off a wave of anti-Japanese sentiment in the United States and ensured renewed enthusiasm for more protectionism. The day after his visit, European leaders threatened both Washington and Tokyo not to conclude any bilateral deals at their expense.

Also as the year started, the Big Three evidenced little capacity to come to grips with the deteriorating situation in the former Soviet Union. Secretary of State James A. Baker hastily called a conference in Washington of nations around the world to coordinate humanitarian aid to the new republics. German resentment ran high because of a feeling that Berlin had been carrying far more than its rightful share of the financial burden while Washington was grandstanding and trying to look like the leader of the worldwide effort. Japan lacked enthusiasm about any help to the former Soviet Union because Russia had still failed to return the islands that Stalin captured from Japan during World War II. The fact was that each of the Big Three was totally preoccupied with its own special situation. American policy was driven by its farmers wanting Uncle Sam to guarantee sales to Moscow; Germany was being pushed by its banks worrying about debt defaults in the republics; and Japanese nationalists wanted their territory back. Lost in the bickering was any concerted response to the evaporating hopes for democracy and capitalism in the vast Eurasian landmass between Europe and the Pacific Ocean.

Finally, as the first full year after the collapse of the Berlin Wall ended, economic conditions in all of the Big Three were deteriorating. The

American recession lingered, with massive job layoffs being announced by one major blue chip company after another. Growth projections in Japan were being revised downward with each passing week. The German Bundesbank raised interest rates to thirty-year highs, thereby guaranteeing a slowing not just of the German economy but of all of Europe. In this situation one might have expected the Big Three to huddle, since, intellectually at least, they all understood that the fate of each was dependent on the other. Instead, as 1992 began, aside from expressed concerns about their individual situations, there was total silence.

We assumed that in the post–Cold War era, Japan and Germany would naturally take on more responsibility for global peace and global economic management.

America, of course, had numerous reasons for promoting shared responsibilities among the superpowers. On one level, Washington sought to make virtue out of the inevitable, knowing that Japan and Germany were acquiring greater influence and importance. But at a more pragmatic level, the United States needed the help of Tokyo and Berlin to finance its deficits, and it wanted their money to offset its own declining contributions to worldwide economic development. To judge by the rhetoric, Japan and Germany bought the idea. After all, they had long ago outgrown the role of nations in the process of reconstruction and were prepared to exercise some largesse towards others. Japanese statesmen such as Prime Minister Kaifu talked about Japan's "fulfilling its international role." Germany's President Richard von Weizsaecker said that "Germany's responsibilities have grown and will be shouldered." German Foreign Minister Hans-Dietrich Genscher declared, "A united Germany will carry greater weight and with it we shall not strive for greater power but will be conscious of the greater responsibility."[3]

As the Cold War ended, Americans were concerned that Japan and Germany might become *too* assertive. The divisions at the 1990 Houston Summit underlined the potential problem. "The talks," wrote *The New York Times*'s columnist Leonard Silk, "demonstrated the depth of conflicts among [the Big Three]. Self-interest and the more equally distributed economic power are pulling them apart . . ."[4] Robert D. Hormats, vice chairman of Goldman, Sachs International observed, "Both [Japan and Germany] came to Houston, told the United States what they planned to do, and told us to take it or leave it. This is the new architecture of the economic world."[5]

In fact, we misinterpreted what was happening. Yes, Tokyo and Berlin were speaking their minds more forcefully. But they were focussing on very specific issues of urgent importance to bring about order and stability in their backyards. This was not a grab for global power or responsibility.

There are many reasons why Japan and Germany may not take on the international burdens that Americans expect them to. First of all, unlike America or Great Britain, neither Japan nor Germany has any tradition of undertaking global commitments peacefully. In fact, as late industrializers with militarized societies, each burst on the world stage with a fierce momentum that made them destabilizing forces. Both Tokyo and Berlin, moreover, have become highly successful nations without taking on global responsibilities. Why would they want to change a winning hand? While Americans like to believe that other people would see the world as we do if given the freedom to do so, in the case of Japan and Germany this supposition is not true. There is no equivalent in these two nations for the American projection of universal values or universal missions. For Japan and Germany, global responsibility may mean keeping their own houses and their own backyards in order, and not much more.

In Germany, for example, public opinion is at best ambivalent about new international responsibilities. In the first wide-ranging survey of German attitudes after unification, for example, 75 percent of those polled rejected a new international role for their nation. In fact, the three countries that most Germans saw as a model for their own nation were Switzerland (40 percent), Sweden (30 percent), and Japan and Italy (10 percent each). America rated 6 percent.[6]

As for Japan, its hide-under-the-table behavior in the Uruguay Round trade negotiations shows how difficult it is for it to be pro-active. And its repeated failure to get legislative approval to contribute men and women to international peacekeeping operations, despite the exhaustive efforts of former Prime Minister Toshiki Kaifu and his successor, Mr. Kiichi Miyazawa, reveals the sentiment of the population about contributions other than money.

Of course, just because Tokyo and Berlin do not want to be drawn into greater global responsibilities does not mean that they will be able to avoid heavier involvement in their backyards. They may do so because they see a dangerous vacuum of leadership, or because they want to protect very specific national interests. But they are unlikely to move one inch more than they have to.

Germany, for example, has been drawn into Eastern Europe and the former U.S.S.R. more deeply than it ever contemplated because of fears of instability. In response to strong domestic sentiment in Germany, Hans-Dietrich Genscher, the German foreign minister, spearheaded European recognition of the Baltics and the breakaway Yugoslavian republics. Fearing economic chaos on the Continent and hordes of refugees on its borders, Germany was the country that proposed that a special European peacekeeping force be established. Germany was the most vociferous among the major western nations and Japan about pumping aid into the Soviet Union. "Because of weight and where it stands," warned the *Economist*, "Germany cannot be a Switzerland—an introverted hedgehog in a turbulent world, quietly getting fatter."[7]

As American security interests become less pressing, Japan will also be sucked into a vacuum. Already it has played a key role in the Cambodian settlement, and Asian nations are looking to Tokyo for help with an eventual Korean unification. Japan is by far China's major foreign benefactor, and has been way out front of the United States or Europe in developing political and economic links with Beijing after the Tienanmen Square killings. And Japanese companies are establishing extensive control over the entire East Asian region. With all this, Tokyo cannot help but get more involved politically and economically. Like Germany, it will approach its new responsibilities reluctantly and defensively, particularly in the military arena, where it may be a long time before Japanese politicians agree to send troops abroad.

We believed that America would continue to be the leader, and Japan and Germany, while contributing more to the common effort, would remain followers.

Despite all the literature bemoaning a U.S. decline, most Americans have not bought the argument. In September 1991, President Bush told a nationally televised audience that, "America must lead again as it always has, and only it can."[8] Indeed, Americans are conscious of their economic potential, confident of the nation's military capabilities, and aware that our other assets such as a universally appealing ideology and an ability to manage multilateral diplomacy have no real equal among nations. Behind this, of course, lie forty-five years of history in which we saw ourselves as the undisputed leader of the free world, a nation above all others in moral standing and military and economic clout. After all, in World War II, and in the Korean and Vietnam wars, we not only paid for our own troops but we footed the bill for most of our allies. It's a long way from this to the "tin-cup diplomacy" that characterized the Gulf War, and the implications are not easy to digest.

It is fair to say that neither Tokyo nor Berlin has challenged the principle of American leadership. Japanese officials always say that they prefer to follow American policies, although they are quick to add they want much more consultation and coordination. While German leaders are less explicit about subordinating their role to Washington, it is difficult to find one who has said that Germany should supplant the United States as the prime power. But what we may have failed to anticipate is that just because Japan and Germany do not aspire to leadership doesn't mean they will be willing followers. They might, for example, have a much different notion of what the preconditions for "following" are. America seems to want to tell others what to do, have them finance U.S. adventures, and otherwise stay quiet. But Tokyo and Berlin want a say in decisions. To them, being a follower means participating in the decisions from the beginning. Mr. Kohl has minced no words on the subject. If Germany is to take on more responsibility, he said, "ways will have to be found to bring German views more strongly to bear on decisions of [the U.N.] and the Security Council." Yusuke Kashiwagi, chairman of the Bank of Tokyo, has characterized the 1990s as "the decade in which Japan will have to learn to speak up and assert itself."[9]

It is possible, as well, that Japan and Germany have some distinctly different interests from the United States. As creditor nations, for example, they are bound to see the global financial picture differently from the world's largest borrower. As up-and-coming members of the global financial institutions like the International Monetary Fund (IMF) and the World Bank, they could well challenge the way America has run the organizations for its own foreign policy purposes. As regional powers, Tokyo could well see its stakes in China or in the two Koreas in significantly different terms than does the United States. The same is true of Germany and the nations to its east, including the former U.S.S.R.

There's another way to think about the flawed assumption that America would lead and the others would follow that doesn't entail Tokyo's and Berlin's deliberately and overtly defying the United States, but defying it nonetheless. This is the concept of "dead weight." Japan and Germany might simply refuse to budge on certain issues. In 1990 they did this in the Uruguay Round. They tried in the Gulf War, until

Washington pulled out all the stops. Acting as dead weight need not be a deliberate policy of active opposition, nor would the leaders in each society necessarily see this as a desirable outcome. But it just may happen, because of political polarization within each government over internal differences, or because of different perceptions in Tokyo and Berlin over their long-term interests.

We assumed that the military alliances between Washington and Europe and between Washington and Tokyo would remain intact.

Of course there would have to be modifications, particularly given the dissolution of the Warsaw Pact, but our assumption has been that such modifications would occur within the existing framework. After all, for many years and for most Americans it has been an article of faith that NATO was an essential political instrument for America to remain centrally involved in Europe. And in the Pacific, the U.S.–Japan Security Treaty has been the keystone of the ties between the two nations, taking precedence over all the disputes over textiles, automobiles, semiconductors, and currencies.

Today the entire question of security ties has to be revisited. Both formal alliances are under great strain. NATO is in disarray because of the disappearance of its *raison d'être*—the Soviet military threat. America's views and objectives are only one of many perspectives on how to proceed in the future. Washington has demanded that NATO remain the prime vehicle for transatlantic security cooperation, but some Europeans, especially the French, would like to create a separate European dominated force, which, while not replacing NATO, would surely make it less relevant. Others, like the U.K., are vehemently opposed to such radical change. Germany seems uncomfortable with any of the alternatives; it is torn between not wanting to send German troops into battle under any circumstances, preserving some U.S. presence, and creating a European force. Nevertheless, towards the end of 1991, France and Germany did agree to form a new European defense force. "A united Europe is unthinkable in the long run without a common European defense," said Chancellor Kohl.[10]

Germany and the United States have begun to talk about some type of association agreement between NATO, Eastern Europe, and the former Soviet Union—thereby evidencing the total transformation of what the security pact might become. Other discussions have focussed on giving NATO a role in migration problems or conversion of defense industries to civilian use. Could it be any clearer that NATO has lost its way and that new, centrifugal forces are at play?

Major changes are also in store with respect to the U.S.–Japan Security Treaty. It is increasingly hard to explain why America should expend its own limited resources to defend one of the wealthiest nations and its number one trade competitor, especially when no major threat to Japan can be identified. From the standpoint of many Japanese, the rapid changes in Asia—including the lessening of the Soviet threat, detente between the two Koreas, peace in Cambodia, normalized relations with Vietnam—also call into question the need for the treaty. Beyond Asia, moreover, Japan does not want to be dragged into what it considers to be American escapades like the Gulf War unless it is sure such efforts are in its interest; this, too, could cause Tokyo to distance itself from close security ties with Washington. Finally, the Security Treaty once symbolized America's determination to stay involved in Asia. This was particularly important when the U.S.S.R., China, and Vietnam were aggressively exporting communism. In the years ahead, the bona fides of such determination will not be troops or aircraft carriers, but American products, American capital, and American firms.

This much *is* certain: in the mid-1990s large numbers of American troops will be coming home from Germany and Japan since the rationale for keeping them abroad is now too tenuous for both the U.S. Congress and for the proud and powerful host countries to accept. From more than 314,000 troops in Europe in September 1990, the United States was down to about 260,000 by 1991 and is aiming for 150,000 by mid-decade. In the Pacific, American forces numbered around 140,000 in 1990, and significant reductions are also taking place. The full withdrawal from Germany is apt to come when all the Soviet forces leave, which could be very soon. The return of troops from Japan is likely to be accelerated by growing trade problems and the deteriorating relations that will result, as well as by increasing protests by the people of Okinawa, where many of the U.S. troops are based.

In retrospect, the Gulf War is not as good a precedent for the coming world order as is the civil war in Yugoslavia. The war against Saddam Hussein was the last great conflict of the old era. It is unlikely to be repeated, not only because of its unique black-and-white nature, and not only because of the oil factor, but because the United States is unlikely to shed American blood without the full support of Japan and Germany again, including their participation on the ground. Yugoslavia, on the other hand, is more representative of the regional tensions that could characterize the mid-to-late 1990s, and in this conflict there was not even a hint of U.S. military involvement. It was a crisis for Western Europe itself to handle as best it could, but in the end, alone.

Beyond these kinds of stand-offs, moreover, is the prospect of more intervention in the internal affairs of nations where human rights are grossly violated, or where the specter of nuclear blackmail arises. Such situations could occur if nationalist movements get out of hand, or if economic instability creates exceptional political turmoil and a spate of new, ruthless dictators. As in the Gulf, or in Yugoslavia, of what relevance is NATO or the U.S.-Japan Treaty to these kinds of problems?

In 1991, both Germany and Japan advanced ideas that left Washington cold. Germany recommended that a special peacekeeping force and security council be set up to deal with Yugoslavia and similar crises to its East. Japan made proposals for security consultations in Asia, including discussions of Japan's role. In neither case was the United States consulted in advance. It seems clear that while Berlin and Tokyo are taking steps toward a more independent security stance, the United States is being pried out of its primary geostrategic position in both Europe and Asia.

We assumed that the energy and the aggressive tendencies of Germany and Japan, which were evident in the early part of this century, would be submerged and contained within multilateral frameworks.

American policy toward West Germany since 1945 was to enmesh it in NATO and the European Community. This served several purposes. It placed West Germany within a web of commitments that would force it to take account of its neighbors' needs and to see international cooperation as being in its own interest. In addition, it allowed other nations to keep close tabs on West Germany's policies. Two trends now call into question the continuing likelihood of Germany being tied down by others. One is that NATO is withering. The other is the changing character of the European Community. In both cases, unification upset all the old assumptions.

Regarding the E.C., in particular, the prospect is for the Germanization of Western Europe rather than the Europeanization of Germany (although there will be some of both, of course). Rather than be tied down by European integration, Berlin is going to have a broader playing field and greater influence than it has had since World War II. Germany already dominates monetary policy and its influence will only grow as time goes on. In addition, many of the nations clamoring to join the E.C.—including Sweden, Austria, Hungary, Poland, and Czechoslovakia—will have a strong affinity for Germany's unique style of economic and social policy, combining as it does entrepreneurship, order, and extensive welfare benefits. Germany will have the strongest voice in the E.C. when it comes to dealing with Eastern Europe and the former Soviet Republics, including what to do about aid and refugees. In the end, Germany is likely to push all E.C. policies in accordance with its own national priorities—as it has already done in monetary affairs and with regard to Yugoslavia. And in the end, as well, the E.C. will likely become the vehicle for legitimizing German leadership in Europe by giving it the means to exorcise the ghosts of the Third Reich. "The united German republic," wrote foreign policy scholar Stanley Hoffmann, "may well be able to attain just enough integration to serve the interests of German farmers, businesses, and services, just enough diplomatic coordination to provide Germany with a seal of European legitimacy, but also enough freedom of diplomatic maneuver to prevent unwelcome constraints in foreign policy and defense." [11]

As for Japan, it has never been integrated into multilateral alliances at all. From 1945 onward, Tokyo's major link to the international system has been its exceedingly close bilateral relationship with the United States, ties that were both military and economic. As the underpinnings of the U.S.–Japan Security Treaty weaken, the bilateral relationship will revolve increasingly around economic issues. It is no secret that the growing Japanese presence in the American markets, the Japanese dominance of high technology sectors, the American requirement for Japanese capital, and the growing political frustrations in the United States about being able to penetrate the Japanese markets have all put massive strains on bilateral ties. In the years ahead Japan is likely to become more assertive in articulating and pursuing policies that lessen its need for a close U.S. connection. This will include deepening its ties in Asia, diversifying its trade and investment towards Europe, and striking out on its own when it comes to relationships with China and the former Soviet republics. As was reported by the Japanese Foreign Ministry in its 1991 Annual Report, "With the disappearance of the East-West confrontation, it cannot be denied" that the U.S.–Japan alliance "is becoming less persuasive among the public." [12]

Global economic institutions will also experience erosion from centrifugal forces of the Big Three. GATT, for example, is being challenged by the growth of regional trade blocs in North America, Europe, and East Asia. New regional financial institutions such as the European Bank for Reconstruction and Development will be challenging more universal bodies like the World Bank. In each case Japan and Germany will be playing the paramount roles in their respective geographic spheres, thereby increasing their resistance, or indifference, to U.S. pressure.

Despite a brave face, Washington is clearly worried. At the NATO Summit in November 1991, President Bush demanded immediate assurances that the United States was not "superfluous." On a trip to Japan the same month, Secretary of State James Baker went to great lengths to assure his hosts that America intended to remain an active power in the Pacific, an effort that would have been totally unnecessary only a year ago.

We thought that after the Cold War, the liberated communist nations would follow an American model of politics and economics, as would most of the Third World.

This, too, seemed a given. For forty-five years there were really two competing systems in our minds—democratic capitalism and communism. The first was championed by the United States, inculcated in the two other most powerful and dynamic nations of the free world—Japan and Germany—and more or less embraced by many Third World nations. On the other hand, communism, both its political and economic dimensions, was totally discredited. What we did not envision was that there could arise another form of competition, this time among different kinds of capitalist systems. When the world was divided in two, these distinctions did not seem so important, nor were they as pronounced as they may become. But the differences may go to the heart of what countries will be looking for in the future.

The capitalist systems of America, Germany, and Japan differ significantly in many crucial respects: in the priority given to individual freedom versus the cohesion of their societies and in the relationship between government and business. While most of the nations struggling to shake the yoke of communism are enamored of the American Dream, it is by no means clear that they will want or be able to use the freewheeling

American system. The more tightly woven and highly organized societies of Germany and Japan—both of which have so clearly demonstrated the ability to revive their nations from total collapse—may prove much more relevant and attractive once the immediate euphoria of newfound freedom wears off.

Americans have assumed, moreover, that in an interdependent world there would be economic convergence on the American model. But this might not be the case. The formerly communist nations behind the iron curtain are more likely to emulate the mixed capitalism of Western Europe, the most successful case being Germany. The "Asian tigers"—Taiwan, Singapore, South Korea, Thailand, Malaysia—are already following the path of Japan. America's market system once produced unprecedented prosperity, to be sure. But for nations struggling to get on their feet, for those worried about explosive pressures of unemployment, for those trying to foster investment rather than consumption, for those looking for proven manpower training programs, for those desperate for stable banking systems that can provide long-term capital, for those who want the best way to develop technology for commercial application, is the United States likely to be the most practical model?

Why does it matter that the old assumptions cannot be trusted? It means that we have to go back to basics. We have to accept that the Cold War era was a unique period, and that the changes that will now occur will go well beyond what America has been willing to consider. It's not simply that there is no common enemy like the former Soviet Union; not simply that Japan and Germany will be more assertive; not simply that we're in for tougher economic competition. The roots of the world as we have known it are being pulled up. The definition of interests, friends, foes are all changing. "There is a pervasive sense that the world is on the threshold of a new era," wrote Zbigniew Brzezinski in late 1991.[13] And so we are. But as the old framework shatters, the forces of divisiveness, not of cooperation, are gaining momentum. The events of the past two years are enough to focus our minds, but more telling evidence is to be found in the underlying pressures that will drive the societies of the Big Three in different directions. These include not only historical events but how we have interpreted them—in particular, how America has viewed Germany and Japan over time, and what it means for the future.

CHAPTER II

Germany and Japan in the American Mind

For most of the last hundred years, Germany and Japan have been at the heart of America's international concerns. For much of this time the two countries have been American obsessions. Americans have seen them as fierce economic competitors, but also as promising markets. We have seen them as military threats, and, more recently, as key allies. Both nations have sent millions of their people to live and work in the United States, bringing their literature, architecture, and cuisine with them. Germany and Japan are the only industrial nations that America occupied with soldiers, the only societies that the United States tried to regenerate from the ashes of war and remake in its own image. In no other countries has the United States held such hopes and fears, so consistently and for so long. We hoped that both would adopt American consumerism and democratic traditions, and that "they" would become just like "us." We feared that these two nations, with their cohesive societies, their awesome efficiency, their willingness to make national sacrifices, and their perceived need for expansion beyond their borders would present perilous challenges to our way of life.

America is the only nation that often talks about Germany and Japan in the same breath. England and France do not, because their relationship with Germany has been much closer, for bad and for good. The same goes for Russia. China's interaction with Japan, on the other hand, has been far more intense than with Germany. Because American geography forces us to look both west and east, because our history has involved us in both European and Asian wars, because of the responsibilities we undertook after World War II in both Europe and Asia, and because of the truly global role we've played since 1945—because of all this, no other nation has been so preoccupied, and *equally* preoccupied, with both Germany and Japan as the United States has been.

Both nations declared war against America in 1941, and we fought each with equal tenacity. But Germany and Japan represented more than a military challenge; in the American view, they operated according to principles and standards that were threateningly different. Here were rival societies with a different and more highly organized type of capitalism than we practiced. Here were two countries bursting onto the world stage with enormous force and speed. Here were societies where government ruled with an iron fist and where individual citizens were subordinated to national aims in a way Americans found offensive. Here were the only two nations in this century whose megalomania caused them to take total leave of their senses and whose disastrous miscalculations caused them to attempt to change the existing world order by force, resulting in the deaths of some fifty million people.

For Americans, Germany and Japan represented something else, too. They became a mirror in which we saw ourselves. "When World War II was over," wrote David Halberstam, "we were rich and confident in a world that was poor and pessimistic."[1] Germany and Japan, more than any other two nations, created within us a sense of omnipotence. Following the war, the U.S. Occupation of both countries influenced our perceptions of ourselves and our role in the world. It is because of the total and unconditional defeat of Germany and Japan that America grew to believe that war worked, that it was worthwhile—in contrast to the conclusions we drew from World War I, which had fostered deep disillusionment. America always saw itself as a generous country, and the way we befriended our former enemies reinforced our self-image of being magnanimous people. In our minds, the occupation was not just a total success, but tangible evidence that other people—proud people who had in the past been fierce warriors and highly competitive businessmen, and who gave the world great cultural gifts—could be remade in our image.

Up until the time we occupied Germany and Japan, there had been a strong strain in American thinking that by ruling over others, we would corrupt our own democratic institutions at home, that in the words of Carl Schurz, the famous antiimperialist, a democracy could not for long "play king over subject populations" without distorting its own democratic principles. The two occupations, however, proved otherwise; they were intoxicating wine. Had there been just one success, just Germany or just Japan, perhaps America would have thought the circumstances were too unique to replicate. But in our minds we transformed Germany *and* Japan, we succeeded in Europe *and* Asia, which meant we could replant the American Dream *anywhere*. No wonder we thought we could bring democracy and free markets to Latin America, Africa, and Vietnam.

After World War II, and long after the U.S. occupation of both countries, West Germany and Japan remained key American concerns. Throughout most of the Cold War they were, in their respective parts of the world, the nations we were most worried about protecting. As American and Soviet troops faced one another along the border that split the nation into western and eastern halves, West Germany was the true dividing line of the Cold War and Washington left little doubt that Americans would again be willing to die to protect "our half." Japan, on the other hand, was the only industrialized democracy in East Asia; in our eyes it was the showcase for what American-style democracy and free markets could do for a nation. It was like an unsinkable battleship in the Pacific Ocean on which we could rely.

PARTNERS AND RIVALS

Economically, these two countries were of overwhelming importance to the United States. As early as the 1960s they were shaping up to be America's fiercest trading competitors and fastest growing markets. Two decades later they were to become Washington's most important creditors. This transformation in economic relationships was to create contradictory feelings in many Americans: on one side, pride and satisfaction that we turned these erstwhile enemies into reliable allies; on the other, deep concerns that we helped engineer their ascendance while our own society was in growing disrepair.

It was the latter fear that seemed to prevail as the Berlin Wall crumbled and the Cold War ended. When the United States hassled over currencies and interest rates, it was the German mark and the Japanese yen that we focussed on, and our antagonists were the Bundesbank and the Bank of Japan. When the Uruguay Trade Round collapsed in December 1990, both Germany and Japan were in the forefront of opposition to U.S.

demands. When we talked about economic systems that were different and threatening to our own, we were talking about our two allies' tightly woven economies, where government, banks, industry, and labor seemed to work together so well. When Saddam Hussein invaded Kuwait and America mobilized for combat, it was Germany and Japan to whom we looked for large-scale financial help and it was their slow and begrudging response that enraged us.

By the early 1990s Germany and Japan seemed to be entering a new phase. They were feeling freer to be themselves since anytime over the last forty-five years. With no Soviet military threat to bind them so closely to America, centrifugal pressures were gathering force. Chancellor Kohl denied it; intimate ties with America were among Germany's highest priorities, he was fond of saying. Prime Minister Kaifu denied it; he and virtually the entire political-industrial establishment in Tokyo saw no choice but to continue close relations with the United States. Americans couldn't help wondering, however, whether the collapse of the Berlin Wall was also the beginning in a collapse of the post–World War II ties with our two protégés. At a minimum, we were under few illusions that in the New World Order we would wield the same degree of influence as we did these past several decades.

As we look ahead into the mid-1990s and beyond, America's relations with Germany and Japan are again in flux. Nevertheless, Americans will see the future *de novo* but with the heavy baggage of how we have seen two nations in the past. We will have in our heads the lessons of history, and whether or not they are the right lessons for the 1990s, it will be impossible to untangle the future from what happened before.

GERMANY IN THE AMERICAN EXPERIENCE

America's attitudes about Germany have ranged far and wide: from Hansel and Gretel living in a gingerbread house to goose-stepping militarists; from poets and musicians to heinous murderers; from arrogant foes to close friends.

It was in 1683 that the first German settlers set foot on American shores—thirteen Quakers settled outside of Philadelphia in what became Germantown, Pennsylvania. They were the forerunners of some 60 million Americans who, by the 1980s, would claim German ancestry. After the British Isles, the German-speaking countries of Central Europe have supplied the largest contingent of the American population. Americans began to form strong images of Germans in the late 1700s based on the efficient Hessian mercenaries, which the British employed to fight against America's rag-tag Continental Army, as well as from the reputation of Baron von Steuben, who endeared himself to the American cause by becoming the chief drillmaster to General George Washington's troops. Since then German immigration has helped shape American stereotypes of who Germans are—hardworking, highly organized, quality conscious, stubborn, conservative, and deeply devoted to family.

Throughout the nineteenth century German immigrants enriched many aspects of American life. They provided talent for the first American symphony, introduced German educational methods from kindergartens to the reform of higher education, helped develop a good deal of American agriculture in the midwest, and personified—through names like Anheuser-Busch, Steinway, Weyerhauser—diverse parts of the industrial scene. John Roebling (1806–1869) revolutionized the art of bridge building and engineering when he designed the Brooklyn Bridge; Thomas Nast (1840–1902), the great nineteenth-century political cartoonist, gave us indelible images of corruption at Tammany Hall as well as the donkey and elephant as symbols of our two major political parties. Ottmar Mergenthaler (1854–1899) revolutionized the art of printing with new linotype technology. Alfred Stieglitz (1864–1946) was one of the great figures in American photography. Carl Schurz (1829–1906), Robert F. Wagner, Sr. (1877–1953), and Henry A. Kissinger (1923–), became major political figures. German immigrants also provided the nucleus of some of this nation's great financial family dynasties, including the Astors, the Rockefellers, the Morganthaus, the Kuhns, the Loebs, the Lehmans. In the 1930s and 1940s Germans fleeing persecution came to the United States and invaluably enriched American science, including most notably Albert Einstein. Refugees like Paul Tillich and Hannah Arendt also added great depth to the study of philosophy. These names tell only a small part of the story of German contributions to American society. There was, however, also a darker side to the German influx. Before and during World War I, a German fifth column operated in America; before World War II some self-serving Germans fanned the flames of American isolationism in order to help Hitler. But for the most part, the overwhelming part, America accepted Germans with open arms.

Americans tend to think of Germany as a nation much older than our own. In fact, a unified German nation was created only in 1871, almost a hundred years after the proclamation of American independence. For most of the nineteenth century, Washington and Berlin were busy consolidating their own nations, and there was little sustained or meaningful contact between them. But once modern Germany began to emerge under Otto von Bismarck, it seemed destined to share the limelight of the world stage with America. Both were industrializing quickly, both were intent on becoming naval powers, and both were developing according to very different notions of what society should be and how it should be governed. In addition, both nations were searching for export markets, while pursuing protectionist policies at home.

Emerging Problems

The growth of German economic and industrial power in Europe was dramatic: it started late and occurred in a telescoped time period. In the mid-nineteenth century, Germany was well behind England in its industrial modernization. Within a few decades it caught up, and then moved ahead. The implications, at least for the European balance of power, were not lost on some of the keener American observers. After visiting Germany in 1887, Henry Adams wrote, "For the last generation, since 1865, Germany has been the great disturbing element in the world, and until its expansive force is decidedly exhausted I see neither political nor economic equilibrium possible." Four years later, writing from St. Petersburg, Russia, Adams's view had not changed. "Germany, from this point of view, is a powder magazine. All her neighbors are in terror for fear she will explode, and sooner or later, explode she must . . ."[2]

The earliest commercial clashes between Germany and the United States centered on agriculture, reflecting the fact that Bismarck was highly protective of the agrarian lords, the Prussian Junkers, who constituted much of his political power base. For example, American farmers screamed when the Germans prevented the import of U.S. pork in 1883, citing inadequate U.S. inspection procedures. But the United States itself was not pure; in 1890, Congress enacted the McKinley Tariff, a serious blow to German sugar interests.

An early political row came during the Spanish-American War in

1898. When Admiral Dewey assaulted the Philippines, he found a large German squadron anchored in Manila Bay. Its alleged purpose was to grab any territory America did not want for itself. While there was no shooting between the navies, the Americans viewed Germany's intentions with great suspicion. In the Boxer Rebellion of 1900, when the Chinese rose up against foreigners, America saw the behavior of German troops as particularly ruthless, the kaiser having given orders that "Peking must be razed to the ground."[3] And Washington was particularly worried about German immigration to South America, since it seemed that Germany would not only achieve significant commercial penetration but also acquire naval stations.

The first major outbreak of anti-German feelings in the United States took place in the early 1900s, some of it reflected in popular literature. In 1909 diplomat Lewis Einstein wrote a book on U.S. foreign policy warning against German dominance in Europe. Herbert Croly, who would later found *The New Republic*, called Germany "the chief menace to the stability of Europe." In 1912 Homer Lea wrote a book about the upcoming war between Germany and the Anglo-Saxons. In 1913, Roland G. Usher's book, *Pan Germanism*, said "The Germans aim at nothing less than the domination of Europe and the world." In the years preceding America's entry into World War I, public opinion turned decisively against Germany. Germans were seen to be fanning conspiracies in America, and supporting sabotage; among the more famous examples was the bombing of the Black Tom Terminal in New York Harbor, where war materials were stored. But the chief cause of American anger—and a major reason for America's entering the war—was the unrestricted German submarine warfare against British and neutral American vessels, which resulted in the deaths of innocent American passengers.

It was because of Germany that America broke with its isolationist tradition and sent its troops into a European war. When it was over, the Treaty of Versailles proclaimed a new order for Europe, and imposed extremely onerous terms on Germany. In the end, the U.S. Congress never ratified the Versailles treaty, which was seen as an entangling alliance best left to the Europeans. Isolationist sentiment grew in America, and once again the nation turned its back on Europe. It was disillusioned with the results of the war, and preoccupied with the 1920s economic boom and the Great Depression that followed. But relative to the other victors, Washington played a benevolent role toward Berlin. The harsh peace was clearly untenable for the Germans. America took the lead in renegotiating reparations payments, and it granted significant loans to Germany to allow the economy to recover. Owing to its distance from Europe, to its natural sympathy for the downtrodden, and to its admiration for German technological achievements and culture, Americans were the quickest among the allies to forget the horrors of World War I.

But as the 1930s wore on and Hitler rose to power, alarms started to sound again. Americans became agitated over reports of book burnings, purging of German universities, growing censorship in the German media, and other limitations on freedom of expression. They saw that anti-Semitism was growing. The financial community grew nervous when Germany could not repay its loans. When Berlin inaugurated a plan of controlled trade, some of it highly subsidized, Washington retaliated with higher duties on German products. By the time Hitler invaded Poland, igniting war in Europe, most Americans had again turned against Germany. Their basic hope to stay out of the war was strong, but this resolve was shattered when Germany, allied with Japan by treaty, declared war on the United States four days after the bombing of Pearl Harbor. From that day until now, U.S. involvement with Germany ceased to be episodic.

The War and Its Aftermath

The names of major battles fade, but they are recalled in books and movies, and for many Americans they still evoke memories of fierce struggles, great sacrifices, and sweet victories: Anzio, Monte Cassino, Normandy, the liberation of Paris, the Battle of the Bulge, the crossing of the Rhine, the seizing of Berlin. Americans remember paratroopers falling from the sky; tank battles in the heart of Europe; massive waves of strategic bombing; secret agents infiltrating behind enemy lines; partisans in enemy-occupied territories. We think of the "home front"—the industrial machine swinging into action; streets jammed with men in uniform; millions of young women waiting for their husbands to return; families sitting by the radio listening to President Roosevelt or Edward R. Murrow. For America there was never a war like the one fought against Germany—never such a clear cut case of right and wrong, of protecting the national security. It was, in the perception of nearly all U.S. citizens, a just war.

Hitler was viewed as evil incarnate, even before his most horrible atrocities and crimes against humanity came to full light. And when they did, when it was clear what he and German society committed, it was almost too much to deal with. It *was* too much, in fact, and the impact and implications would take much longer than fifty years to digest, as evidenced by the spate of books and articles and first-hand accounts still emerging in the 1990s. The library at Columbia University, for example, lists 656 books published about the holocaust between 1985 and 1990 alone, including scholarly histories, collections of letters and pictures, oral testimony, and memories of survivors. The memories were kept alive not just in books or in recollections of survivors, either. On January 20, 1992, for example, a new memorial was erected in Berlin in the house where the decision to impose the Final Solution was made.

And so America led the allied charge against Germany, forcing it into unconditional surrender, bombing to rubble such cities as Berlin, Hamburg, Cologne and causing significant destruction of smaller cities like Potsdam. Americans were numbed by the statistics and the photographs: ten million homes were destroyed; almost every major bridge became impassable; railways were in even worse condition. In cities everywhere people could be found living in sheds and in cellars, often sick with dysentery and typhoid. In Berlin, the once thriving capital of Central Europe, 149 schools were demolished and Berliners used row boats to navigate the flooded tunnels of the nonfunctioning subway system. To General Lucius Clay, commander of America's occupation forces in Germany, Berlin looked "like a city of the dead." [4]

From 1945 on, Germany became an American preoccupation. Washington worried about yet another revival of nationalism. It worried about the legacy of Nazism. It worried about whether the rest of Europe could recover while Germany remained prostrate. It worried that the post-Hitler political vacuum might be filled by communists. It feared that the imminent division of Germany into two halves—one belonging to the Allies, one to the Soviets—would bear the seeds of another global confrontation. Indeed, for the next half century, almost every aspect of American policy toward Europe—the establishment of NATO, the idea for the Marshall Plan, the encouragement of a Common Market for

European integration, Washington's relationship with Germany—derived from these concerns.

Amid these immediate geopolitical worries was a sense of history—American officials remembered the chaos that had characterized the Weimar government in the years between 1919 and 1933. Washington understood the need to avoid imposing a peace that was too harsh, and the need to help German pro-democratic leaders to deliver a better life for their citizens. As happened after World War I, the United States quickly became Germany's major benefactor, the driving force in promoting its economic recovery. It refused to accept France's call for increased reparations and permanent limits on Germany's industrial capacity. It fought against Moscow's desire to combine massive reparations and strong central control. The aims of the United States were summed up as early as September 6, 1946, by Secretary of State James F. Byrnes. "The American people," he said, "want to return the government of Germany to the German people. The American people want to help German people to win their way back to an honorable peace among free and peace-loving nations of the world."[5] Germany became an American protégé in the emerging Atlantic Alliance. It became a symbol of America's new world outlook.

The Marshall Plan of 1947 helped Germany, along with the rest of Europe, to recover. The North Atlantic Treaty Organization would eventually incorporate Germany into a transatlantic security pact. But perhaps no event so illustrated the intimate German–U.S. relationship as well as the Berlin Crisis of June 1948. Moscow closed the overland routes between the western part of Germany—the zone that the Allies occupied —and Berlin, which was located in the eastern, Russian-occupied zone. (Berlin itself was a divided city, with the western half belonging to the Allies, the eastern half to the Soviets.) American and British transport planes wasted no time in mounting a major airlift—the Berlin Airlift— eventually carrying eight thousand tons of food, fuel, and goods daily. From that moment Berlin became the battlefield of the Cold War. Because of tremendous support and enthusiasm on the part of West Germans and West Berliners, the event also became a symbol to America of West Germany's determination to fight for its right to remain in the Allied camp, and strengthened its own resolve to oppose the Soviet Union.

If the build-up of East-West tensions brought America and West Germany close together, so did the American Occupation of the nation itself. In those early postwar years Germany became an extension of the American political system. American soldiers guarded Germany's borders. Marshall Plan funds provided a good deal of foreign exchange. Washington tried to reform German schools and labor unions, to break up its economic cartels, to write a new constitution. Along with the parallel efforts in Japan, this was the most far-reaching tutelage of one major industrial nation by another ever attempted in modern history.

American involvement concerned not just Germany's future but its past. German tribunals in the American zone tried some 930,000 cases of Nazi war crimes; of these, 9,000 criminals went to prison, 22,000 were barred from public office, 25,000 lost some or all of their property, and more than 500,000 were fined. Although the effort was not sustained, American efforts at denazification were the strictest of all the Allies'.[6]

There was a program to impart American culture, too. Books were translated into German, exhibitions of American art were sent over, and musical and theatrical performances went on tour. "American houses" were set up in major cities, and educational exchange programs were quickly established for German students who wanted to study in the United States. Germany was on its way to becoming the most Americanized nation in Europe, a development reflected in close personal ties between Konrad Adenauer, West Germany's first postwar chancellor, and various American ambassadors, secretaries of state, and presidents. Adenauer's successor, Chancellor Ludwig Erhard, carried on the tradition.

America, Britain, and France officially recognized the German Federal Republic on September 21, 1949. American-German ties continued to grow, but the intimacy of the immediate postwar years, and the senior-junior relationship became somewhat more balanced. One of the most pivotal events occurred not in Europe but in Asia, when North Korea invaded South Korea on June 25, 1950. Fearing the onset of a communist offensive around the world, America redoubled its efforts to accelerate Germany's integration into the West, militarily and economically. From this point onward, many of the restrictions levied by the Occupation on defeated Germany were relaxed. Moreover, the Korean War itself caused an economic boom in Germany as steel firms and others became suppliers to the U.S. defense forces.

U.S.–German Relations in the Cold War

One constant refrain during the Cold War years was the tension between Washington's preoccupation with the Soviet threat and West Germany's less singular and more complicated agenda with the U.S.S.R. America's focus was exclusively on containing Soviet aggression, and Europe was the potential battlefield. While West Germany never wavered from being on Washington's side, it was more reluctant to antagonize Moscow for fear that this would impede the ultimate objective of prying East Germany loose and achieving unification. At the other extreme, Bonn worried that the United States might make a deal with the Soviets that would entail giving away East Germany in return for the Soviet Union's agreement to pursue detente. Bonn was also reluctant to have the United States station nuclear missiles on its soil, since in the event of a war Germany would clearly be the first target. The U.S.S.R. was on Germany's doorstep; from the late 1960s on, therefore, Bonn, far more than the United States, became a strong proponent of *ostpolitik*—more normalized relations with the East, a policy strongly advocated and persistently pursued by West German chancellor Willy Brandt. "If one asked a typical citizen of the Federal Republic to list the beneficiaries of detente," recalled American Ambassador Arthur F. Burns, "he could point to the normalization in and around Berlin, to improved personal contacts between the citizens of the two Germanys, to the return of several thousand ethnic Germans from Eastern Europe . . . On the other hand, a typical American citizen, if asked to identify how detente had affected his life, would be hard put to respond."[7]

While Washington always shared with Bonn the goal of reincorporating its eastern portion, there was some ambivalence as well. At times, the United States worried that a reunified Germany could once again become a threat to its neighbors and an unstable element on the Continent. At other times, Washington feared that a united Germany with roots in both the West and the East would opt out of the Cold War altogether by assuming total neutrality.

Economic tensions also marred U.S.–German relations during the Cold War. America subsidized German recovery by providing generous foreign aid and unilaterally opening its markets to German goods. This became less palatable as the German economic miracle proceeded. As Germany recovered, however, it became more and more enmeshed in the European Common Market, so that U.S. dealings on trade and finance frequently meant having to deal with several West European nations as a group. In the 1970s, in particular, skyrocketing energy prices and inflation caused Washington to lean hard on Germany, at that time the world's second most powerful economy (still ahead of Japan), to expand its economy as a stimulus for U.S. exports. But Bonn was opposed to growing too fast for fear of undermining price stability. In 1978, however, under severe pressure from Washington, it accelerated its growth engines. As Bonn had warned, inflationary pressures were ignited in the Federal Republic and the experiment failed. It was a powerful lesson for Germany. Never again would it accede to similar American demands—which were, nevertheless, still made almost every time U.S. growth slumped badly.

In October 1987, another major brouhaha occurred, again over interest rates. The United States accused Germany of maintaining a monetary policy that was too tight. America's objective, once again, was for Bonn to stimulate its economy in order to boost U.S. exports. When it appeared that Germany would not budge, U.S. officials hinted that they would publicly express a view that the dollar should be pegged at a lower rate, thereby threatening the German market with lower-priced American products. The financial markets were greatly disturbed about an apparent breakdown in cooperation between these two key nations; these fears surely contributed to the stock market crash on October 19 of that year.

In the 1960s, 1970s, and 1980s, Bonn's economic strength also was cause for Washington to demand more burdensharing in the security arena. Why should the United States have to pay the total amount for the stationing of its troops on German soil to protect German citizens, as well as to ensure western security, many Americans asked? In American eyes, Germany never contributed enough to the common defense, but no one was willing to rupture the alliance over this or any other issue as long as the Soviet threat existed.

In fact, from the late 1960s, the views of Bonn and Washington were also diverging on a variety of foreign policy issues outside of Europe. Bonn did not support America's involvement in Vietnam in the 1960s, nor did it endorse President Carter's cutting off grain shipments to the U.S.S.R. in the late 1970s after the Soviet crackdown in Poland. Germans resented President Carter for tying foreign aid to human-rights issues, with the attendant risk of antagonizing Moscow, and the likelihood of achieving little, in the German view. Bonn was incensed when President Reagan demanded that Germany abrogate natural gas contracts with the Soviet Union in the 1980s, and regarded Reaganomics and the deficits and debt it spawned as irresponsible, not only for America but for the world economy, too. Every time America demanded Bonn do more to create global growth, the reply was, "What are *you* doing about your growing deficits and your undisciplined policies?"

Finally, the Cold War period was punctuated by lingering and unending American concerns about the Nazi atrocities. For many, it was important that the horror never be forgotten, and that Germany openly come to grips with it. As time went on, there was more and more discussion in Germany about the holocaust. But whenever it seemed that Germany was facing up to its past crimes, there was a desecration of a Jewish cemetery or synagogue, or another splinter party glorifying the Nazi era. And every time, old wounds were reopened. A particularly tense incident took place when President Reagan was invited to visit the cemetery at Bitburg, where forty-nine members of the German storm troopers, the Waffen S.S., were buried along with many other Germans. Many Americans were outraged. Eighty-five members of the U.S. Senate and 257 members of the House of Representatives urged the president to change his itinerary. *The Washington Post* observed: "Nazi Germany was not, as Mr. Reagan seemed to suggest, the handiwork of 'one man' and his regime or even hundreds or thousands. It remains, in the recollection and understanding of those who dare to recollect and understand, a terrifying—and endlessly instructive—monument to what can happen when a people, for the most part, let it happen."[8] Still, the issue remained. Former Ambassador Burns said, "We cannot expect our German friends, especially those born during the past half-century, to live with a sense of personal guilt on account of the Nazi crimes; and we certainly should avoid subjecting every German action to a special test of moral purity. Nevertheless, there is no way for the German nation to escape the historical burden of responsibility for the holocaust. The German people cannot be proud of Beethoven and forget Hitler's crimes against humanity."[9]

As the 1980s drew to a close, America's relationship with Germany exhibited the ambivalence and contradictions that will be projected into the 1990s and beyond. We worried about Germany's growing trade surpluses, which, as a percentage of G.N.P., were as large as Japan's. This did not stop America from rejoicing when they watched German citizens dancing atop the Berlin Wall. But even *that* event raised a host of inconsistent feelings in the United States. While President Bush and most Americans were wholeheartedly supportive of Chancellor Kohl's efforts to accelerate the timetable for unification, many Americans wondered where Germany was now headed, and whether the darker side of its history would again emerge. Lead stories in America's top magazines captured the feelings. "The Germans: Should the World Be Worried?" asked *Time* magazine on November 20, 1989. "Can Germany Be Contained?" asked *Newsweek* on July 30, 1990. These concerns were mixed, uneasily, with Germany's reluctance to play more of a role in the Gulf War.

The Cold War years were indeed an extraordinary period for U.S.–German relations. For most of this time America was committed to defending West Germany with its troops and with nuclear weapons at the risk of its own destruction. But Germany was the battlefield between the United States and U.S.S.R. at the risk of *its* destruction. In this environment all economic and political squabbles were ultimately containable, because they were subordinated to the issue of mutual security.

JAPAN IN THE AMERICAN EXPERIENCE

From the beginning of their history, Americans have had a much vaguer idea about Asia than about Europe. "There is certainly nothing to compare with the intricate web of bonds that tie [the American] in so many ways to Europe and Europeans—his near or remote origins, cultural roots, language, religion, history, picture of the world," wrote Harold Isaacs.[10] Asia, in contrast to Europe, had symbolized a sense of the remote, the exotic, the unfamiliar, the inscrutable. School children have at least passing familiarity with the Magna Carta, Shakespeare, the French Revolution, Julius Caesar. Their memories of Asia are vaguer and filled with distorted images—Chinamen with pigtails and bound feet, peasants with lamp shades for hats, Japanese with buck teeth. Only a few names like Confucius or Genghis Khan are recognizable.

Asian geography has also been a mystery to most Americans. While the outlines of a map of Europe seem vaguely familiar, Asia and Oceania were uncharted territory to most students. "The average American," wrote author William Manchester about the era of the Spanish-American

War, "didn't know whether the Philippines were islands or canned goods." During World War II, Americans were totally unfamiliar with the geography of the Pacific battlefield. Most of what they knew was from movies. Few ever heard of Yap, few knew the difference between New Caledonia and New Guinea. "The U.S. Navy," said Manchester, "began the war using eighteenth-century charts . . . Often the only way MacArthur's soldiers could find out where they were was by capturing enemy maps."[11]

Nevertheless, America's emergence as a world power was linked at least as much to Asia as to Europe—perhaps more so. Among America's earliest diplomatic initiatives outside the western hemisphere were Commodore Perry's opening of Japan in 1853 and its demand for an Open Door to China in 1899. Shortly afterward Commodore George Dewey steamed into Manila Bay, opened fire on Spanish ships, and laid claim to the Philippines as America's first colony. Indeed, it was the annexing of the Philippines that placed the American flag in regions where it was vulnerable to intimidation or attack by other powers, where security was no longer insured by geography, and where it was essential to build a big navy. In 1905, President Theodore Roosevelt helped negotiate an end to the Russo-Japanese War; it was America's first major role as an international mediator. It was the Japanese attack on Pearl Harbor that finally mobilized Americans to enter World War II—the one event that irrevocably thrust America onto the world stage and that led it to become a global superpower. America fought its first bloody war against communists in Korea. A decade later it tried again in Vietnam.

Indeed, America's outlook on world affairs was inordinately shaped in Asia. Europe represented the "old," Asia the "new." Europe was the corrupt society we left behind; the Pacific presented us with the challenge to conquer new frontiers. The "heathens and peasants" across the Pacific were thought to be more susceptible than the Europeans to American exhortation about Church, family, education, good government, free markets.

Establishing Contact with Japan

American attitudes toward Japan have alternated between fear and admiration, between mistrust and benevolence. Japan evokes images of strong American personalities—Commodore Matthew Perry breaking down the doors in 1853, Theodore Roosevelt sending the Great White Fleet as a demonstration of American power in 1907, Secretary of State Henry Stimson refusing to recognize Japanese conquests in Asia in the 1930s, Franklin Roosevelt declaring war following the Japanese attack on Pearl Harbor, General Douglas MacArthur acting as regent during the American occupation.

Unlike Germany, moreover, America faced Japan across an ocean with no one in between. Contacts were not diffused by neighbors. The relationship began in the middle of the nineteenth century with great intensity, and for nearly a century and a half there has been no let-up.

From the beginning, America tried to break down barriers. Even before Commodore Perry there were repeated attempts by American merchants to trade with the Japanese, who repelled them with cannon and gunshot, diverted them to ports where they were blockaded or sequestered, and always barred them from meeting anyone important. When, on July 8, 1853, Perry arrived, signalling that America would not be deterred, the Japanese were horrified. According to Japanese sources, "The whole city was in an uproar. In all directions were seen mothers flying with children in their arms, and men with mothers on their backs. The tramp of war-horses, the clatter of armed warriors, the noise of carts, the parade of firemen, the incessant tolling of bells, the shrieks of women, the cries of children, dinning all the streets of a city of more than a million souls, made confusion worse confounded." [12]

America's interest in Asia and Japan was always heavily commercial. The American imagination was fired up by the writings of Marco Polo, who described fabulous riches and a way of life that was "a mixture of extravagance and wickedness." Indeed, commercially and morally, Americans saw the opening and reforming of Japan as part of its own inexorable destiny.

America also had a missionary purpose. At first, the goal was to bring Christianity to Japan. One of the earliest American geography texts, first published in 1784, described Japan as the "grossest idolaters and irreconcilable to Christianity." [13] Not long after, America wanted to reform Japan more broadly. After Perry concluded his mission, Secretary of the Navy James C. Dobbins said that the new treaty would "advance the cause of civilization, liberty and religion." A Boston newspaper wrote that "it was time the Yankee schoolmaster was sent." [14] These sentiments foreshadowed America's bold experimentation during the Occupation, and even America's current attack on Japanese customs and institutions that affect international commerce. We have always tried to change Japan.

Americans nevertheless admired Japanese art and architecture, including the screens, the fans, the lacquerware. In 1876 the Philadelphia Exhibition of Japanese Art and Architecture drew millions of visitors. "Huge crowds waited for hours to enter the Japanese house, made of fine-grained wood mortised, dovetailed, beveled, assembled without a single nail, decorated with lattice work, sliding panels, and black tiles with elegant white trim, all set on the grounds of a delightful garden of dwarfed evergreens and bonsai trees," said one observer.[15] In 1886, Edward S. Morse published *Japanese Houses and Their Surroundings* with illustrations and technical details. Tiffany & Company sold Japanese articles. Americans admired the way Japan was able to refine Western technology. Japan's achievements were "extraordinary, surpassing in some particulars those of the nations of the West . . . They imitate perfectly our manufacturers," said the American Annual Cyclopedia in 1861.[16]

America soon became Japan's benefactor. In 1883 it helped Tokyo revise a series of one-sided treaties that favored foreign countries. In the late nineteenth century, the United States helped Japan develop its navy, selling it ships and sharing construction techniques. Japan bought its first submarines from America. Washington supplied advisors to help with engineering, agricultural production, and the practice of diplomacy. America was not Japan's only friend and teacher—Germany did a lot, too, especially in areas like medicine, military training, and civil service organization—but the United States was heavily and directly involved. Even as late as 1905, America tried to help Japan in its international conflicts, this time acting as a mediator to end the Japanese-Russian hostilities at the Portsmouth Peace Conference.

Early Trouble Spots

Offsetting America's admiration and its good will was a darker side to the emerging relationship, a side that was, on balance, to become the over-riding factor. Even from Perry's day, the image of Japan as vindictive and deceitful was growing in America. Perry's men found the Japanese to be "the most polite people on earth"; yet Perry was deeply frustrated by what he considered to be their "outright lies, evasions, and hypocrisy." [17] Perry himself argued that it was useless to reason with the Japanese unless persuasion was firmly backed with force. One of the first major misunderstandings between the two countries occurred on the heels of the Perry mission. The U.S. government thought that American families would be able to live in the city of Shimoda for the purpose of facilitating trade. When Americans began to arrive, however, the Japanese sent them home, saying the treaty clearly implied that only Japanese nationals could handle cargo. Such differences in interpretation were echoed throughout the history of U.S.–Japanese relations, from disputes over the naval balance, to tensions over China, to different views over trade agreements. The American traders left in a huff, returned to California, and organized the first anti-Japanese lobby. A spate of anti-Japanese editorials appeared. Suits were filed against Japan.

The journals of Townsend Harris, America's first consul to Japan, reveal enormous frustration, too. He was kept waiting for fourteen months, for example, before he could get a meeting with the shogun he had come to see. His description of one incident is revealing. "I have received a circular from the United States Patent office asking for a variety of information about cotton. Today I have received [the reply from the Japanese government.]," he wrote in his journal on May 14, 1857. "It is a beautiful specimen of Japanese craft, cunning and falsehood. Their great object appears to be to permit as little to be learned about their country as possible; and, to that end, all fraud, deceit, falsehood and even violence, is justified in their eyes." [18] These early impressions helped set the pattern for a good deal of American thinking until this day.

Indeed, acrimony was building from the start. In 1852 a California newspaper said, "Japan must be compelled to contribute her share into the great treasury of knowledge. She must give more than her meager mite of lacquered ware, elaborately carved images and similar specimens of curious manufacture." [19] In 1894 the U.S. Senate held hearings about the problems of exporting to Japan. Two years later the National Association of Manufacturers Report entitled "Commerce and Industries of Japan" concluded that Japanese industriousness and wage scales created a situation where nothing but total protection could keep out Japanese products. America was complaining about Japan's disregard of its copyright laws, including incidents where Japanese businessmen used well-known American trade names like "Colgate" to sell their products, without having any relationship with the U.S. company.[20]

Every one of these problems was to be a theme throughout the twentieth century. In fact all the contradictions imbedded in the way Americans saw Japan from the beginning were destined to survive through the years. When Sheila Johnson, writing about American views of Japan in 1988 said, "The favorable Asian stereotype includes such attributes as patience, cleanliness, courtesy and a capacity for hard work; the unfavorable one emphasizes clannishness, silent contempt, sneakiness, and cruelty," she could have been paraphrasing the thoughts of Commodore Perry or Townsend Harris.[21] So could Ruth Benedict, in her classic post–World War II sociological analysis of Japan that influenced generations of Americans. "The Japanese are," she said, "to the highest degree, both aggressive and unaggressive, both militaristic and aesthetic, both insolent and polite, rigid and adaptable, submissive and resentful of being pushed around, loyal and treacherous, brave and timid, conservative and hospitable to new ways."[22]

Collision Courses

Until 1941, there were three fundamental problems between the two nations—an incompatible drive for security in the Pacific, including the conflict over control of China; the U.S. prohibition of Japanese immigration; and tensions over trade policy.

The first occasion when a modern American warship faced its Japanese counterpart was in 1893, ironically not far from Pearl Harbor. America wanted to annex Hawaii, and the Japanese vessel was there to protect Japanese citizens who had already begun to migrate to the islands. Japanese assertiveness caused American nationalists to take note. The United States, however, was already embarked on its path to global power. As a result of the Spanish-American War and the subsequent treaty with Spain, Washington annexed Hawaii, the Philippines, and Guam, making it a Pacific power. It immediately embarked on a program of naval expansion to protect its new possessions, moving from having the fifth largest fleet in the world in 1901 to the second largest, next to Great Britain, by 1909. The implications of the dramatic buildup were not lost on Japan, which itself had had designs on parts of China, Korea, and Formosa.

By the end of the first decade of the twentieth century, many Americans were nervous about Japan's growing power. Japan's victory over China in the Sino-Japanese War in 1894, giving it rights to certain territories, was noted with alarm. Senator Henry Cabot Lodge said that the Japanese "have just whipped somebody and they are in a state of mind when they think they can whip anybody." Japan's victory over Russia in 1905—the first time an Asian power had defeated a European nation in the modern era—established Japan as a major force in the Pacific. By 1908 scholars like Harvard's Archibald Cary Coolidge were predicting that America and Japan were on a collision course. American authors were quick to sensationalize the potential problems. In 1909 Thomas Millard's *America and the Far East Question* accused Japan of robbing the United States of its rightful markets; in that same year E. H. Fitzpatrick wrote *The Coming Conflict with Japan or the Japanese-American War.*[23]

Though a honeymoon of sorts occurred during World War I, when Japan aligned itself with the Allies and took over German possessions in Asia, it was not long before relations turned sour again. In July 1918, both the United States and Japan (among other nations) intervened in the Russian Revolution in Siberia. But America wanted Japan to limit the size of its intervention force to no larger than its own, and it wanted Japan to leave Siberia at the same time it left. Tokyo refused on both accounts. A much bigger problem grew out of the Treaty of Versailles, when the United States voted to nullify Japan's territorial gains as an ally during the war and America refused to agree to Japan's request to insert language into the treaty acknowledging that all nations were racially equal. From Tokyo's perspective, America was building up its navy to confront Japan; it was trying to prevent Japan from satisfying the same imperial goals that the European powers had been able to pursue; and it was fanning racist tension.

Finally, the growing American uneasiness about Japan's intentions in Asia and America's own expansionist ambitions caused the United States to propose a series of agreements up through the late 1920s trying to limit the naval-armaments race in the Pacific by freezing the status quo. The intent of such efforts as the Washington Naval Treaty of 1921 was to restrain Japanese expansion. However, the formulas tended to be ridden with loopholes and ambiguities. From the American perspective, none worked satisfactorily, and frustrations grew.

In 1931 Japan invaded Manchuria. Shortly thereafter it moved into other parts of China. America refused to recognize these territorial acquisitions, and the League of Nations condemned Japan's action. Tokyo withdrew from the League rather than capitulate. As the years progressed, Japan moved deeper into China, butting up against American interests in preserving open markets and freedom of action for missionaries. Eventually, American citizens in China were mistreated, and American business felt threatened. China became a microcosm for all that was going wrong between Washington and Tokyo.

Throughout the thirties, in fact, mutual paranoia was growing. The American press hinted that Japanese agents were being stationed in Mexico, that secret fortifications were being built in the Pacific, and that Japan was eyeing Alaska. Japan had the jitters, too. When, in 1932, National City Bank of New York asked its Japanese branches to collect photographs of their surrounding business districts, Japanese newspapers warned that the United States was gathering information for a bombing raid.

Trade issues also plagued U.S.–Japanese relations. America resented the surge of Japanese imports into the United States in the 1920s and 1930s, and Japan eventually suffered from its dependence on imports from the United States, from which it was buying more than 80 percent of its autos and lumber, 70 percent of its building materials, and 50 percent of its oil. When the U.S. stock market crashed in 1929, the New York silk market collapsed with it and Tokyo, which was selling the United States 90 percent of its silk, was clobbered. American tariffs were then raised, with extra duties from 5 percent–200 percent applied to Japanese products. [24]

Finally, there was the explosive immigration question. By the 1890s Japanese immigration in the United States was growing steadily. By 1905 the American Asiatic Exclusion League was organized, and in 1906 the San Francisco Board of Education ordered Japanese and Chinese children excluded from regular schools. Tokyo was incensed, protested vehemently, and agreed to voluntarily stop the flow of people if the school board rescinded the order. But American xenophobia continued unchecked. In 1913 California barred Japanese from owning land or leasing it for more than three years. In 1924 U.S. legislation once again banned

Japanese immigration. By the time Japan bombed Pearl Harbor on December 7, 1941, United States–Japanese relations had deteriorated beyond repair.

World War II and the Occupation

World War II in the Pacific—Pearl Harbor, Corregidor, Bataan, Midway, Iwo Jima, Coral Sea, Guadalcanal, Leyte, Los Banos, Okinawa—brought different images to the American mind than did the war in Europe. While Germans were seen as being like Americans, Japanese were perceived quite differently. America's harsh treatment of people of Japanese descent reached its apex during World War II when thousands of American citizens of Japanese ancestry were interned in barbed wire camps—among America's greatest civil rights infractions. Suffice it to say, Germans were never rounded up.

The sneak attack on Pearl Harbor, which President Roosevelt called "unprovoked and dastardly," reinforced American views that the Japanese are deceitful. The prevalence of jungle warfare in the South Pacific conjured up feelings that the United States was fighting a barbaric, uncivilized enemy. In his book on the Pacific War, John Hersey quotes an American soldier. "I wish we were fighting against the Germans," he says. "They are human beings, like us . . . But the Japs are like animals. Against them you have to learn a whole new set of physical reactions. You have to get rid of their animal stubbornness and tenacity. They take you to the jungle as if they had been bred there, and like some beasts you never see them until they are dead." [25]

Hollywood reinforced the idea of Japan as a cruel and ruthless people, devoid of scruples. In movies such as A *Prisoner of Japan, Menace of the Rising Sun, Remember Pearl Harbor, The Beast of the East*, the same themes prevailed: the Japanese were ruthless savages, fiendish and diabolical, usually operating in the jungle where deceit, brutality, and torture were the way of life. Unlike descriptions of Germany, no distinctions were made between good and bad individuals. Germany was generally treated as a problem of evil government, but in American eyes the Pacific War was seen as being fought against an evil race. [26]

Many of these images were soon superseded by a new image of a mushroom-shaped cloud. On the morning of August 6, 1945, an American B-29, the *Enola Gay*, opened the atomic era; a few hours later, some

78,000 people lay dead or dying in Hiroshima. On August 9, a second bomb was dropped on the city of Nagasaki, killing 25,000. On September 2, 1945, Japan formerly surrendered. It was the way the war ended that allowed many Americans to feel a sense of sorrow and pity for Japan. The atomic bombing remained a powerful image in the American mind, representing the dawn of the nuclear age with all that entailed for the potential destruction of the planet.

The Occupation was the most concentrated period of foreign influence ever experienced by Japan. As in Germany, America had found a new social laboratory, a frontier to be conquered, a deferential student who would have to listen to Washington's ideas on politics, economics, and culture. And, indeed, Washington endeavored to remake the nation from top to bottom: a new role for the emperor, a modern constitution, land reform, police reorganization, educational decentralization, trust busting—we tried to do it all. As in Germany, America became a benevolent conqueror, supplying aid and food, and canceling reparations. In a far-sighted gesture of magnanimity, MacArthur refused to treat the emperor as a war criminal, despite pressures from the United States and its allies. When Washington seemed to be leaning toward putting the emperor on trial, MacArthur's stand sent this message: were he to proceed, he said, he would need at least one million reinforcements to contain the guerrilla warfare that could break out.

Compared to Germany there were significant differences in the nature of the Japanese occupation that affected how policies were actually implemented. Hitler had committed suicide, and his aides had fled or were discredited. There was no postwar government in Germany, which meant the allies had to administer everything themselves. In Japan, however, the government continued to function throughout the Occupation, and several members of the wartime cabinet even made the transition to the postwar administration. The result was that from the beginning American demands in Japan were filtered through Japanese politicians and bureaucrats, a situation that certainly moderated the way change took root. Unlike in Germany, the British, French, and Soviets played virtually no role in Japan; America assumed all responsibilities, and one man, General MacArthur, towered over the whole process. As during most of the century, Washington and Tokyo were dealing intensively with one another—with no one in between.

From an American standpoint, the Occupation was a great success.

The behavior of the Japanese was at great odds with the fanatical resistance that America had expected—a fear borne of wartime kamikaze pilots and similar images in the American mind. Japanese cooperation was in fact so far reaching that American views were changing rapidly. In less than a generation, wrote Harold Isaacs, "Americans [were] called upon by events to leap from images of wanton Japanese murderers of Nanking and the Bataan Death March to new images of reformed sinners and earnest democrats, from bloody-handed rapists and sadistic captors to the delicacy of flower arrangements and Kabuki plays." [27]

America and Japan signed a peace treaty in San Francisco on September 8, 1951. During the Occupation and afterward, America and Japan had to come to grips not only with the aftermath of war and the future of Japan, but with the horror of Hiroshima and Nagasaki—the unique horror that America unleashed. The overwhelming consensus of American opinion was that President Truman had little choice if he wanted to end the war without massive U.S. casualties. Nonetheless, Americans were moved by the human tragedies. John Hersey's story *Hiroshima*, which provided a careful reconstruction of the bombing and its aftermath as it was experienced by six survivors, took up the entire August 31, 1946, issue of *The New Yorker*, and the same story was reprinted in its entirety in several American newspapers. During the week of September 8, 1946, the ABC radio network canceled regular programs and had actors reading from Hersey's book, which itself went through fifty printings. Norman Cousins, editor of the *Saturday Review*, brought female victims of the bombing from Japan to the United States for plastic surgery, and these so-called "Hiroshima maidens" won many American hearts. On many anniversaries of the bombing, articles, books, and television specials kept alive the memory of what happened.

As in Germany, the emerging contest between America and the Soviet Union was to drive U.S. policy in Japan. The confrontation in Europe and the outbreak of the Korean War gave the Cold War a global dimension, with Japan being seen in Washington as an essential democratic bulwark in Asia. From this U.S. vs Soviet perspective, all else followed: whatever political and social reforms America wanted to impose had to take a back seat to quickly rebuilding Japanese strength. Because of the Korean War, for example, the United States allied itself with the conservative forces in Japan who represented, more than the others, historical continuities. America did an about-face and allowed the Japanese authorities to clamp down hard on labor unions and left-wing parties. It permitted a slowdown in reform efforts to decentralize education, management of the police, decartelization of the industrial conglomerates. As in Germany, the Korean War created an economic boom for Japanese industry, whose gears began to turn in order to provide equipment and provisions for U.S. forces.

Postwar Tensions

Japan's recovery from devastation, like Germany's, is now legendary. But with recovery came a series of new problems between America and Japan. Trade tensions were a constant theme, interspersed with a variety of other policy crises. First came disputes over the surge of Japanese exports of cotton and tableware in the 1950s. Then, in 1961, U.S.–Japanese relations were shaken badly but temporarily when the U.S.–Japan Security Treaty came up for renewal. Many Japanese were opposed to the treaty, and the renewal caused the greatest mass uprising in Tokyo since the 1918 riots over rice prices. A planned trip by President Eisenhower had to be cancelled. And although the treaty was finally renewed and the crisis blew over, the turmoil raised fears in the United States about Japan's political stability and about its loyalty to the West.

In the 1970s, there were additional economic and political flashpoints: disputes over textiles and apparel; problems with steel and autos. America returned Okinawa to Japan in 1971—removing a major political irritant to Japan—but in the same year it shook the world monetary system when it announced without any warning that the dollar would no longer be backed by gold. Shortly afterward, the United States suddenly slapped an export embargo on soybeans—a Japanese staple—in response to rising prices in the United States. President Richard M. Nixon's visit to China in 1972 also stunned the Japanese. Shortly afterward, the energy crisis drove a wedge between the two countries; Washington felt that Japan was too soft on OPEC, while Tokyo resented America's inability to constrain its own energy demand.

By the 1980s Japan had become America's number one trade nemesis. It had become America's major creditor, too, accounting for some 30 percent of all purchases of U.S. Treasury obligations. Japanese investors purchased landmark real estate in Los Angeles, New York, and other cities. Honda, Nissan, and Toyota made dramatic inroads into the U.S.

auto industry. Japanese electronics firms—Hitachi, Toshiba, NEC—became household words. Japanese semiconductor firms came, seemingly from nowhere, to challenge Silicon Valley. Sony and Matsushita ventured into Hollywood, purchasing Columbia Pictures and Universal Studios, respectively. Japan was seen as the up-and-coming technological superpower, threatening U.S. dominance. A crisis flared in 1989 when America wanted to share the manufacture of the FSX fighter plane with Tokyo and withhold certain advanced technology from the Japanese. American executives studied Japanese management; American professors studied Japanese industrial organization; labor unions studied Japan's collective bargaining. By the beginning of the 1990s, every aspect of American life had some connection to Japan.

The U.S.–Japanese relationship was, once again, poised for big trouble as trade problems escalated against the backdrop of recession and declining competitiveness in America. In addition America had not forgotten that Japan had been slow to help out in the Gulf War. The combination of tensions augured a new stage in the U.S.–Japanese relationship, one embodying virtually all the historical themes. The trade and financial challenge was raising the most fundamental questions about American dependence and even its national security implications. Washington seemed desperate to find ways to force open the Japanese economy for American products from auto parts to supercomputers, including mounting a major attack on the Japanese system of doing business at home. Whereas trade and national security policy between America and Japan had been kept on separate tracks in the Cold War years, now they were seen overlapping. Why were our troops protecting our major trade rival, Americans began to ask? Why wasn't Japan transferring to us the advanced technology they were developing in the same way we once gave them the benefits of our scientific genius? Why wasn't Japan using its wealth for more than its narrow self-interest? American preoccupations with what Japan should do and how it should change became increasingly intense, and the pressure unrelenting.

Germany and Japan—with no other two countries have America's relationships spanned such a gamut of issues and emotions. Of course there are significant differences between America's relationship with Germany and its ties with Japan. The cultural affinities with Germany have been much stronger, stemming in part from the impact of massive German immigration into the United States. Americans know the names of Germans who had a major influence on America, but, when it comes to Japan, we remember mostly the Americans who had an impact on it. Germany has never appeared as closed off to Americans as Japan, nor have Germans appeared as difficult to understand.

Compared to Germany, Americans have always had a greater expectation of what we could accomplish in Japan, and consequently they have had greater disappointments. Because Japan was not surrounded by powerful neighbors, we believed our diplomatic goals could be achieved with fewer complications; this, too, aroused great frustration when results were not forthcoming.

In the last decade Japan has had a much greater impact on American thinking than Germany. Its economic penetration of the United States was far more extensive than Germany's, as was its resistance to U.S. exports and investment. Japan was becoming identified with Americans' insecurity about the future, while fewer such links were made to Germany. Japan was seen as a truly unique force in the world, whereas Germany was viewed as part of a much more familiar Europe.

Despite such differences, however, there has been an inexorable pattern of competition between America, on one side, and Germany and Japan on the other. The first half of this century revealed how intense this could be; the second half was an anomaly because of the peculiarities of the era—the devastation of war, the requirements of recovery, the need to rely on Washington for military defense against the Soviet Union.

The last forty-five years, moreover, reflected a similar pattern in the relationship between America and its two allies. During this time, bilateral ties in each case were unequal, with America dominating militarily, economically, and psychologically. These were also relationships in which economic tensions, while increasing, were subordinated to military alliances, thereby making it much easier to contain economic conflict.

Nevertheless, from an American perspective, Germany and Japan are apt to be linked in our minds for many years to come. As in the past, they will be our principal challengers, if not militarily then certainly in the economic and social arenas that now count for so much. As in the past, Americans will develop many close personal relationships with Germans and Japanese, there will be a great deal of positive interaction and much mutual admiration—but as always, Americans will fear that these two nations are seeing the world and their interests in ways that are inconsistent with American goals.

Americans will be highly ambivalent about their two foremost competitors, just as they have always been. We know that the world is getting smaller and that we will be interacting more and more with Berlin and Tokyo. But we will not be able to decide whether we want Germany and Japan to be strong or weak; whether we want them to be assertive or docile; whether they should remain pacifist or send troops into conflict. We will want them to use their clout to help solve global problems, but we will worry about where the exercise of that power will lead. We will clamor for them to define their vision for the world, then argue that because the vision is not exactly our own, it is a dangerous one.

In the 1990s, Germany and Japan, more than any two other nations, will be part of the debate about how America approaches its domestic problems. Some in the United States will blame their nation's problems on Tokyo and Berlin—especially Tokyo. But many will be more balanced and more reflective and will ask: how do their education systems work? How do they provide health care? Why do we have so many banking problems compared to them? Americans will want to improve their lives in any case, but an added motivation and a political rallying cry to action will be, "We have to become more productive and efficient in order to compete with the world's two most successful countries."

The truth is that for most of our history, Americans have been uncomfortable with Germany and Japan except when there was little interaction or when America was clearly dominant. Neither of these situations describes America's relationship with Germany or Japan today or in the years ahead. The challenge for America is going to be to live with nations that are fundamentally different, without viewing every challenge as a provocation, and without creating the wild gyrations of emotion that characterized the past. This will not be easy, to say the least, because we are about to see the unleashing of drives in Berlin and Tokyo that, because of their Cold War constraints, have been submerged for many years. In fact history has been in a deep freeze since 1945, and the thaw is now occurring before our eyes.

CHAPTER III

Different Historical Legacies

For most of the past fifty years, the different legacies of America, Germany, and Japan had only a minimal impact on their relations with one another. The reason was quite simple: Germany and Japan were obliged to follow American dictates. But now that the Cold War is over, it is natural that Berlin and Tokyo will feel freer to be themselves, freer to revert to deep-seated political and economic patterns. And it is likely that this will result in severe strains in their relationships with the United States and with one another.

There are ideas and practices in all societies that are deeply ingrained and help explain how they see themselves and why they behave as they do. These practices help us to understand why some are stronger economic competitors than others, why some are more afraid of inflation than of unemployment, why they hold differing notions about economic or physical security. The way a nation sees itself and the way it has conducted its affairs over time become particularly important during periods of stress and uncertainty, when there is a strong and natural desire to return to national roots as a psychological anchor point.

If we go back to the historical and intellectual origins of the Big Three —to the American Revolution of 1776, to Bismarck's consolidation of the German Empire in 1871, and to Japan's Meiji Restoration in 1868 —we notice many of the drives and values that still exist today. We see how these three societies balanced the rights of individual citizens with the notion of the broader national community; how they defined their economic objectives; how they saw the applicability of their way of life to other nations; what they most wanted and what they most feared. "The entire man is, so to speak, to be seen in the cradle of the child," said Alexis de Tocqueville, the nineteenth-century French philosopher. "The growth of nations presents something analogous. To examine the oldest monuments of their history I doubt not that we should discover in them the primal cause of the prejudices, the habits, the ruling passions, and, in short, of all that constitutes what is called the national character."[1]

THE AMERICAN EXPERIENCE

For over two hundred years, the hallmarks of the American experience have been remarkably consistent. America has placed individual freedom above almost any other value. It has harbored great suspicions about the concentration of public and private power. It has been an open society with great opportunities for upward mobility. It has assumed a mission of extending its social values and political institutions across ever-expanding frontiers. It has fostered an environment in which government and business are generally adversaries. It has seen itself as a rich country, physically secure, and, as a result, it has been a highly confident society. "The national myth," wrote Frances FitzGerald, "is that of creativity and progress, of a steady climbing upward into power and prosperity, both for the individual and the country as a whole. Americans see history as a straight line and themselves standing at the cutting edge of it as representatives for all mankind. They believe in the future as if it were religion . . ."[2] Not one word of this description, as we shall see, is applicable to Germany or Japan.

American traits can be attributed to many historical factors, but three of the most pivotal were the circumstances surrounding its birth as a nation in the eighteenth century, the subsequent conquest of the frontier over the next hundred years, and the impact of American industrialization on government-business relations.

Individualism

The colonists who came to the new world were looking for political and physical space. Their voyage to Virginia, New York, or Massachusetts was itself a claim of independence. Some arrived with recollections of their families being persecuted and with a determination to rid themselves of similar tyranny. By the mid-1700s, the colonial settlers were already reacting to what they saw as distant and unfair British rule—from "taxation without representation" to strangling commercial restrictions. Influenced by the great European liberal philosophers—John Locke, David Hume, Adam Smith, and others—they were already beginning to formulate ideas that were to influence the republic for the next two centuries. These included the opinions that concentration of power in the hands of a few men is bad; that while government is necessary, the people must have the right and the means to alter it or to abolish it; that the collective welfare is best achieved by every person pursuing his self-interest; that national wealth comes not from government regulation but from unleashing the energies of individuals through free markets. When the War for Independence began, its purpose was clear: to sever the colonies from an imperial power whose rule made it impossible for the colonists to exercise freedoms they demanded.

America seemed so big and so distant from Europe that the temptation to turn its back on the old world was reinforced by the feasibility of doing so. In addition, individualism was able to flourish because of certain conditions that did *not* exist. There was no feudal structure in place— no monarch, no military, no aristocracy. There was no shortage of land, hence no need for a government strong enough to apportion it. There was little concern with invasion from abroad, hence no need for a professional army. Indeed, liberal ideas flourished in a rich material setting where the normal constraints of organized society were less present than in any European nation. "Americans," said Toqueville, "were born equal without having to become so."

While there were debates over *how* to create a society where individual freedom was the highest priority, the objective itself was never in doubt. And the themes that emerged in the eighteenth century—those spelled out in the Declaration of Independence, the Constitution, and the Bill of Rights—have been the predominant themes ever since. They emerge most clearly in those eras that have defined America—the years of Thomas Jefferson, Andrew Jackson, Abraham Lincoln, Theodore Roosevelt, Woodrow Wilson, Franklin D. Roosevelt, John F. Kennedy, Ronald Reagan. Whether Democrats or Republicans, whether favoring a weak government or a strong one, they have all nourished our belief in individual liberty and dignity.

Americans worship individual achievement as no other society does.

We know who invented the cotton gin, the light bulb, the telephone, the personal computer; we know who discovered the vaccine to eradicate polio. Although many of these inventions were the result of joint efforts, we cherish the vision of lone individuals working in solitary confinement, achieving the big breakthrough against all odds.

The American system has rested heavily on the notion of contractual relations for protecting individual rights against arbitrary power, by the state or by anyone else. It is a system designed to regulate conflict— between individuals, between individuals and the government, between the government and industry, between management and labor. It is based on the notion that only through a confrontation of competing interests can the truth be known and justice attained. The arena of conflict is generally the courts, because under the American system law is the protector of individual rights. Moreover, much of our law is above the state. It safeguards inalienable individual rights that the government cannot give or take away. In fact, there is no "state" as such, no central authority in which sovereignty resides. Sovereignty rests only with the people.

Individualism has meant more than freedom of choice or freedom from harassment. It has implied unlimited opportunity. Abraham Lincoln grew up in a log cabin and became president. John D. Rockefeller began as a clerk earning four dollars per week. The dream of unlimited opportunity was planted in millions of American minds between the Civil War and the mid-twentieth century in the rags-to-riches stories by Horatio Alger.

In the American tradition, government has a very limited role. In fact, the Constitution creates a system of checks and balances and a clear separation of power among the executive, the Congress, and the judiciary —all designed to minimize the scope of government's intrusion into people's lives. The more diffused government power is, the better.

America's traditional attitude toward business has been an extension of the individualist philosophy. Companies should compete in the marketplace with minimal interference from public institutions. Their prime objective is to satisfy the individual consumer, or the individual shareholder—only after that comes management, labor, the local community, the nation. Consumer protection has been carried to lengths not seen anywhere else. Antitrust has been a recurring force in American politics. Regulatory policy is conducted by multiple agencies fighting with one another. In matters of commerce, national policies are often undercut by the tug of war between Washington and the states and between the Executive Branch and the Congress.

All of this is not to say that the exaltation of individual freedom was without controversy. From the republic's earliest days, there were strong undercurrents in support of a broader concept of national interest. "The public good," wrote Thomas Paine, "is, as it were, a common bank in which every individual has his respective share." If the "bank" is in disrepair, he argued, individuals, too, will be hurt.[3] James Madison decried the unequal distribution of property for which unrestrained individualism could be at least partially blamed. He argued that equality was a prerequisite for good, democratic government.

American-style individualism had particularly harsh critics in the late nineteenth and early twentieth centuries when unbridled capitalism collided with a rapidly changing society—one that was becoming more industrial, more national, and more stratified into social and economic classes. In these new circumstances, the Jeffersonian vision of decentralized, self-reliant communities had little relevance to the problems of sweatshops, the rise of big corporations, the need to respond to nationwide financial panics, or our growing involvement in world affairs. Still, the notion that individuals should be free to live their lives without government interference remained deeply rooted.

In the twentieth century individualism could not stay pure. Progressives, for example, were a vital force in American politics, hoping to rationalize American industry not through competition in free markets but through tripartite boards in which representatives of government, business, and labor would organize production. The two Roosevelts also brought the power of government to bear on many aspects of American society through trust busting and the growth of federal regulation. During the Great Depression, government intervened to rescue the country. Although many of the results were later voided by the Supreme Court, these collectivist efforts carried over into the Cold War and Great Society eras, when government's influence in America expanded dramatically. But despite all this, America has remained a society that cultivates the idea of "self." Even as the government bureaucracy grew, it never achieved a comfortable role at the center of society, and antistatist yearnings never ceased to exist. Generation after generation, Americans have not been comfortable with an activist government, nor with subordinating individual freedom and satisfaction to *anything*. For much of the twentieth century, in fact, America has looked at extreme forms of any antiindividualist philosophy as its enemy. It fought fascist totalitarianism as represented by Germany and Japan in the 1940s. And it fought the Cold War against a perceived communist threat.

The Frontier

Beyond the strong influence of the Founding Fathers, American values were shaped by the experience of conquering the frontier and settling it. Originally, the idea of frontier was physical—Columbus discovering America, the Pilgrims landing on Plymouth Rock, Lewis and Clark finding their way to the great northwest. But for America it was far more than territory gained; winning the frontier became a state of mind.

As the thirteen colonies expanded westward, Americans had a sense of bringing civilization to the wilderness. They transplanted their political philosophy and institutions. They annexed territories with great physical wealth and extended their markets. "Go west, young man, and grow up with the country," exhorted Horace Greeley. And many did—pathfinders, explorers, crusaders, reformers, those looking for a new start. "Their destiny was manifest: they were driven westward by the hand of God, and they carried with them all that was best of civilization, education, improvement, republican government, and democratic ideals," said historian James Oliver Robertson. "They filled a vast and 'empty' continent with the virtues and institutions of the freest people on earth. This is the myth and the dream."[4]

America's natural inclination to see itself as the best of all societies was clear even before the Republic was founded. John Winthrop, the first Governor of Massachusetts, talked about the new world as being an example to mankind, a "city upon a hill." Later, in 1776, Thomas Paine called America "an asylum for mankind." Moral superiority came naturally, and generation after generation became eager to spread the American idea to an ever larger territory.

The frontier meant emancipation. It encouraged self reliance, improvisation, and entrepreneurship. It created the environment for mobility—and mobility meant opportunity. In the new territories, unregulated trade flourished. Immigrants were easily assimilated because they could settle in virgin territories without disrupting established communities.

When the continental frontier was settled, the process was not over. "Movement has been the dominant fact," wrote Frederick Jackson Turner in the classic 1893 study of the American frontier "and, unless this training has no effect upon a people, the American energy will continually demand a wider field for its exercise."[5] Beyond the California coast lay the Pacific Ocean and the Orient. Beyond that lay the opportunity, following World War II, to transplant the American way of life to Germany and Japan, and, later on, to much of the Third World. "Whether it was 'taking up the white man's burden,' providing 'oil for the lamps of China,' freeing Cuba from Spain, 'making the world safe for democracy,' . . . or 'nation building in Vietnam,' America's mission . . . has become—with the disappearance of the American wilderness— something to be carried out in the larger wilderness which is not America," wrote Robertson.[6]

But Americans saw the extension of their ideals as different from classic imperialism. They always believed that they were sharing their ideals, not imposing them. They always felt that they were expanding not out of grievance, envy, or greed but because it was their destiny and that of those they came in contact with. In the twentieth century, this translated into an American tendency to think, speak, and act in spectacularly universal terms. Woodrow Wilson attempted to export a distinct vision of American society that emphasized free trade and ethnic pluralism. Americans made a similar, and far more successful, attempt to recreate the United States abroad when President Truman pledged to provide political, economic, and military aid to anticommunist governments threatened by foreign invasion and internal insurgency. Presidents John F. Kennedy, Lyndon B. Johnson, and Ronald Reagan were willing not just to provide aid but to fight wars and destabilize communist regimes when the threat was not to American territory but to American values.

Industrialization and Government-Business Antagonism

Along the path of American history there developed a deep antagonism between government and big business—something not found in virtually any other industrial society. This tension began toward the end of the

nineteenth century, and it can be attributed in large part to the fact that
the U.S. pattern of economic development was different from that of
other industrial nations. In all others, big government preceded big business or arose along with it. In America, the opposite was true: for the
most part industrial development was managed and financed by the private sector at a time when the government was small and weak. By 1910,
for example, railroad companies were employing over 100,000 people
each, the American Tobacco Company had capital of almost $500 mil-
lion, and the United States Steel Corporation had been created by
J. P. Morgan in a series of mergers valued at $1.4 billion. Not only was
the government ineffective and imbued with a hands-off ideology, but
there was no other countervailing power—no aristocracy, no military
class, no church, no guilds. As a result, by the last two decades of the
nineteenth century, there was a powerful public reaction to this one-
sided concentration of corporate power. It resulted in a stream of regulatory legislation (such as the Interstate Commerce Act, or the Sherman
Anti-Trust Act) that, in its focus on restraining big business, had no
equivalent in other nations. "With the rise of big business," said Harvard
professor Thomas K. McGraw, "the term 'private enterprise' acquired a
different meaning. It brought, without any question, that very centralized
power against which the Founding Fathers had fought their revolution."[7]

Big business resented the intrusion. It had grown up with an unusual
level of autonomy, and it alone had created the industrial state. Government, it argued, should therefore continue to stay out of its affairs and
let the market regulate itself. But pressure for government action was
fanned by public suspicion and by a press that became obsessed with
what it saw as a "public-be-damned" attitude of big business. The tension
between public and private sectors ebbed and flowed. But a consistent
habit of cooperation never developed and, compared to other industrialized societies, there has been, at best, an uneasy relationship between
business and government throughout this century. This is especially true
of how big business has viewed Washington. Wrote political scientist
David Vogel, "The most characteristic, distinctive and persistent belief
of American executives is an underlying suspicion and mistrust of government."[8]

As the postwar years progressed, American business passed through
several stages. Not all were characterized by opposition to Washington,
however. For example, after World War II, major American firms—

IBM, General Electric, the Ford Motor Company, Westinghouse—came to symbolize the American dream of a better life, and often worked closely with Washington to keep the economy expanding. In the 1950s, 1960s, and 1970s, the big firms were symbols and instruments of American power abroad, reinforcing U.S. foreign policy. But by the 1980s the multinationalization of American business was being seen as a problem as well as an opportunity. Among rising concerns were that some companies were becoming divorced from the American economy. Many were producing abroad, investing their profits abroad, hiring abroad. It was a complicated picture, of course, but this much was clear: many of the big U.S. multinational companies were acting as individual units without any particular allegiance to their home nation. They were acting in the American tradition of exploiting new frontiers with little obligation to national community. "I was asked the other day about United States competitiveness," said the president of NCR Corporation, "and I replied I don't think about it at all. We at NCR think of ourselves as a globally competitive company that happens to be headquartered in the U.S."[9]

GERMANY AND JAPAN

Germany and Japan arose in different circumstances. But before examining each nation individually, some general observations can be made that apply to both and that distinguish their self-images and historic patterns from those of the United States.

For both countries, the welfare of the group—the nation, the community, the firm—has traditionally overshadowed the importance of the individual. The critical social unit in each society is not the person but the family, the town, the company. While individuals in both nations have extensive rights, this has been consistently true only since 1945, and even now German and Japanese citizens are far more conscious than Americans of their obligations to improve the welfare of the groups of which they are a part.

In contrast to America, Germany and Japan can be categorized as communitarian societies. This is more than just a catchy label; it reflects a distinct premise about the purpose of the state and the responsibilities of its citizenry. In communitarian societies, the underlying philosophy is that the individual is an integral part of the whole, and that one's best chance to develop fully is in the context of the state's goals. In an individualist society, on the contrary, each person is regarded as already fully developed, and his or her problem is to protect what he or she has from being taken away by the state. One reason for these fundamental differences is that neither Germany nor Japan experienced a true democratic revolution, in which the rights of individuals emerged as a top priority in society, as happened in France and America. There were democratic undercurrents, to be sure, but they were either too weak to have a major impact on the population or else they were repressed by the government. From such divergent starting points stem different approaches to political and economic institutions.

For Germany, even before nationhood in 1871, the constituent parts of the German-speaking peoples were organized in terms of rulers and subjects, with kings, princes, or bishops reigning over them. In Japan, going back centuries before the modern era, there were emperors or shogun with similar functions. From early on, the government in both societies derived its powers not from its citizens but from the idea of a state that existed above and apart from the people. Today Germany and Japan are representative democracies, but this form of government is not deeply ingrained from a historical standpoint.

For both Germany and Japan, the emergence of tightly knit, hierarchical societies—under both civilian and military rule—stemmed from circumstances that were totally different from the American experience. Both were feudal societies since the Middle Ages. By the time Bismarck forged the German nation and Japan opened its doors to the world after two centuries of seclusion, both nations were well behind England, France, and America in becoming modern industrial states. In order to catch up, strong authoritarian government emerged to marshal the energies of society. Social solidarity was essential, since political tensions would undermine the people's will to work for the state. There was a remarkable similarity in the needs identified by Bismarck and the Meiji leaders to build a nation. In each case, accelerated economic development was to be the means.

Both nations developed in a different geopolitical setting than America. Both felt encircled, crowded, resource poor, and vulnerable. Both were worried about their neighbors. Germany, always at the crossroads of Europe, had a long history of being invaded and ruled by its neighbors; at times, wrote political historian David Calleo, it became "a sort of athletic field for playing out the various dynastic ambitions of the ancient regime." [10] Japan, although an island, had long felt vulnerable to neighbors such as China and Russia. Indeed, in both countries, nationalism developed in reaction to external threats, real or imagined.

While Germany and Japan both lacked the natural resources they needed to be industrialized states, they were energetic and efficient enough to produce finished goods far in excess of what they could consume. At an early stage, therefore, the world market weighed heavily on their consciousness; access to raw materials and overseas outlets to sell their products became obsessions. Economic considerations thus often dominated foreign and security policy, and there ultimately arose in their minds a need to match their economic aspirations with political control over foreign territory. They never became effective colonial powers like Great Britain or France, however, possibly because they started so late, and this surely contributed to their inflamed frustration in the 1930s.

The combination of economic pressures, geographic constraints, and the absence of an individualist philosophy led to the development of many similar ideas and economic institutions in Germany and Japan. Neither Germany nor Japan believed in the idea of a self-regulating market. The interests of the state were more important than the individual profit motive. The natural anarchy of true capitalism was seen as dangerous to orderly economic development. Banks, industrial concerns, and the government forged close relationships in order to support one another. Large-scale organizations, with long-term planning horizons, typified both nations, as did heavy involvement by the state. Cartels were not just prevalent but encouraged. Industrial and financial concentration served another purpose too: Germany and Japan, both fearful of social unrest, and both feeling vulnerable to the destabilizing impact of the business cycle, found the combination of big business and big government helpful in controlling economic cycles.

For both Japan and Germany, in marked contrast to America, the frontier represented a line of trouble and a reminder of their limitations. "The American frontier is sharply distinguished from the European frontier—a fortified boundary line running through dense populations," wrote Frederick Jackson Turner. "The most significant thing about the American frontier is that it lies at the hither edge of free land." [11] In Japan's case, the frontier was summed up with an old proverb, "One step ahead is darkness." Neither Japan nor Germany saw the frontier as an opportunity to spread their way of life; on the contrary—to the extent that the frontier had to be confronted, the stakes were power, security, and markets.

In the late nineteenth and early twentieth centuries, the need to make up for lost time led Germany and Japan into conflict with the existing industrial powers, many of whom sought to hold their expansion in check. Germany and Japan wanted extended empires, but being latecomers, their ambitions became a threat to the established order. The particularly compressed timetable during which they burst on the world scene caused their behavior to be seen as dangerously aggressive by their neighbors. This led to resentment in Berlin and Tokyo, to bitter national grievances, to a sense that they were unfairly being singled out, and to the unending quest to find their rightful place in the sun.

In this century, Germany and Japan have had to adjust to cataclysms that America has never known. Both experienced total military defeat, including bombing, famine, the collapse of trade and currencies, and hyperinflation. Both responded with spectacular national mobilization to overcome and even surpass their previous economic achievements by margins that no one could have foreseen. It is impossible to gauge the impact of these singular achievements on their national psyches, but it is unlikely that less organized societies could have responded the same way.

Finally, despite their admirable records since 1945, Germany and Japan, among the democratic societies that govern the world today, bear the heaviest historical burdens. America with very few exceptions (slavery, the internment of Japanese-Americans, McCarthyism, for example) rejects almost none of its past. Berlin and (to a lesser extent, perhaps) Tokyo are horrified about large parts of theirs.

GERMANY'S PAST

Before it was unified as one nation under the Prussian crown in 1871, Germany existed as a group of separate principalities, cities, feudal kingdoms, and medieval estates, together with a few states, the most powerful being Prussia. While the German groupings were united by language and, to some degree, by culture, there was no single political leader or dynasty who ruled, no capital city that served as a central site for politics, finance, or the arts, no German-wide legal framework for business. For a good deal of its history, in fact, this conglomeration of German entities was consumed by religious war and was the battleground for wider European struggles.

The German states and territories had been in tremendous ferment during the first half of the nineteenth century. After the French Revolution, there were great liberal movements agitating for more popular participation in government. These reached a height in 1848, but ultimately failed. From then on, conservative authoritarianism was to characterize Germany for the next several generations.

There were several reasons why the ideas of the French Revolution did not take hold in Germany, aside from the fact that there was great resistance on the part of the entrenched conservative powers. The liberals were not radicals but reformers. They did not seek to overthrow the existing German leaders—the conglomeration of princes, kings, and noblemen—but only to get their permission to establish a new system. They feared lawlessness and instability, and were preoccupied with orderly change. The reformers, moreover, were convinced that liberalism required a unified Germany with a strong central government. But they could not agree on how such political change should come about. There were too many questions that could not be answered. What were the true borders? Should Austria, for example, be included? What about the German ethnic groups living to the east? Finally, the liberals lacked a political center. In fact, due to the pre-existing fragmentation of the German territories, there was not one revolution but several, all occurring without coordination and hence lacking the force of one powerful effort.

The collapse of the effort was to have formidable consequences for German history. "That the outcome was failure again underlined the different patterns of political development in Germany and Western Europe," wrote historian H.W. Koch.[12] While some of the liberals went into radical opposition, others were co-opted by the conservatives, and some easily slipped back from the role of "citizen" to that of "subject" of their respective kings, princes or other rulers. Many adopted a disdain for politics altogether, and much of the middle class, defeated in its political aims, channelled its energies into commercial affairs. Consequently, in the next twenty years the Prussian economy soared. Germany's flight from politics and its near single-minded focus on economic progress foreshadowed its pattern of development after World War II.

Prussia and Bismarck

Following the failure of the liberal revolution, Prussia, under the political leadership of Otto von Bismarck (appointed to the position by King William I in 1862), proceeded to unify Germany step-by-step. First he went to war with Denmark in 1864 and annexed the duchies of Schleswig and Holstein. In 1866, he crushed Austria in the Seven Weeks' War, solidifying Prussia's dominance of the North German Confederation. Then in the Franco-Prussian War of 1870–1871, he defeated France and absorbed the southern German states of Bavaria, Wurttemberg, and Baden. Bismarck's military victories fired the German imagination. Prussia became the nucleus of the new German Reich and all of Germany was swamped by the Prussian spirit. The Prussian character—rigidly authoritarian, antiliberal, spartan, militaristic, awesomely efficient, and protectionist—would become integral to the evolution of Germany for at least the next eighty years.

In creating the modern German state, Bismarck allied himself with the conservative landholders and the big industrialists. He fostered a social system based on class distinctions and aristocratic privilege. Although he was not unreceptive to many of the cries for social justice, Bismarck fought against political participation and popular rule. His political objective was unencumbered control. In the words of the German sociologist Max Weber, "Bismarck left behind as a political heritage a nation without any political education, . . . a nation without any political will, accustomed to submit, under the label of constitutional monarchy, to anything which was decided for it . . ."[13]

Indeed, nation building for Bismarck was always a heavily economic concept. He was acutely conscious of the economic basis of state power. His objective was to link authoritarian political rule with economic nationalism. The success of the strategy depended on continual economic success, since there would be few political institutions to absorb the shock of an economic crisis. Growth became the central consideration, the sine qua non for national integration and political order.

Germany was far behind its competitors in modernization, and Bismarck's philosophy had an element of urgency behind it. He saw a powerful central government with supporting institutions in business and finance as the way to catch up. Industrial development *was* power, and achieving it required eliminating divisive politics. This was accomplished in several ways.

First, the actual constitution of the state would make Bismarck himself responsible only to the emperor and not to the Reichstag (parliament). Sovereignty resided not with the people but above them. The parliament would have control of the budget, but otherwise its effective role was limited to being a safety valve for discontent and a mirror for public opinion. Second, Bismarck promoted big business syndicates, trusts, and cartels, and other arrangements that concentrated economic power and fostered mutual interests between the state and commerce. At the same time, he supported the formation of large industrial associations to circumvent parliament and to handle issues before they became politically explosive. These included the League of German Iron and Steel Industries, and the central Association of German Industrialists.

A third dimension to Germany's approach to economic development was the marriage of banks and industry. Big banks took large stakes in Germany's companies, creating a unique concentration of capital and technology that was managed in the interest of stability and national development. Fourth, not only did the state support the industrialization process, but it directly participated in it through the creation of nationalized industries. These included mines, blast furnaces, railroads and canals, and banks.

Finally, Bismarck built the first modern welfare state. Among its purposes was to encourage workers to identify with the state rather than with their socialist political leaders. He introduced insurance schemes for accidents, sickness, old age. He reduced working hours for women and children. He constructed special schools, hospitals, and churches for the workers.

One man whose philosophy heavily influenced Bismarck's commercial policy was the German political economist Georg Friedrich List (1789–1846). List had challenged the orthodoxy of free trade as espoused by Adam Smith. While he advocated the abolition of the tariffs among the states of Germany, this was to be combined with a strong protective trade policy for German interests vis à vis the outside world. His argument was that England could afford free trade only because its manufacturing industries were the world's best, but that a latecomer like Germany would catch up only if it could import raw materials cheaply and develop its native industries behind protective walls. Tariffs, said List, could be an investment in national productivity; they might result in a short-term cost, but in the long run the nation will have developed critical capabilities it would otherwise not have had. For List, free trade was an abstraction; like so many other German philosophers of the nineteenth and twentieth centuries, he was preoccupied with the importance of state power.

Bismarck's policy was also influenced by a prolonged economic depression in the late 1870s. At the urging of his conservative supporters, he forcefully embraced a protectionist trade policy for Germany for both agriculture and industry. Together with his progressive social legislation, Bismarck thus married nationalism and liberalism, while attempting to submerge democratic government. The result was economic order, national industrial power, and a total absence of democratic political institutions.

German growth between 1850 and 1913, a period dominated by the Prussian ethic, was phenomenal by any measure. Domestic production grew by 500 percent; per capita production by 250 percent. Between 1871 and 1913, coal production jumped from 29.4 million metric tons to 191.5 million metric tons.[14] By 1910 Germany had outstripped Britain in iron and steel production. In the chemical, electrical, and optics industries, German firms burst onto the world stage challenging their British, French, and American counterparts. Germany's industrial revolution, said scholar Ralf Dahrendorf, "occurred late, quickly, and thoroughly."[15]

Scholars still debate how the German industrial revolution occurred without an independent pluralist social and economic order, as had been the case in America, England, and France. Sociologist Max Weber said Germans willingly subordinated themselves to the ethic of national purpose. Dahrendorf explained that the liberal principle was crushed under the state goal of reducing social conflict via every conceivable institution —from paternalistic cartels to social welfare programs. Historian Thorstein Veblen spoke of the Prussian feudalistic spirit. David Calleo, an American professor of political economy, surveyed all past theories and concluded that Germany's late start in industrializing resulted in a compression of the normal economic development period, which simply foreclosed the possibility of a strong liberal movement. Whatever the explanation, there is little disagreement that Bismarck's legacy had an overwhelming impact on German life until 1945.

World War I and Versailles

In the years between Bismarck's retirement in 1890 and the outbreak of World War I, Germany's growing economic power became ever more consolidated and organized—bigger firms, bigger banks, heavier government involvement. Berlin searched for new markets, while the old agricultural class at home succeeded in protecting its own farms with high tariffs. Rapid economic development was accompanied by the buildup of a world-class navy—Prussian militaristic traditions would allow for no less—and the combination of its new economic and military clout put the nation on a collision course with its neighbors. In 1907, the Kaiser captured the mood. "The more we are able to wrest for ourselves a prominent position in all parts of the world the more should our nation in every class and industry remember that the working of Divine Providence is here manifested. If our Lord God had not entrusted us great tasks He would not have conferred upon us great capacities."[16]

Indeed, Germany was determined to find its rightful place on the European continent and the more established powers were determined to resist. In 1914, it took but a spark to ignite World War I.

It was Germany's humiliating defeat in World War I that sowed the seeds for a much greater disaster some two decades later. In the 1919 Treaty of Versailles, German territory was confiscated, massive reparations were demanded by the victorious powers, severe limitations were placed on German rearmament, and allied troops were to occupy the left bank of the Rhine for fifteen years. The limitations on German sovereignty were bad enough for Berlin; but the forced admission of war guilt was at least as difficult, since many in Germany genuinely felt that no single nation was responsible for starting the Great War. The terms became too much of a burden for the Weimar government to absorb both financially and politically. For fourteen years, grievances and resentment mounted, and government after government fell—twenty-one cabinets and thirteen different chancellors ruled and at no time were there fewer than ten political parties. Foreign powers were blamed for all the nation's political and economic problems.

During the 1920s, hyperinflation overran economic life. Official print-ing presses simply couldn't print enough notes, and special facilities were set up in local communities to stamp banknotes. Wives picked up their husband's checks at the factory to spend them immediately, before the money became worthless. This was to be Germany's first of two such experiences—the other being after World War II—leaving an uncom-promising conviction since the late 1940s that, at all costs, inflation had to be rigidly controlled.

In the late 1920s came the collapse of international trade, and the rise of protectionism everywhere. Germany was hit worse than any of the other continental economies because it relied on exports not only for everyday life but to pay its wartime reparations. By the early 1930s the government could not endure all the pressures.

The irony is that World War I did little to change the old order. The same old feuds flared, the same old faces appeared. The ruling aris-tocracy, the Prussian bureaucracy, the military, the trusts, cartels and syndicates, the close ties between government and business, the social welfare ethnic—all were still there. It was not long before Ger-many's nationalist right wing was calling again for a return to great-power status.

The Nazi Era

When Adolf Hitler came to power in 1933, his Third Reich pledged to regenerate the German spirit, the German economy, and Germany's role in the world. Hitler's National Socialist Workers Party—the Nazi party—evolved into an extreme form of fascism. It embraced an ideology that was hypernationalist, antiparliamentarian, antiliberal. Its objective was national social integration through one party, using whatever means were practical including paramilitary violence.

The Third Reich carried Bismarck's initiatives to monstrous extremes. It brought together many of the strands of German thought that had been in the air since the nineteenth century: Germany as deserving a place among the world's great powers; Germany as having a glorious past; Germany as a state that guaranteed prosperity for its subjects; Germany as a single community with shared values and traditions. "If Nazism did not exist as the only possible response to the German past," wrote histo-rian Harold James, "it nevertheless grew out of a wish to reformulate national traditions and identities in a period when economic aspirations attached to the national unit had so clearly been disappointed." [17]

Hitler mounted Germany's most extreme experiment in central economic planning, aimed at industrial self-sufficiency, full employment, and the wherewithal to rebuild military capabilities. He set out to enlist the German economy in his own service, not necessarily to change its structure. He argued that all economic interests must be harnessed for the state. Hitler's policies included gigantic public investment programs focussing on transportation, synthetic fuels, steel, chemicals; a high agricultural tariff and an attempt to achieve national self-sufficiency in food supply; ruthless suppression of independent labor organizations; regulated trade with other European countries; and an attempt to develop a separate trading bloc that would enlarge Germany's political and economic control over Eastern and Southeastern Europe.

Historians have debated the degree to which German business backed Hitler willingly. Some say business promoted Hitler, others that it cooperated with him to protect itself only when it became a matter of survival. Whatever the case, fascism could easily be imposed on the structure that already existed, one which was highly concentrated, subject to control through its own hierarchical network of associations, accustomed to collaborating with the government, and historically supportive of the identity of its interests with those of the state. Business leaders, moreover, like the officials of the Third Reich, shared the historic German longing for order and stability, for social harmony, and for the suppression of social conflict.

We know the rest—Hitler's secret rearming of Germany, the reoccupation of the Rhineland in 1936, his support for the fascists in the Spanish Civil War, the invasion and annexation of Austria in 1938, the dismemberment of Czechoslovakia in the same year, the secret pact with Stalin, the invasion of Poland in 1939, the historically unparalleled acts of genocide. All would instigate a war that would bring an end to Germany's dreams for many decades, if not longer. What Bismarck had unified in 1871 was now shattered. Within a few years, Germany would be partitioned into western and eastern states as a result of the Cold War.

Post–World War II

Germany's recovery from ruin did not occur overnight, but by the early 1950s, the so-called economic miracle, the "Wirtschaftswunder," was underway. Between 1950 and 1963, total industrial production almost tripled, auto production increased twenty-fold, exports soared, per capita income doubled.[18] Once again Germany was coming from behind to emerge as Europe's strongest economic power. By the early 1960s, Germany was the second largest exporter in the world, after the United States, and the third largest producer of steel.

German policies were critical to its resurgence. Of particular importance was the currency reform, which extinguished the postwar hyperinflation; the removal of price controls on many products; a tough fiscal policy; a relentless focus on exports; tax incentives to save, reinvest, and sell abroad. In addition, Germany fashioned a labor policy, which resulted in extensive cooperation from the unions—overtime earnings were tax exempt, generous pension benefits were extended and adjusted for inflation, and housing subsidies were offered.

How did it happen? There was no one factor. Hard work, discipline, and the influx of German refugees from Eastern Europe eager to work all helped immeasurably. There was the enforced modernization of German industry due to wartime destruction. Foreign aid through the Marshall Plan was a big boost. But it was also the intensifying Cold War that quickly transformed Germany's relationship to the West from foe to friend and forced the Allies to shift the thrust of their Occupation policy from holding Germany down to building it up.

The German policymakers and their American advisers were determined to dismantle, decentralize, and democratize the prewar economic institutions that had given Hitler such concentrated control and power. They insisted on creating a strong federal structure in which the various regional entities had substantial control of their policies and a major voice in national policy; they created an independent central bank and removed price controls; they tried to undo the heavy concentration of industry including industrial-financial conglomerates.

Without question, much progress was made, but it would be wrong to say that many of the historical legacies did not remain. "When the Germans began to construct their economy," wrote Oxford Professor Andrew Shonfield in his classic study of modern capitalism, "they built upon the familiar structural foundation and plan, much of it invisible to the naked eye, as if guided by an archeologist who could pick his way blind-folded about some favorite ruin."[19] The government continued to play a major role in the economy, if not always in Bonn then at the regional level. Economic concentration, while vastly diminished from years before, remained impressive; to take one example, the three big banks—Deutsche, Dresdner, Commerz—were dismantled after the war but were reconsolidated as early as the late 1950s. The tight relationship between banks and industry continued as a pillar of the economy. Industrial associations continued to wield strong influence over the economy. Exports remained a paramount national objective. Bismarck's emphasis on social welfare remained a paramount objective. The new Germany was clearly sired by the old.

On the political front, Germany's primary goal was to integrate itself into the west. It joined the European Coal and Steel Community, the Common Market, and NATO. German leaders, wrote Dahrendorf, were preoccupied with "creating the conditions for putting the ship of state on a steady course by joining it to the European fleet, and making sure there were no shortage of provisions."[20] Also crucial was keeping alive the dream of reunification with East Germany. As relations with Western Europe became tighter, Germany's interest in all of Eastern Europe and the U.S.S.R. began to revive. Geographically and politically, the nation was, as it had always been, at the center of Europe.

Looking back over the years between Bismarck's Germany and today, several themes emerge that clearly distinguish German from American thinking. In Germany individualism has never been a driving force—the state or nation always came first. Germany's frontiers always represented a problem for itself and its neighbors. For most of its history, it has been a closed and introverted society, aloof from its neighbors, characterized by high levels of economic and industrial concentration. The emphasis was on control and stability, consensus and harmony; the diversity and anarchy of real capitalism was always seen as dangerous to society. Unlike the United States, Germany never argued that there was or should be a dividing line between public and private interests; German industrialization was almost always the result of cooperation among financial-industrial conglomerates, on one hand, and public authorities, on the other. State socialism of one kind or another existed from Bismarck onward, with the biggest exception being the Nazi period.

JAPAN'S LEGACY

Japan's mindset—communitarian values, a tightly woven culture, xeno-phobia, its vision of merged public and private interests—goes back centuries. However, it was during the Tokugawa Era (1600–1868), when the nation was virtually sealed off from the rest of the world, that these attitudes and practices were consolidated into the Japanese national character. Japan was heavily influenced by Chinese Confucianism, which had been imported and adopted hundreds of years before and was an ideology based on a society of rigid hierarchical structures. Loyalty was prized, as was adherence to tradition and discipline. The duty of individuals was to work in order to benefit society as a whole. Some of the popular expressions of the Tokugawa Era foreshadowed much of what Japan was to become. "Let the producers be many and the consumers few. Let there be activity in the production and economy in the expenditure." "If man's desires are given rein, then their authority could not be endured . . ." "If each part of a whole fulfills its function, all will go well. If any part is out of kilter the whole system is apt to be upset." [21]

In the Tokugawa period, Japan was a grouping of many clans, albeit with some degree of centralization. Feudal domains created their own closely knit communities, often forging strong identities as a result of their geographical isolation and their occasional clashes. Commitment to a clan or family took precedence over any universal value, and the emphasis on group cohesion and harmony constituted its own morality. The group took full responsibility for the individual, and everything the individual did reflected on the group.

During this period, land was not owned by individuals, but by family clans. The rights to till the land passed from generation to generation. Moreover, while in European feudalism there were contractual ties between lord and vassal—a reflection of Roman law—in Japan the lord-tenant relationship was based on the assumed benevolence of the master. The lord had the right to unlimited loyalty, and in return he had the implicit obligation for the welfare of his subjects. The contract was moral, not legal. In fact, laws were few; each situation was judged on its unique merits.

During the Tokugawa period, the idea of a national economic policy was poorly executed. Episodic attempts were made at taxation, price fixing, and supervision of industry, but whatever was tried was aimed at maintaining the status quo, rather than at economic development. Commerce itself was not highly valued in society. In the Confucian tradition merchants had low social status, since they were seen as exploitive and had a reputation for living by a double standard—honesty within their own group or clan, and unscrupulous behavior to people outside.

During the Tokugawa seclusion, Japan shut out most of the outside world with the exception of very limited trade with China and the establishment of a small Dutch trading post on a small island in the Bay of Nagasaki. But by the mid-1800s, the Japanese were becoming aware of European conquests in East Asia. When Commodore Matthew Perry of the U.S. Navy arrived in 1853 with his "black ships" and demanded that Japan open its borders to outside trade, the shogun realized that the world was changing and that they would be no match for western ships and cannon. The opening of Japan forced its society to pull together, not just to handle the foreign invaders but to develop the capacity to deal with other countries on equal terms. But the Tokugawa system was too set in its ways to adapt to the new world and fifteen years later was overthrown by the samurai, the old warrior aristocracy, on behalf of the young Emperor Meiji.

The Meiji Restoration

A new policy—called the Meiji Restoration—created the central authority and the modern state of Japan. The word "restoration" is significant. Led by the upper classes, this was not a social revolution but rather a controlled movement to keep many of the old ideals, values, and institutions, to restore certain traditions that had been forgotten, and then to graft new structures on the old foundation. Japan harkened back not just to Tokugawa days but even earlier—to Chinese traditions of education and a skilled civil service. It then adopted features of modern European government, including many of the policies then being implemented by Bismarck in Germany.

From the outset, the Meiji rulers were preoccupied with motivating the population to work as one nation. Consistent with Confucian thought, those who supported "people's rights" were considered to be selfish and undermining the worthy cause of nationhood. The Meiji government feared disunity and social disorder; it disdained and discouraged political opposition and parliamentary procedures. Some dissident political groups did emerge, but they were not political parties in the Western sense with public platforms, ideologies, or objectives of broad representation. Instead, they were small elite factions, held together by personal relationships. Time and again, the Meiji rulers were able to overwhelm their opponents who called for greater representation and less corruption. The idea of a government devoted to the national interest and general welfare, rising above the factionalism of party politics, was decisively imposed.

The Meiji government created a state by restoring the glory of the emperor and making him the symbol of the nation, although the cabinet and the emperor's court held real power. The Constitution of 1889 was seen as a gift from the emperor, and it stated that the emperor was supreme, sacred, and inviolate. While the Diet had the power to restrain the cabinet by rejecting legislation and withholding budget approval, form and substance diverged. There was no pretense that the new government represented the will of the people. In fact, two powerful institutions developed, neither authorized by the constitution. There was a council of elders, the so-called *genro*, which acted as a powerful clique and chose the cabinet ministers. And there was the military, which was given the mandate for strategic affairs. It, too, had a de facto veto over cabinet selection.

Japan was eager to import Western ideas that could benefit the nation. In 1871, it sent its first mission abroad—the Iwakura Mission. Its objectives were to study other countries' constitutions and laws, their systems of trade and finance, their schools, and their communications infrastructure. The mission was a huge success in terms of gaining access to new technology and learning new ways of organizing administrative systems for government, the military, and the education system. But Japan avoided importing ideas and institutions that would have fostered individual rights, due process, and free markets and could have undercut the order and stability it so prized. Tokyo's view of life in the West was described in the Iwakura report. "The people of Europe in general live a life of greedy competition," it said. [22]

The Meiji rulers gave education a very high priority and built a universal education system, centrally controlled and administered, to train people for service to the state. They also stimulated and subsidized the modernization of the industrial sector, investing in mining, railroads, and chemical factories, to take but a few examples. The government gave loans to samurai to start up agricultural enterprises, silkworm rearing, and tea growing. It set up a national tax system, built roads and ports, tied the nation together by telegraph, and adopted legal and medical systems from abroad, mostly from Germany.

The samurai group played a major role in economic development. As a class they were educated, socially connected, and devoted to the emperor and the state. Unlike the merchants, they behaved like quasi-government officials, and acted with a sense of public responsibility.

At the time of the Meiji restoration, the imperial government owned a lot of the nation's businesses. But by the late 1870s, a new strategy was adopted, and the political leaders began turning over businesses to private families, helping them to accumulate capital in the process. Part of the government's effort entailed selling pilot plants and granting exclusive business licenses. As a result, many of the companies believed that while they had the rights to private ownership, they were responsible to the government and operated for national purposes, and a loose working relationship grew between the government and business.

The Meiji leaders created a national banking system, and designed it to be a handmaiden to the creation of powerful industries. Government-supported regional banks gave special help to industries and sectors considered important to national development, such as textiles and shipping, and provided low cost loans to firms helping the government to acquire technology from abroad. Early on, there was a heavy emphasis on exports, since foreign exchange would be required to purchase the raw materials that Japan needed but did not possess.

Early Twentieth Century

By the late 1890s, Japan was already forging a relationship between government and business that was unique among industrialized nations. Public officials and private firms were locked in continuous consultations to exchange information and plan strategy. Conferences were arranged to deal with specific industry problems. The government encouraged businesses to create large scale organizations to be its counterpart in various areas. Originally established on a regional basis, they later became national in scope and represented such industries as textiles, electrical engineering, metals, beer, iron, steel. Industry groups were not limited to manufacturing; publishing and finance were organized, too.

By 1915 one large umbrella group, the Japan Industrial Club, was formed to represent firms spanning several industries. It formulated policies for the iron and steel industries, which it subsequently presented to the government. It recommended the removal of tariffs on certain imported equipment, exemption from certain taxes, limits on imports of iron and steel products, and the creation of a government sponsored committee to plan for the future of the steel industry. The government set up a special committee, composed of officials and business leaders, to study the report. Ultimately it approved most of the recommendations. It was almost the exact procedure used to formulate policies today.

Although foreign advisors were consulted for precise tasks, they were almost always sent home after limited periods of time; and although foreign trade expanded, industrial development—in stark contrast to the history of almost every other major country—was achieved with virtually no foreign capital.

Despite Japan's rapid progress, a sense of vulnerability pervaded the society. The great typhoons and earthquakes took their toll in lives and in terms of the way Japan viewed itself. But so did the humiliation of foreign arrogance in the 1860s, the heavy dependence on imports of raw materials, and the exclusionary racist policies abroad. Repeated humiliation at the hands of foreigners was, in fact, to have a large impact on Japan's psyche. In the late nineteenth century, Japan struggled to build itself up militarily. Its objective was to be on an equal footing with the European powers, including the ability to compete for overseas territories that brought with them markets, resources, power, and status. In 1895, Japan defeated China in a contest over Korea, winning in the process the Liaotung peninsula of Southern Manchuria. Despite the national disgrace of being forced by Russia, France, and Germany to disgorge the spoils of war that it had just won, Japan continued its drive to be a great power. In 1905 it won such status with its victory in the Russo-Japanese War.

During the first two decades of the twentieth century, the thrust of Japanese policy was to create an industrial order at home, and, to the extent possible, throughout East Asia. This was achieved with a combination of state power and private initiative. For most of this period, government allowed business fairly free reign, although it was generally operating behind the scenes to stimulate consensus and coerce holdouts and mavericks.

Government and business had many common goals, such as enhancing the nation's productive capacity, but the real community of interest was in facing what they saw as a hostile world. In 1922, for example, the Japan Economic Federation was formed, overshadowing the Industrial Club. Its goals included many lofty national objectives, plus planning "for the unification of our opinions toward the outside world." [23]

It was in the 1920s that a formal industrial policy began to emerge in full force. Export associations were established to control volumes of trade and prices. Joint public-private forums were established to oversee special loans to industry. The government began an exhaustive compilation of industrial statistics and started to gather intelligence on foreign markets. Tokyo tried to copy elements of the German example of government-sponsored trusts and cartels as a means for promoting a stable economy, controlling the direction and pace of reforms, and moderating what it believed to be destructive cut-throat competition at home. In 1931 the Industries Control Law was passed; this sanctioned cartel arrangements among businesses, allowing them to fix levels of production, establish uniform prices, limit new entrants, and control marketing for particular industrial sectors. [24]

But Japan's trade problems grew, with imports expanding rapidly and exports running into competition from European nations, now quickly recovering from World War I. Business groups asked the government for assistance in the consolidation of certain industries to effect large scale production, including help in closing inefficient factories. They sought long-term, low-cost financing. They wanted the government to do more by way of predicting future supply-and-demand conditions. Business even made recommendations for streamlining and reorganizing the government bureaucracy to increase its effectiveness. Kawai Yoshinari, a top executive of the Tokyo Stock Exchange, wanted the government to lead and control the economy, "standing on a peak with a fair and comprehensive perspective." Kuhara Funanasuka, founder of the Nissan Company, wanted government to help fine tune the nation's competitiveness. He even proposed that the government should coerce firms into donating 50 percent of their profits to investments in industries that could crack open foreign markets. [25]

The 1930s saw a continuation of the growth of industrial policy jointly managed by government and business. As before, primacy was placed on control—at times business felt suffocated by too much government intervention; at times the bureacrats demanded a tighter grip. The notion of an industrial policy was not based on protectionism or any other particular philosophy. There was no Adam Smith in the wings, no Frederick List. What mattered was what worked, even if it meant import liberalization combined with heavy export subsidization, or some other eclectic approach.

Joint business-government arrangements never worked particularly well. Bureaucratic infighting reduced the government's efficiency, as did the growing power of the financial-industrial conglomerates called *zaibatsu*. But government bureaucrats were gaining valuable experience in understanding how industry worked.[26] Equally noteworthy was the resistance to the tenets of free market economics. Said one of the most influential business leaders in Meiji Japan, Shibusawa Eiichi: "Although people desire to rise to positions of wealth and honor, the social order and the tranquility of the State will be disrupted if this is done egoistically. In order to get along together in society and serve the State, we must by all means abandon the idea of independence and self-reliance and reject egoism completely."[27]

The Path to Pearl Harbor

Japan's perceived need to control foreign markets and raw material sources was but one of the factors on the tragic road to World War II. The notion that Japan was unfairly being frozen out of the imperialistic scramble of other great powers and the fierce nationalism of the military and its followers also helped provoke its invasion of Manchuria and China, and later its occupation of Indochina. Japan's road to war reflected its sense of vulnerability. Its inability to find diplomatic compromises reflected its true outsider status vis à vis Europe and America.

The preparation for war brought public and private interests together as never before. With the outbreak of worldwide protectionism in the 1930s, Tokyo believed that international trade was becoming a form of warfare. A consensus had emerged that the global trading arena would treat Japan's exports with hostility, and Japan thought it had to develop a country-by-country strategy, including retaliating against those who discriminated against Japanese products. In 1933, for example, high level talks between government officials and business executives resulted in the

"Law to Protect and Regulate Trade," legislation that resulted in Tokyo's raising tariffs against Canada and Australia as retribution for new duties imposed on Japanese products. From this point on, new laws were passed throughout the 1930s giving the Japanese government tighter control over trade as well as over specific industries. The Steel Industry Law, the Aircraft Manufacturing Law, the Machine Tool Industry Law, the Shipping Industry Law—all were designed to provide special government financing, taxes, and protective measures for individual industries.

Commercial policy became part of a virulent nationalism. Big business cooperated with the military in China and Manchuria, working hand in glove to organize the East Asian sphere for Japan's benefit. This entailed careful planning of which industries to develop, and how to protect existing companies at home that might be threatened. The experience of colonizing Manchuria was especially important as Japanese business and military, working together, constructed massive hydroelectric power facilities and did extensive land reclamation. Manchuria, in fact, was a laboratory for experimenting with new industries with advanced technology, such as the production of aluminum.

As the 1930s ended and as the war approached, Japan's internal government/industry tensions over who had control of the economy were resolved in favor of the government. New heights of centralized control were reached. Tokyo moved to establish a new trade ministry to coordinate all industrial policy, and to oversee the growing number of export and import associations that were now operating like cartels, arranging cooperative purchases of supplies, setting prices, allocating export by destination, and controlling imports to balance trade nation by nation. Special cabinet boards and ministerial committees drew a tighter ring around economic policy. Subsequently there emerged an "economic general staff" made up of military officials and also bureaucrats detached from the main economic ministries.

As the war came closer the government established "control" associations—government-industry cartels. Companies were categorized into licensed companies (Nissan, Toyota for example) or national purpose companies (Japan Steel) and overseen accordingly. An Industrial Facility Corporation, belonging to the government, was established to purchase or lease idle factories and convert them to munitions production. New laws made it illegal to open a new business without government license, and the government gave itself authority to order any enterprise to convert to munitions production. In fact, the national general Mobilization Law gave the public authorities carte blanche to do anything they wanted. Policies of totalitarian control encompassed industry but went well beyond, to education, labor, the press—anything remotely relevant to the war effort.[28]

The war was, of course, a disaster for Japan. Its economy was crushed, its national spirit destroyed, and its image in Asia and elsewhere set back for perhaps a century. When unconditional surrender came, Japan's destiny was shakier than at any time in the modern era.

After 1945

Following the war, Japan's number one objective, like Germany's, was economic reconstruction and the paramount task revolved around getting the nation back on its feet and regaining pride, sovereignty, and economic solvency. In this task, the experience of government-business cooperation, including the experience of total state control over the economy during the war, greatly benefitted the nation. "The managers of the postwar economic 'miracle,' " wrote Professor Chalmers Johnson, "were the same people who inaugurated industrial policy in the late 1920s and administered it during the 1930s and 1940s."[29]

After 1945 there were significant structural changes in the economy, including the breakup of the *zaibatsu*—the financial-industrial conglomerates—and the emergence of labor unions. Still, in many important respects Japan's industrial policy did not change dramatically from earlier days: government and business leaders collaborated closely; energy was focussed on priority sectors for investment; exports were among the top priorities; imports were strictly regulated. All foreign investment, including investment by anyone who wanted to license technology in Japan, needed permission from the government. Tariffs and import duties were manipulated to favor certain industries essential to the recovery. Foreign exchange was rigorously controlled and used for priority industries. The government retained authority to create cartels for the purpose of restructuring industry. Government-owned development banks operated alongside a rigorously compartmentalized and regulated banking system. Savings were encouraged by tax-free accounts in the post offices and channelled into government approved investment. Government subsidies were rampant, including tax exemptions for exports, research and development, and the building of infrastructure essential for industrialization. "The effectiveness of the Japanese state in the economic realm is to be explained in the first instance by its priorities," Chalmers Johnson wrote in 1982. "For more than 50 years the Japanese state has given its first priority to economic development."[30]

Not until the 1980s did many features of the Japanese economic structure begin to change. As many corporations became prosperous global giants, for example, their ties to commercial banks began to weaken. There were the beginnings of a consumer movement. Cries for reform began to be heard—political reform, more economic liberalization, more inclusion of women in the work place. Yet these stirrings were taking place even as a number of historical continuities remained in evidence.

First, government and business continued to operate by consensus. Heavy-handed control was not required. Business's willingness to work together with government helped ensure that the bureaucracy itself could remain small. It did not need to own companies, it did not need to implement policies.

Second, the history of the last one hundred years is a history of experimenting with ways to control the economy, and this is still true. At times there was totalitarian control, at times it was enough for the private sector to exercise control itself; at times there were cartels, and at other times there were simply intertwined relationships among firms. The modus vivendi changed but not the underlying philosophy that business existed for a purpose well beyond any one institution's profits, and certainly not for the gratification of individuals within the business. Japan evolved a unique model of capitalism based on pragmatism rather than ideology, and on a sense of shared economic nationalism rather than the pursuit of private economic gain.

Third, there has always been a high strategic content to industrial policy, a thrust that continues unabated in the 1990s. During this century, Japan has sought to move its economic base from agriculture to labor intensive industry, and later from capital intensive manufacture to information technology. For generations Japan's leaders have been thinking in terms of consolidating industries, channelling investment, building up savings. No other major noncommunist country has ever presumed to have such deliberate control over the economy or been so successful at achieving it.

Fourth, although there is a legal basis for Japanese policies, most have unfolded according to informal understandings between government and business. This has made for quick and efficient administration, albeit with enormous possibilities for informal bargaining, quid pro quos between the government and business, and decision making that often defies understanding by foreign observers. In this area, too, Japan stands alone in its legal informality, even today.

Fifth, Japan's constant experimentation with industrial policy resulted in economic institutions and policy procedures that simply did not—and do not—exist anywhere else in the advanced industrialized world. This has included the centralization of all trade and investment policy in one ministry, the informal guidance of the ministries in place of detailed published rules and regulations, and the close interrelationships among firms. It also included the placement of ex-ministry officials on the boards and in senior management of Japan's major companies—a type of network that extended the ministries' reach and further blurred the distinction between public and private interests.

Finally, Japan has been highly insular in its approach to the outside world. A major distinction between Japan and Germany is that while both have pursued highly nationalistic economic policies, Japan has consistently carried control over foreign transactions to much greater extremes, as can be seen from its record of meager imports and incoming foreign investment.

The historical legacies of the Big Three are reflected in the way they are organized today. No one would argue that political, economic, and social patterns have not changed over the years, or that in the mid-1990s America, Germany, and Japan behave just as they did in the nineteenth century, or, for that matter, in the mid-twentieth century. But strong links to the past exist. And they are very different pasts, each of which has ingrained in the three societies different institutions, different drives, different preferences. In times of economic boom and political stability, these differences will matter much less than when times are tough. They would also be less important if each of the three were on more-or-less equal competitive footing for the industrial revolution now occurring. But economic growth is slowing, ethnic and regional tensions are flaring, and not all types of capitalism are similarly suited for the twenty-first century. There are thus important reasons to take a closer comparative look at how each society is functioning now, particularly with regard to economic policy.

CHAPTER IV

Different Kinds of Capitalism

Now that there is no common military threat, as economic competition heats up among the Big Three, it will matter less which nation has the warheads than which one saves and invests the most. In place of East-West tensions we will see competition among the various kinds of capitalism. Time and again, the different systems will be measured against such criteria: Which kind of capitalism creates the most rewarding jobs? Which builds wealth and distributes it most equitably? Which gives its citizens the greatest sense of personal security? Which provides the greatest chance of fulfilling the potential of individuals?

No three countries better illustrate the contending models of highly successful capitalism than America, Japan, and Germany. They differ in many respects—in the role that government plays, in attitudes toward industrial and financial concentration, in the relationship between industry and banking, in their attention to manpower training, to take but a few examples. Far more important than any one or two distinguishing features, however, is the fact that the various parts of each model—from the kinds of business organizations they have developed to their tax regimes—fit together into a coherent system that reflects the way each society developed over the long term, including the legacies of history just discussed.

America is more purely market driven than the other two. It might be labeled a liberal market economy. In neither Japan nor Germany, for example, are the ownership rights to companies so likely to be bought and sold; in neither country are workers thrown into the marketplace like commodities, to take their chance in the job market (as opposed to being placed in positions for which they have been trained or will undergo lifetime training). It is not that the Darwinian American system doesn't have rules—some would label it the ultimate regulatory state—but it is a nation consumed by laws designed to ensure fair play, not to create any particular economic outcome.

Germany is frequently called a social market economy. More than the others, it practices capitalism with a conscience, meaning that alongside its capitalist structure it has the largest government-backed social insurance programs for its citizens. Policy objectives are far less neutral than in the United States—less focussed on fair play than on ensuring that the values of nationhood and community are furthered.

Japan might be labeled a developmental economy. Its government is nowhere near as hands-off as in America, but neither does it sponsor the extensive social welfare programs of the German government. Instead, it is highly active in the promotion of national goals through the manipulation and development of the industrial structure itself. Relative to the United States and Germany, Japan is less preoccupied with laws and relies more on custom and guidance from the bureaucracy.

Japan and Germany practice a much more organized type of capitalism than does America. In the United States, for example, it is expected that private and public interests will clash. Americans would be highly concerned if this perpetual struggle at federal, state, and local levels ceased to exist. But in Germany and Japan there is concern that such clashes would foster chaos and instability. Both countries, therefore, display a much greater harmony among the component parts of capitalism—government, business, and labor—than is found in the United States. Another major difference is that Germany and Japan each, in different ways, are more deliberate in their strategies for investing in human capital, especially in training and developing their work forces. As a result of these factors, Japan and Germany are in a better position than America to design and implement cohesive national commercial strategies.

None of the three models is pure, of course. America is taking up some Japanese management techniques and studying Japanese-style relationships between major companies and their suppliers. Germany is privatizing many parts of its state-owned industry. Japan's financial system is undergoing some deregulation and is looking more like America's.

This said, however, because the models have deep roots in their respective societies, it would take a long time, and the withering of many institutional and philosophical continuities, for them to lose their distinctions. A few simple examples illustrate the gaps that would have to be closed for the three systems to lose their unique features.

ORGANIZING FOR ECONOMIC POLICY

In any nation, economic policy is heavily influenced by the institutions that have evolved to carry it out. The American experience has led to a set of organizations in both the public and private sectors that is haphazard in its overall design, and underpinned by a system of checks and balances. As we have seen, neither Japan nor Germany has had a remotely similar historical experience, and hence in neither Tokyo nor Berlin could there occur so many challenges from within the public sector itself without bringing down the entire government. In neither does a supreme court play as prominent a role as it does in America. In neither nation do individuals and private groups have so many channels to legally and effectively challenge government activities.

As much as Americans complain about Washington's ineffectiveness and bungling, they are not uncomfortable with the fragmentation, overlap, and competition within the organs of government since such obstacles keep public officials and agencies from becoming too powerful. Japan and Germany, however, have consistently supported efficient public sectors on the theory that strong nations need strong, effective government.

To take a few examples, trade policy in the United States is the purview of at least six cabinet officers and countless congressional committees, whereas Japan and Germany handle it all in much more streamlined fashion within their executive branches and with very little parliamentary participation. The regulation of the U.S. financial system is overseen by the Federal Reserve, the Department of the Treasury, the Federal Deposit Insurance Corporation, the Office of the Comptroller, the Securities and Exchange Commission—none of which is in charge. In Japan, there is only one regulator, the Ministry of Finance, and in Germany, the Ministry of Finance and the Bundesbank share oversight responsibility. Unlike Japan and Germany, moreover, the United States has no effective department for science and technology policy, despite its increasing importance. In fact, America has never given attention to forming a first-class civil service in the way that Japan and Germany have, and Americans have never given the respect to any one organ of government as has Japan in the case of its Ministry of International Trade and Industry or Ministry of Finance, or Germany, in the case of the Bundesbank. Indeed, Americans have settled for what one British observer called "a loose confederation of more or less hostile bodies." [1]

Japan and Germany have not only taken a more positive view of the role of government than has the United States, but their private sectors have been more organized as well. Of course, America has its National Association of Manufacturers, its Chamber of Commerce, its Business Round Table, its special industry groups like the Semiconductor Industry Association or the Motor Vehicle Association. But for the most part these are weak umbrella organizations. They may oppose or support government policy with public statements and studies, and they may do a lot of lobbying, but their relationship is generally much more at arm's length with the public sector than are organizations in Japan and Germany. Partly as a matter of attitude and partly due to antitrust law, unlike their foreign counterparts they are not geared to exchange business information or to develop joint strategies, nor, as a general rule, do they pool resources to upgrade the technical skills of workers in particular sectors.

Almost all the features of the institutional structure of Japan are at the other end of the spectrum from the United States. Instead of three co-equal branches of government, Japan's civil service has ruled. It makes executive decisions, writes legislation, and arbitrates among conflicting interests. The legislature and the courts serve mainly to legitimate the bureaucracy's direction. As part of its normal government operations, the Japanese bureaucracy maintains close links to the business community and is a powerful force for bringing together groups with differing interests and for finding common ground.

Typically the government in Tokyo does far more than set the policy framework with the basic budgetary and monetary tools. It also sets the long-term direction of individual industries by preparing studies, coordinating discussions, and creating consortiums for research and investment. Government and business do not, however, exist in perfect harmony. The bureaucracy provides "guidance," which business or labor often dislikes or resists. Government itself is often divided, too—indeed, the infighting among Japanese departments can be fierce. But there is an overarching belief that the fate of everyone in the country is bound together, and that the public sector must work closely with industry toward common objectives for the nation. One of the prime goals, if not the overwhelming one, is success in the global marketplace. Indeed, building a society that is economically superior on the world stage pervades the entire web of public and private institutions.

Two government agencies play a particularly strong, supporting role. The Ministry of International Trade and Industry (MITI) has historically been charged with making Japanese industry competitive globally. Its true power rests not on reams of legislation, but on custom and the broad acceptance by industry that an intermediary between the private and public sectors and an organizer for strategic policy are essential. Equally powerful is the Ministry of Finance (MOF). Although theoretically Japan's counterpart to the U.S. Treasury, there really is nothing like it in America. Not only does the MOF coordinate all financial policy but it writes the national budgets, collects taxes, issues stock when government-owned firms, such as the former national telecommunications company, are privatized, and oversees the management of huge public sector pension funds. It also has traditionally played a leading role in industrial policy and in manipulating credit, taxes, regulations, and the currency in conjunction with broad industrial goals.

The idea of drawing a line between government and business is alien in Japan. While both MITI and the MOF are alleged to have lost some of their clout in recent years because of the deregulation of Japanese industry—a trend that is sure to continue—this does not necessarily mean the government has lost its strong influence. When top MITI and MOF officials retire, for example, they often take senior positions in firms whose activities are overseen by the agencies they came from. These links are a far cry from America's revolving door, in which former officials use their government connections for personal gain. In Japan, the former MITI or MOF men never fully retire in spirit, and their ties to their old agencies create strong two-way loyalties. Large private associations like the Federation of Economic Organizations *(Keidanren)*— which is akin to a Chamber of Commerce for many of Japan's largest firms—and the Federation of Employers *(Nikkeiren)* also work closely with the government. Their role and power bear little relationship to their American counterparts. The *Keidanren*, for example, is often a genuine partner with government in developing and implementing policy. It employs ex-MITI officials and routinely exchanges staff. It is even organized along the same lines as MITI.

Throughout Japanese industry, there are deliberation councils, cabinet advisory councils, industrial rationalization councils, industrial structure councils—all dedicated to close cooperation between government and business. Numerous standing advisory councils in the private sector continuously interact with government agencies. Sectors like steel, shipping, and computers all have their own associations, which bring together officials from government, labor, and academia. The primary issue is nearly always how to foster greater competitiveness in the world market.

An analysis of Germany today must focus on what was recently West Germany, since it is the West German system that is being imposed on the reunified country. Even though Germany's structure differs from both the American and Japanese models, it is much closer to the latter. Industry, labor, and the financial establishment have maintained a large degree of organizational concentration, and in two key respects—the inclusion of labor organizations in national policy deliberations, and the assumed responsibility for social welfare programs—Berlin is even more expansive in its aims than Tokyo.

The concentration of power in the German government is much less than in the United States or Japan. Today the federal bureaucracy employs only 10 percent of all the nation's civil servants, with the rest working at the state, or *Länder*, level. Compared to the American system, German federalism is an intimate and highly cooperative structure, with a clearer delineation of responsibilities. Thus far government still maintains significant ownership stakes in industry, however, with public bodies in the West alone holding about 7 percent of all German stocks, including 52 percent of Lufthansa, and large positions in the Bundesbahn (railways) and Telekom (communications).[2] The *Länder* also have ownership shares in industry. Lower Saxony, for example, owns 20 percent of Volkswagen. The concentration of state ownership in what was once East Germany is, of course, much larger, but Berlin is determined to privatize as much as possible.

It is the well-organized private sector that is the prime motor for communitarian policies in modern Germany. Four major banks dominate finance. They invest in German companies, their representatives sit on the boards, they have a direct stake in the nation's industrial strength—all of which produces tighter relationships between finance and industry than exist in America. Most of German industry falls under the Federation of German Industry (BDI—*Bundesverband der Deutschen Industrie*) and the German Chamber of Commerce (DIHT—*Deutschen Industrie und Handelstag*). There are many trade associations that actively help companies to strengthen their competitive standing. Labor unions are powerful, but in addition there are extensive institutional ties between labor and management.

Like the Japanese, Germans have great respect for their public institutions. The best example is the Bundesbank. (In America, by contrast, most people know little about what the Federal Reserve does, let alone have an informed view about its relationship to the administration or Congress.) The central bank is revered and its independence from the government is strongly and widely supported by the population. It alone is entrusted with safeguarding the value of the German currency. When inflation begins to accelerate, the Bundesbank tightens interest rates and slows the economy. At times it may have to boost the value of the German mark and possibly slow German exports (by making them more expensive). These critical policy issues, which affect almost everyone, are the functions of any central bank. What is different in Germany is that there is a strong consensus that whatever the Bundesbank does, its judgment is respected. Its authority in monetary policy is virtually unquestioned in national and international circles, and the German government and parliament almost always defer to the bank's formulation of monetary policy strategies. (One major exception was the way West and East Germany were joined in monetary union. Chancellor Kohl overruled the Bundesbank's objections to the rate of exchange between West German and East German makes.)

The institutional networks of Japan and Germany give these societies a mechanism to anticipate future events of importance to industry and to the nation. In both countries, such networks enable industries to marshal resources beyond the reach of individual companies. The big American firms can do some of this themselves. But it is doubtful that they are in a position to compete with the more elaborate and cohesive efforts abroad. Moreover, each U.S. firm plans only for itself. There is virtually no consideration of broader questions about the industry, the community, the nation.

CARTELS AND MONOPOLY

There are few aspects of a society that reveal more about the role of individual vs community than its attitude toward industrial size and concentration. The relationship among American firms has been heavily influenced by an antitrust policy whose roots go back over a century. Sometimes the Justice Department has attempted to break up alleged cartels on the basis of price fixing, even if the prices were shown to be reasonable. Sometimes the criteria were merely a company's size and its potential to fix prices. In the 1960s and 1970s many of the most illustrious American companies—IBM, Kodak, AT&T, and others in the food and retailing industry—were all under investigation. President Reagan's administration was noticeably more lax about antitrust, but even so, America's concerns about economic concentration have no parallels in Japan or Germany (even though their laws are similar to ours because of the influence of the American Occupation). It is no wonder that American firms generally keep at arm's length not just Washington but also each other. This is true even of big companies and their suppliers.

As part of their industrial culture, both Japan and Germany have historically been far more comfortable with all manner of tighter industrial ties. For Japan, cartels and industrial combinations go back to Meiji times. MITI, for example, has power to form and administer cartels for many purposes—to reduce excessive competition, to phase out a dying industry, to nurture an up-and-coming business. Japan has formed cartels in order to flood foreign markets with low priced products (steel rods, cotton weaving), to assist industries in recession (aluminum, fertilizers), and to promote businesses of the future (space technology, advanced telecommunications). Japan has also formed cartel-like arrangements to slow exports via "voluntary" quotas on automobile sales to the United States and Europe.

In Japan, moreover, groups of big companies *(keiretsu)* with interlocking relationships among buyers and suppliers are often seen as the best way to promote efficient production, gain market share, spread the risk of investment, and ride out the ups and downs of the economy. There are at least six major *keiretsu*, including such well-known names as Mitsubishi, Mitsui, and Sumitomo. The affiliated companies of major groups may be legally independent, but there is considerable coordination of their activities, and there is extensive vertical and horizontal integration within the group. They often use the same banks, sell to one another at favored prices, share information, hold one another's stock, and pool investments. In addition, close relationships that exist among the executives of the companies enhance the collection of market intelligence.

Here are a few examples of how *keiretsu* work. Mazda is part of the Sumitomo *keiretsu*. Others in the Sumitomo family of companies hold 60 percent of Mazda's shares. Mazda holds 20 percent to 40 percent of the equity of its fifteen suppliers. Those suppliers own a sizeable stake in *their* suppliers. Another case, from the computer industry: between 1975 and 1987, *keiretsu* companies bought 54 percent of their total computer purchases from companies belonging to their own groups, even though for a good deal of this time Japanese computer firms were not at the forefront of the industry. A third example—personnel. In many of the *keiretsu*, top management from the key twenty or so companies meet weekly, sometimes in the form of a "President's Club," to exchange information. This pattern is mirrored at several lower, operating levels—marketing, research, planning, supply. Finally, there is group loyalty. A Mitsui building is likely to be built by a Mitsui construction company, using Mitsui steel and Mitsui elevators, and leased to Mitsui companies by Mitsui real estate brokers.[3]

These interlocking affiliations are a vital element in the stability of everyday life in Japan, not to mention a competitive weapon in the global economy. Size per se is not bad. On the contrary, being big is considered a major advantage. Price fixing is not bad either, so long as it enhances the strength of the company. Japan has an antimonopoly law, to be sure, but it is the creation of the American Occupation in the late 1940s and it has, to date, not been seriously applied. In fact, Tokyo's Fair Trade Commission has had a low status in the Japanese bureaucracy, and is easily intimidated by big business. A good deal of attention is being given to these issues in Japan now, and other countries are pressing Tokyo to dismantle many of its tightest structures. Slowly, a policy is emerging to open up the economy. But it will take a long time.

Germany, too, has not been averse to combinations that represented the values of order, security, control, organization, discipline. In fact, German cartels date from the combinations in the metallurgical and coal industries in the last century, later extending to chemicals, electricity, steel, and many other sectors. Records show, for example, that there were 14 major cartels in Germany in 1871, 1,500 cartels in 1918, 2,700 in 1931, and 6,000 by 1945.[4]

After World War II, an anticartel office was established, and has pursued its task with enthusiasm. Nevertheless, it still battles against a deeply ingrained tradition. The office, in fact, can be overruled by the Federal Economics Ministry if there is an overall economic advantage to the country or other overriding public interest. This happened in the late 1980s when Daimler-Benz proposed a takeover of Messerschmitt-Bolkow-Blohm (MMB), a marriage of West Germany's largest industrial group with its leading defense and aerospace conglomerate (and with an additional element being the strong participation of Deutsche Bank, Germany's largest financial institution). The cartel office vetoed what would be almost a corporate state-within-a-state; but the government allowed the merger to go through.

The tightly woven fabric of German society is seen in other areas, too —in the emphasis on long-term, negotiated price and supply arrangements between companies and their suppliers, and in the concerted effort on the part of local government, business, labor, and universities to make investments in the local communities and regions in which they are located.

ATTITUDES TOWARD TRADE

Until recently, America has never attached overwhelming importance to exports. The domestic market was big and profitable enough. Japan and Germany have held different attitudes. For over a century, they have given primacy to selling products abroad. Since 1945, in particular, exports have been an important engine for recovery, and for earning critical hard currency. Tokyo, however, has exhibited a fundamental difference in the philosophy behind its trade policy than Berlin. In fact, Japan is a true anomaly.

In America and Germany, the purpose of trade has been to increase wealth for producers *and* consumers. In Japan, however, the benefits of international commerce have been heavily skewed to producers in order to enhance their market share, and, secondarily, their profits. As a result, the emphasis of trade policy has not been on providing more goods at lower prices to consumers, but almost entirely on achieving industrial dominance for firms. At the end of 1991, for example, the Economic Planning Agency estimated that prices of goods and services in Japan were on average 32 percent higher than in New York and 24 percent higher than in Hamburg, Germany—a fact attributed to too few imports and too many monopolies.

In no other major industrial democratic nation is the structure of trade so imbalanced. Japanese exports tend to be highly concentrated in a narrow range of products where overwhelming global penetration is achieved: textiles in the 1950s, steel in the 1960s, automobiles since the 1970s, and now semiconductor devices. America's and Germany's export profiles are far more diverse and balanced.

Japan also imports a much lower level of manufactured goods in comparison to its G.N.P. than does America or Germany. In 1987, for example, manufactured imports as a percentage of the nation's economic output was 2.4 percent. For the United States, the comparable figure was 7.3 percent and for Germany 14.4 percent.[5] Moreover, Japan's intraindustry trade is unusually small. America is both a major exporter and importer of food; the same can be said of office equipment or almost every other industry in which the U.S. exports. Germany sells Volkswagens to the world but also imports Hondas, Renaults, Fiats. The purpose of such two-way trade within a particular industry is to widen consumer choice, and to gain all the efficiencies that can come from ever-increasing specialization. In recent years, however, the extent of such intra-industry trade in Japan has been less than half that of either the United States or Germany. Imports have consisted of those products in which Japan had virtually no production, such as petroleum; or where an industry has yet to develop, such as large commercial aircraft; or where relentless political pressure is being applied by other nations, such as semiconductors.[6]

INDUSTRIAL POLICY

Does the United States have *any* industrial strategy? Since the late 1940s, there has certainly been an emphasis on building up a military-industrial complex. Included have been projects such as the various programs to explore outer space. Relationships between business and the Pentagon have also been elaborate, with one benefit being spillovers of technology to the civilian sector. In addition, defense spending was a prime ingredient in America's overall economic policies. On more than one occasion, the Pentagon turned on its spending spigot to boost the economy when conditions were weak.

Another aspect of an industrial strategy can be found in the way the U.S. has applied trade protection to some of its ailing industries. In the 1980s, for example, it pressured Japan to limit its exports of cars and created an elaborate scheme to slow the imports of steel and machine tools from abroad. But these measures fell far short of deliberate and positive industrial strategies, and they were achieved in a typical American way—by domestic interest groups with enough power and money to get Washington to listen. They may have been industries that had strategic value, but that was not the criterion. In fact, American protection has always been half-hearted insofar as any desire to cure fundamental problems is concerned. When Congress raised import barriers, there was almost never a requirement for the protected industry to take measures on its own to rejuvenate itself while shielded from foreign competition. Thus, what happened with autos or steel was not an industrial policy as such, but a way to quiet a political uproar.

America's individualist creed has always held that free markets are the best determinant of public interest, and that Washington should intervene only when the political pressure from aggrieved parties leaves no other choice. To the extent that the United States has an industrial policy, it is therefore an accident. This is not unnatural for a country whose market spans a continent and that once believed it had the luxury of near self-sufficiency. The rationale is in the tradition of antigovernment bias, and accords with the deep-seated U.S. preference for keeping the public and private sectors as separate as possible. There is also another important reason for America's approach: the purpose of economic policy is to satisfy the consumer, not the producer. The implication is that the best industrial strategy is to ensure that goods of all varieties are available from any destination at the lowest possible cost. There is no feeling that the United States ought to have any particular industry for strategic reasons, so long as consumers can get the products they need. As far as Washington is concerned, growing tomatoes and building computers have equal weight.

Japan's approach differs dramatically. Its industrial strategies have a lot to do with its being a set of islands dependent on trade for most raw materials. Since 1945 these policies have followed a clear pattern. At any given time a few key industries are targeted for high priority. Outsiders are then prevented from entering the Japanese market in these sectors, but domestic companies are allowed to compete with one another ferociously. Indeed, the intensity of the internal competition has made the home market a product laboratory, producing a mindboggling stream of new products, each quickly modified in response to consumer reaction and desires. Once producers have their product fully developed, they launch a massive export drive. Only after the industries have achieved major global market penetration are foreign competitors allowed into Japan. By then, Japanese companies have a considerable head start and have achieved tremendous economies of scale.

Germany's approach to industrial strategy has also been powerful and coherent. German companies have sought to dominate only a few niches, such as high precision tools or specialty chemicals, but on a global scale. Big banks, industry associations, labor, and universities are all geared to assist in the development of these niche businesses. It is a strategy that fits in with the extensive network of middle-sized family-owned firms that are able to maintain exceptional quality control and where pride-of-product and emphasis on technical perfection are passed from generation to generation. The niche strategy is also important in light of Germany's high wage rates and generous vacation schedules; the more unique a product is, the higher prices can be charged to offset other costs.

Germany's regional policies are a good illustration of the nation's approach to economic matters. The government's policy—mostly local government—has been to take a long-term view in stimulating new investment in depressed localities and industries. Among the incentives are tax allowances and outright grants. Between 1982 and 1990, for example, a regional program was instituted to find alternative employment opportunities outside the iron and steel industries. Shipbuilding, footwear, and coal mining are other industries that have received direct assistance. Outside the United States, most industrialized nations have some programs like these, but the German approach has been viewed by its European neighbors as particularly extensive.

Germany has had much better results than the United States in dealing with declining industries. A good example is the Ruhr Valley, where old steel factories have been replaced with new industries in electronics and aerospace, and where environmental cleanup has proceeded at a fast pace. In fact, the entire question of how America, Japan, and Germany approach declining industries is reflective of the way the three societies function. Japan takes a community approach, using cartels, subsidies, managed takeovers, and targeted investment from government owned banks. Germany, as described, takes a different but quintessential community approach, too. America, however, has virtually no public policies to deal with the situation—virtually no adjustment assistance for workers, few exemptions from antitrust legislation, few strategic subsidies. All is left to the market.

FINANCIAL SYSTEMS

In America there are more ways to raise, lend, and invest money than in either Japan or Germany. The driving philosophy in the United States has been twofold: to try to maintain the freest possible markets (recognizing that all banking has to be regulated to a great extent) and to accommodate the consumer. The American system is both more flexible and more volatile than its counterparts. As in other areas of American life, change—sometimes dramatic change—is accepted as the price of choice.

Stability and predictability are key in Japan and Germany and their systems have been designed to cushion change. Historically their financial systems have been very heavily regulated, including being closed to participation by foreign firms. They have been controlled not to please consumers, but to build up powerful, competitive industries.

Taxes, Interest Rates, Currencies

America has typically taxed its citizens on their savings, while allowing them to deduct the interest cost of borrowing from their taxable income. The effect is to discourage saving and to make borrowing more attractive. The opposite has generally been the case in Japan and Germany where the tax systems reward saving rather than borrowing. America has also been more willing to tax long-term capital gains than either Japan or Germany, thereby failing to encourage investment over current spending. In 1989, for example, the U.S. long-term capital gains rate was 33 percent, whereas in Japan it was 1 percent of the sales price or 20 percent of the net gain, and in Germany there was no tax at all. [7]

America has had a more cavalier attitude toward fluctuations of interest rates and currency values, in line with its greater regard for market forces. Its generally benign neglect of the value of the dollar has been due to its small amount of international trade relative to the size of the economy. If the dollar went up or down, not many Americans were affected. Japan and Germany have had much less reverence for market forces. For the sake of order and stability and also to foster long-term investment, they have placed a high priority on stable interest rates and currencies.

America does not favor inflation, of course, but for the most part it has accepted some steady price escalation in the interest of growth and job creation. Since 1945, Japan and Germany have been much more intolerant; for both, and especially for Germany, inflation is seen as a disruption in stability and predictability. Tokyo and Berlin have preferred to address employment problems more directly with policies for job security and unemployment compensation.

Banking, Stock Markets, and the Market for Corporate Governance

In America, most major companies are owned by a broad spectrum of investors—individuals, insurance companies, pension funds, and other institutions. Issuing shares to the public through the stock market has been the primary means of raising large amounts of capital for long term expansion. Bank lending, on the other hand, has provided short-term credit. In Japan and Germany, stock markets have played a much less significant role in overall economic development. Big banks have provided long term loans for most capital needs, and they have also made direct investments in companies, something U.S. banks are generally prohibited from doing.

Underlying these differences is a crucial distinction: in America, the ownership and the management of public corporations are distinct groups, whereas in Japan and Germany the lines are far more blurred. In America, owners have a distinctly financial interest; in the other two nations they have both a financial and long-term strategic interest. Public shareholders in America have no particular loyalty to the companies of which they own a small piece. They hold paper certificates and their major interest is in financial returns, including current income from dividends. An individual's investment is made for his own enrichment, not for the company, or the community, or the nation. Institutional shareholders are generally professional investors—they have little interest in the affairs of the companies issuing the stocks or bonds they hold, except for the firms' profitability. The boards of directors of these American companies understand that their primary responsibility is ensuring that stockholders get the highest possible returns—or risk being voted out, or sued.

The idea of what a company represents to society is very different in Japan and Germany, where it exists for both economic and social purposes. There is the concept of stakeholders—an idea that includes shareholders, management, workers, suppliers, and the surrounding community, all of whom have legitimate interests in a company's future. Individual shareholders are treated far less deferentially than they are in the United States; often, for example, they do not have access to financial information that American investors would take for granted. (In Germany, for example, some estimates show that only 10 percent of the companies that are obligated to report annual results actually do so.) Japan and Germany look at investments in the shares of companies differently, too. Rather than judging the attractiveness of dividends, historically Japanese and German investors have considered stocks as being akin to low-interest bonds, with their value accruing over time. This is consistent with the long-term view.

Japanese and German corporations are in a position to pursue broader communitarian goals because they are controlled by relatively few institutions. In Japan, most shares of a company are not freely traded. Instead, some 60 percent to 70 percent are typically held in the friendly hands of other companies or banks (often in the *keiretsu*.) In Germany, banks do not have large ownership positions, but together with friendly companies account for well over half the shares that can be traded. Companies issue a variety of classes of stock with different kinds of voting rights that substantially dilute the impact of the votes of public shareholders. Generally, many shareholders give the big German banks their proxy votes, so, in fact, banks have voting control that greatly exceeds their direct ownership stakes. In addition, the idea of a house bank—a primary supporter of a company—is well established. The big three banks have seats on the supervisory boards of the nation's biggest firms. They even own stakes in one another.

The closer relationship between finance and industry in Japan and Germany accounts for a critical structural distinction between them and the United States. In America it is easier for financial and industrial interests to diverge as in the case of the 1980s' leveraged buyout craze when investment and commercial banks dismantled American companies simply for short-term profits to themselves. This could never have happened in Japan or Germany. (Corporate America was also responsible since many executives were happy to trade the long-term future of their companies for immediate financial payoffs.)

In America, takeovers are easy because shareholders almost always vote in favor of deals that offer them a higher price. The impact on workers, suppliers, the community, or on the nation's competitiveness has not been a decisive consideration, since in the United States the company is valued as a bundle of financial assets that belong only to its immediate owners. The management of a company is typically preoccupied with boosting its share price. Often this is reason enough to conclude a merger. It is also the reason why companies so often spend their retained earnings to repurchase their own shares instead of making new investments in facilities or people. In those instances where management is strongly opposed to a merger, it does everything it can to avoid it, including taking on heavy loads of debt to make itself unattractive. Such is life in corporate America.

When takeovers occur in Japan and Germany, they are arranged so that all constituencies are considered. Neither the boards of directors nor the managements of these companies is under anywhere near the same pressure as their American counterparts to impress the stock market.

In both countries, moreover, hostile takeovers are easy to prevent. The concentrated shareholdings ensure that unless all parties agree, a prospective raider can rarely acquire enough of the company to take control. In Japan, for example, the bulk of shares of many companies is owned by affiliates in the *keiretsu*. In Germany there are obstacles too, including restrictions limiting the voting power of any single shareholder to 5 percent to 10 percent regardless of the size of his stake; the two-tier board system in which a supervisory board must appoint the firm's management, and the requirement that 75 percent of the shareholder votes must be marshalled to oust the supervisory board; and the strong role that German labor unions play on the supervisory boards.

A good example of how the German system can work is the attempted takeover in 1991 of Continental AG, Germany's largest maker of tires, by Pirelli SpA of Italy. Germany's top industrialists coalesced behind Continental to oppose the bid. The defense was organized by Deutsche Bank, a top executive of which was head of Continental's supervisory board. Companies like Daimler-Benz, whose supervisory board was also chaired by Deutsche Bank, closed ranks and bought Continental's shares. Other major German companies—BMW, Volkswagen, the Allianz insurance group, many of whom had executives once tied to Continental—also joined forces to prevent Pirelli from succeeding. This concerted effort mirrored the procedures used in the 1970s to block the Shah of Iran's attempt to buy a significant stake in Daimler-Benz. At that time German companies formed a new holding company to buy a blocking minority of Daimler shares.

Short- vs Long-Term Horizons

In America, because stock markets are short-term oriented, a company's stock often fluctuates when quarterly earnings reports are released. This puts companies with major requirements for additional physical plant and infrastructure or for research and development—where the payoff may come only after many years—at a significant disadvantage vis à vis their foreign rivals. The reason is that in Japan and Germany, since banks are the major providers of capital, and since a corporation serves broader global needs, long-term capital has been easier to raise. Because firms are freed from the short-term constraints of having to achieve a return on investment, they can focus on profitability and market share over time.

Due to the heavy involvement of banks in industry, the bankruptcy rates in Japan and Germany tend to be lower than in the United States. Being not just lenders but shareholders, banks can monitor the real performance of the very companies with which they have relationships. They have the opportunity to act as inside advisors and are in a position to roll over loans if necessary in a process that is much smoother and less confrontational than the American Chapter 11 process. Because there are fewer losses as a result of bankruptcies, the overall risk of lending is reduced. This is one reason why the cost to Japanese and German companies of acquiring funds has historically been lower than the cost to American firms in the United States—a major competitive advantage.

The traditions and culture in Tokyo and Berlin have resulted in attitudes toward economic risk and failure that are far more conservative than in America. It is no mystery that their financial markets have been more tightly regulated. Nor is it a surprise that while the American bankruptcy code is designed to give failed risk takers a second chance, in Japan and Germany bankruptcy carries a debilitating stigma and great personal shame.

Different attitudes toward risk have an impact on how new ventures are created. In the United States, venture capital to fund risky start-ups has provided opportunities for entrepreneurs, including those operating out of the proverbial garage or basement. This has few counterparts in the capital markets of Japan or Germany, where large companies generally fund their own experiments internally. If projects are successful, they may be spun off.

Differences in capital markets reinforce other differences among the Big Three. America's venture capital markets promote the individual creative genius. However, innovative ideas may not be commercially profitable without additional investment, and obtaining financing for long-term development of new concepts and techniques can be difficult. The rewards are potentially great, but so are the risks.

In Japan and Germany, spectacular entrepreneurial breakthroughs have been less frequent. But because entrepreneurs operate within large, established companies their focus on improving existing products is much more intense, and their long-term funding much more secure than it would be in the United States.

These distinctions are critical in the 1990s. Consumers are demanding increasingly sophisticated products in ever greater variety. Being able to innovate continuously—small but constant improvements—may be more of a competitive advantage than the occasional dramatic discovery, especially if the innovation occurs in a large firm that is in a position to use it immediately and distribute the related product on a wide scale.

Cost of Money

It has often been alleged that American firms have been forced to pay more for raising funds from U.S. capital markets than have their corporate counterparts in Japan and Germany. (Admittedly, the charge is not

as frequently made with respect to Germany, perhaps because less attention has been focussed on German firms, which have not presented as
direct a threat to U.S. industry.) The argument has been that several
aspects of Japan's and Germany's financial systems are responsible for
this competitive advantage, including their more rigorous approach to
inflation and the lower incidence of bankruptcy. The assertion is probably true, although factors included in the calculations are subject to
different interpretations, and the truth is that differences in capital costs
across national borders are a subject of great controversy and dispute.
(Sidney L. Jones, an assistant secretary of the U.S. Treasury in 1980,
once compared the cost of capital issue to global warming. "There is a
vast amount of information available," he said, "but little agreement.")[8]

The most plausible explanation of the situation, however, is that
American firms often pay more for capital—defined as the combination
of debt and equity—than do their Japanese and German counterparts.
And the reasons have less to do with differential taxes than with the
different financial structures in the Big Three. In particular, because
U.S. companies rely so heavily on the capital markets rather than banks,
the providers of capital are more distant from management than are the
banks that have traditionally underwritten Japanese and German firms.
This translates into the providers being less knowledgeable and less trust-
ful of the companies, and hence putting a greater premium on funds.[9]

There is a strong relationship between the cost of capital and all aspects
of competitiveness. More expensive money means a company can afford
less expansion, less modernization, less research. It also means that if
two companies embark on the same project and raise the same amount,
the one with the higher costs of obtaining equity and debt will end up
either paying more, or having to pay back much faster to reduce the
burden of accumulating interest payments. Thus there is a strong bias on
the part of those with high-cost capital for short-term projects. One of
the most notable examples of what can happen is the case of Cincinnati
Milacron, which was the sole remaining American manufacturer of industrial robots when it sold its business to Asea Brown Boveri AG of
Switzerland. The stated reason: it could not make an adequate financial
return given its cost of funds.[10]

All this said, however, as the financial markets in Japan have been
gradually deregulated, the cost of capital has risen. There is a good

chance that even if Japan had an advantage on this score in the past, it may not in the future. The same goes for Germany, where the control and involvement of banks face competition from capital markets. But capital is only one ingredient in the competitiveness equation, and it has never been clear that it is the major one.

HUMAN CAPITAL

Human capital is a clearer story. Nowhere is the difference between the philosophies of the Big Three better illustrated than in their approaches to human resource development. Two of the many aspects of this subject —attitudes toward the labor force, and attitudes towards education and training—show how differently the Big Three approach these questions. In America, management and workers have historically been antagonists, struggling continuously over working conditions, pay levels, and job security. Antiunion feelings run deep among many U.S. business executives, and organized labor has had a long-standing distrust of management. Workers have tended to be excluded from strategic business decisions both at industry and plant level. Corporate management typically wants the flexibility to hire or fire workers depending on economic conditions and its company's own performance. From the standpoint of American society, precarious employment is recognized as a fact of life, and it is often seen as the flip side of a country that places great emphasis on self-reliance, mobility, and freedom.

It has been much different in Japan and Germany, where a company is a crucial element in the fabric of a community, and workers are part of the soul of a company. Skilled labor is considered a precious asset requiring cultivation, support, and continuous training. Manpower policies in Japan and Germany are not identical by any means, but the common point is that workers participate in company decisions. They have a good sense of their employer's mission and purpose, and their involvement enhances motivation. Whereas American workers derive their prestige from their salaries, wages, and benefits, in Japan and Germany status is heavily based on the reputation and performance of the companies of which they are a part. Workers identify with their companies and assume they will spend their productive life with them, which the companies themselves also assume. As a result, employers are willing to make investments in their work force to upgrade skills, and workers are motivated to expend the effort to acquire such skills.

In the United States, labor relations are centered both at the federal and local levels. Aside from national organizations, thousands of local unions bargain over detailed collective contracts with management. In Japan, labor-management bargaining and overall strategy are centered at the firm level. Lifetime job security is often guaranteed by the company. In Germany, unions are organized and centralized along industry lines, and workers have strong representation on supervisory boards of directors, and they have work councils at the factory level. By law, it is extremely difficult to dismiss an employee.

Which system is most flexible, which is most appropriate in a rapidly changing world economy? America's system gives the appearance of being the most adaptable. This may be especially true in the industries that do not require highly skilled labor, such as manufacturing distribution centers or retailing, where the ability to hire and fire in line with business conditions may be an advantage. However, to the extent that the system breeds lack of commitment and underinvestment in training, there will be far less flexibility to maneuver in sophisticated industries where change and adaptability skills are the order of the day.

Japan's system is, however, much more flexible than it might appear. Despite the emphasis on quality production and sophisticated skills, Japanese workers are all trained to be generalists within their own companies, learning all facets of business—marketing, production, planning, personnel. This serves them well when major strategic shifts are required. Equally important, Japanese companies have demonstrated a tremendous ability to make intrafirm and intra*keiretsu* adjustment without laying off workers.

Movement out of one's specialty has historically been more difficult in Germany. The rigidity of Germany's system, in fact, has frequently been characterized as a liability in the fast-changing world economy. Thus far, however, the combination of a successful niche strategy, relentless effort on high quality production, and strong economic growth in surrounding countries—which has translated into demand for German exports—has overshadowed any disadvantages.

In all three countries, general education is a government responsibility —although only in Japan does the national government, as opposed to local officials, take a leading role. When it comes to training workers, however, America leaves the job to individual firms, as does Japan. Germany's vocational training is a responsibility shared among government, business, labor and, to a lesser extent, universities.

General education has a strong tradition in the United States, where it has been the primary means of fulfilling the dream of upward mobility and equal opportunity. And while America still has a strong lead in higher education—putting it ahead in certain fields such as medicine, engineering, and basic science—it has almost no vocational training, which puts it at a great disadvantage on the shop floor.

In Japan's case, vocational training is far more rigorous and takes place in three ways: companies maintain special training centers; workers are encouraged to be involved in correspondence courses at all levels; and workers have "quality circles" to impart knowledge and experience to one another. (Quality circles, like many other business techniques used in Japan, were originally the idea of an American, Dr. W. Edwards Deming, but never caught on in the United States.)

Germany has perhaps an unmatched ability to produce highly skilled workers. Most sixteen-year-olds become apprentices after their formal schooling, which means they receive a mixture of education and training either within their firms or in specialized training schools where the curriculum is designed and approved by government, industry, and labor, and where the costs are shared by national and state governments, firms, industry associations, and trade unions. Over 350,000 companies in 440 different fields participate in the program. Ninety percent of applicants are accepted, and 80 percent get permanent jobs in their preferred vocation. Apprenticeships generally last three years, after which participants must pass a national examination in their fields. The system is designed to produce highly qualified technicians. To take one example, apprenticeships in the field of optics might be offered in up to twelve technical fields (precision instruments, glass making, etc.) and five commercial fields. Promotions require more schooling and more certification. Beyond apprenticeships, individual universities and colleges tend to specialize in fields relating to the needs of local industries.

In Japan and Germany, there is an obsession with training and retraining—with upgrading human capital. In America, the need for improvement is widely discussed, but neither government nor industry has responded effectively.

SCIENCE AND TECHNOLOGY

The primary difference between the United States and its two key rivals in the science and technology arena is that Washington has emphasized so-called mega projects (frequently called Big Science) and basic theoretical research, while Japan and Germany have focussed on developing technology that is directly applicable to commercial competition.

America's priorities stem from several factors. Ever since the government became deeply involved in the Manhattan Project to develop the atom bomb, there has been a consensus that defense-related technology is one of the few areas where government *should* play a role. In the name of national security, Washington was therefore able to focus on almost anything, and it was able to award scholarships for students and to provide all manner of research contracts to universities and companies. While substantial commercial spinoffs came out of these programs, the stated objective was always national defense.

To the extent that industrial companies wanted to develop nondefense-related technology themselves, there was never a national policy to help them. Nevertheless, the vast sums of money that Washington poured into military technology gave American firms who worked with the Pentagon a great edge in the early days of computer and semiconductor development when the defense industry was at the technological forefront of these industries. In the 1980s, the utility of technology transfers from defense to nondefense slowed down when Japan, which had been focussing on strictly commercial applications, began to challenge American predominance in all areas of microelectronics. The weakness of America's approach was evident: defense projects were drawing skilled scientists from the private sector, and diverting American companies from focussing on the commercial technology that was essential to global competitiveness.

Postwar Japan and Germany had a much less onerous defense burden. Their primary efforts were devoted to building economic advantage. In Tokyo, commercial research and development was conducted almost entirely by private firms, although large consortiums under government guidance were formed to share financial risk. All efforts were aimed at product improvement. In Germany, research was a more cooperative effort among companies, public research institutes, private laboratories, universities, and state governments. There, too, the focus was almost exclusively commercial.

Indeed, America remains infatuated with Big Science. At the end of 1991, big research projects planned for completion in the 1990s included the Hubble Space Telescope ($1.5 billion), a program to map human genetic structures ($3 billion), the development of superconducting supercolliders ($8 billion), and the engineering of a space station ($30 billion).

A particularly important example of the kinds of issues that characterize American development of commercial technology is demonstrated by the collapse in June 1989 of the U.S. Memories Project. This was to be a joint venture to manufacture computer chips known as DRAMS— dynamic random access memory chips. The original backers included IBM, Digital Equipment, Hewlett-Packard, and Intel. The reason for forming the consortium was to develop a secure American source of chips, considering that Japan had a 70 percent world market share. The reasons why the venture failed are instructive. The major companies were reluctant to work together. There was a major division within the industry between those who produced chips and those who used them. And the market for DRAMS went from shortage to glut—whether a temporary phenomenon or not, no one knows, but no one wanted to look too far ahead. It was a paradigm of the way American business operates, and it helps explain why Washington and industry have been reluctant or unable to mount other cooperative programs.

Meanwhile, Japanese investment in commercial technology with precise applications has been accelerating at a phenomenal rate. At a time when research budgets of American companies were under pressure because of the short-term demands for profitability, cash-rich Japanese firms were plowing back an increasing amount of their profits into the development of new processes and technologies. Germany continued to focus on upgrading existing advantages, and big efforts are being channeled into major European Community research projects such as Jessi, a research consortium set up by Siemens, Phillips, and SGS Thompson for experimenting with manufacturing technologies needed to produce the next generation of semiconductor memories. There is, to be sure, considerable questioning in Europe about the effectiveness of these programs, but there is at least a strong concern that effective alternates be found to mobilize funds in a highly organized way to compete with Japan.

Another major difference among the three countries is the degree of openness to foreign researchers. The United States and Germany have virtually no barriers. Japan is at the opposite extreme. It was not until 1982, for example, that laws were passed to allow foreign faculty in Japanese national universities, not until 1986 that senior foreign appointments could be made to the national laboratories. The two largest American programs preparing U.S. scientists to work in Japan send fewer than sixty-five people each year. Yet there are more than 300 Japanese researchers at the U.S. National Institutes of Health alone, and an estimated 16,000–26,000 Japanese researchers in the United States, while there may be only 800 U.S. students in all of Japan.[11]

These differences in economic philosophies and structures are critical to the relationships among the Big Three. In fact, if we look beneath the current disputes over trade and finance we will see that many of these arguments are the result of how national economies are organized. Different forms of capitalism will lead to different levels of competitiveness, especially as the third industrial revolution, which is now occurring, accelerates, and different systems have their own strengths and weaknesses. It is too early to say whether American capitalism has lost its edge, whether Japanese capitalism is the wave of the future, or whether Germany's social market model is the one most nations will wish to emulate. But this much is certain: at different times each of the three models will be seen as having a distinct advantage. And as they compete and collide, we will hear cries of "unfair" or just "unacceptable" and we will see new attempts to erect barriers to trade or at least to slow the pace of change. The diversity of the three models is likely to make economic collaboration increasingly difficult, too. Coordination in the future will require that leaders make their institutions bend to a common goal among groups of nations. To the degree that this means putting pressures on long-standing national customs, laws, and preferences, resistance to change will be more and more difficult to overcome.

CHAPTER V

Open vs Closed Societies

For the last four decades, there were two clear visions of how society should be organized. The dividing line ran between democracy and free markets, on one side, and totalitarianism and Marxism, on the other. Now politics everywhere is veering in the direction of democracy, and virtually all countries admire Adam Smith. Does this mean that there will be no major ideological disputes, no fierce competition among political and economic systems? Absolutely not.

We have already seen that America, Japan, and Germany practice different kinds of capitalism, and noted some of the reasons behind their choices. But even recognition of their distinctive systems by the Big Three will not avert the conflicts that are brewing and that could lead to sharp divisions among them.

One problem concerns differences in the degree of openness in each society—the differences in the willingness of each of the Big Three to accept imports of products, foreign investment, and people from other nations. In the first instance, such divergence can become a matter of fairness, because societies that see themselves as more open than others eventually become angry over the disproportionate costs which they believe they bear. The United States, for example, increasingly finds it unfair that other markets are not as open to foreign penetration as its own; the president, cabinet officers, and many prominent congressmen have made the point with increasing passion.

They often point out that Asian and European companies are able to penetrate America's deregulated telecommunications industry or its banking system while the United States is shut out of their more controlled systems. In the 1980s, Europe and most of East Asia enjoyed a business boom, in good part because America was taking almost half of their exports. There were benefits to American consumers, of course. But there were also costs—the ravaging of certain industries, the dislocation of workers, and the cumulative trade deficits that added to the national debt. Other examples of where America believes it gives more than it receives are in affording foreign scientists the chance to do basic research, educating so many engineers from other nations, and taking a share of the world's displaced people. Such lopsided patterns held less significance during the Cold War, when Washington was willing to use its market to facilitate the economic recovery and military protection of its allies, and when American economic confidence was high. But those days are long gone.

Different levels of openness are also raising national security questions. A truly open economy makes little distinction between industries that are strategic and those that merely satisfy consumer demand—between, say, companies that manufacture semiconductors and those that make motion pictures. Over the past few decades America has not worried much about the implications of such openness, because dependence on imports of strategic products was minimal. In addition, Washington was buying from close allies, who were, after all, dependent on Washington for their military protection, thereby making it inconceivable that they would take any measures to weaken America's national security.

Now, however, the mood in the United States is shifting. The degree of imported components necessary for the functioning of the American economy, including defense and other high-technology areas, has been soaring, as has foreign investment in U.S. companies—in such fields as machine tools or electronics—that would have to support the defense industrial base in time of war. And now that the Soviet Union has collapsed, Japan and Germany are seen as rivals as much as friends. Indeed, this national security issue is real, especially to those who recall how America once used its economic clout against its allies, and who worry that the tables could be turned in the future. In 1956, for example, Washington forced Great Britain and France to withdraw their forces from the Suez Canal by threatening to cut off oil supplies to them. In the mid-1960s, to take another instance, the United States forced France to cut back its nuclear arms production by refusing to issue licenses to I.B.M. and Control Data to transfer essential technology to Paris.

Openness may not be uniform, even within a country. A nation may be receptive to some types of penetration and more restrictive about others. Germany, for example, has welcomed imports of manufactured goods, but is less open to foreign investors, and still less open to immigration. Also, a description of the early 1990s is merely a snapshot in time. Nations that allow easy access today may behave much differently under tomorrow's pressures. The United States, for example, may decide that the costs of a wide-open economy are too great, and become more protectionist. Conversely, Japan may liberalize its economy faster than anyone now anticipates. The problem is not just who is open and who is not, but the very existence of different situations at any given time, the pressures on each nation to change, and the tensions involved in trying to deal with these divergent environments in an interconnected world economy.

TRADE

In trade, the potential collision course of the Big Three can be described this way: The United States has become single-minded in its pressure on other nations to further open their economies to its products and services. It is increasingly truculent—prepared to retaliate harshly, to risk escalating trade tensions, and to conclude bilateral deals that are inconsistent with the open multilateral system it vigorously supported during most of the postwar years. Japan, on the other hand, is moving up the competitive ladder with breathtaking speed, resulting in greater export penetration and no offsetting purchase of imports. Germany could become less open to American and Japanese products than in the past, especially if the E.C. turned inward, if it increased subsidies to high-technology firms, or if Japanese penetration of Europe became so intense that it caused Berlin to reassess its policies—all real possibilities.

America's Shifting Outlook

Throughout the postwar period, the prevailing trade theory—at least the theory to which most lip service was given, and certainly the one pushed relentlessly by Washington—was one of free trade on a multilateral and nondiscriminatory basis. That meant two things: governments should get out of the way of trade; and, if a tariff or quota was reduced for one country, it would automatically be reduced for all others. There were many exceptions, but the thrust was clear.

Now American policy is changing. In the 1980s, trade deficits grew dramatically, from an average of about $10 billion per year in the 1970s to $94 billion per year in the 1980s. (America's deficits with Japan were much larger than with Germany—averaging $40 billion per year in the latter part of the decade with Tokyo, vs about $10 billion annually with Germany.) With foreign competition becoming increasingly fierce, Congress grew disillusioned with the GATT, because it felt that other nations were subsidizing their own firms, closing their markets to American companies, failing to uphold patent and copyright laws—and getting away with it. Legislators also believed that foreign firms were dumping products in the U.S. market at prices below what they charged at home. As a result, Congress passed new trade legislation in 1988, ordering the administration to get much tougher in its negotiations. Among the weapons that it put in the President's hands was a provision mandating that Washington retaliate against countries with a record of blocking the import of American products. Retaliation would be justified in a broad variety of situations, leading to a United States which would become increasingly combative. The U.S. administration would be the accuser, the judge and the jury on other nations' trade practices, rather than accepting adjudication under the GATT, as required by international law. This resort to so extreme a *unilateral* approach was seen outside the United States (and also among the trade policy traditionalists in America) as evidence that America was playing by new rules, even though Washington argued that only by prying open foreign markets could it avoid protectionism in America and promote freer trade for everyone.

Indeed, America is in the process of a fundamental shift in philosophy that goes beyond the degree of government intervention in any particular industry. It is moving towards a policy of managed trade—government-to-government agreements to regulate the volume of trade in a particular area. In the past, if tariffs were reduced, if quotas were abolished, or if trade-blocking regulations were removed, this in itself was considered a successful end to a negotiation. What counted was the *process* of trade liberalization. The market would take care of the rest, so the argument went. But with managed trade, Washington is saying something else. It is trying to determine the *outcome*, regardless of how it is engineered. The euphemism of this new approach is "results-oriented trade." For example, throughout the 1980s Washington pressured Japan to "voluntarily" limit car exports to 2.5 million units. It concluded an agreement with Tokyo to guarantee that American firms receive 20 percent of the semiconductor market in Japan (an agreement that was interpreted differently in Washington and Tokyo, leading to subsequent frictions). Managed trade has become contagious; now the European Community is preoccupied with forcing Japanese firms to "voluntarily" restrict their car exports to Western Europe in order not to exceed a precisely specified market share.

Economists would say that the implication of such growing government involvement is great inefficiency and higher prices. But equally significant, managed trade means heightened friction as politicians in one country attempt to determine market trends and officials in other nations argue with these actions. A clear example is America's demand in 1992 to force Japan to accept a certain increase in the imports of American autos and auto parts.

Japan and Europe are already accusing the United States of turning its back on the postwar trading system. America is abandoning its international outlook, they say. They are blunt in their warnings about the political dangers. They are also increasingly frank in expressing their view that America's trade problems are a result of its lack of competitiveness, not the unfair practices of its trading partners.

Meanwhile, America's trade deficit remains high. The problem for it and the world will put great pressure on global trade for years to come. For every year that the large deficit persists America has to borrow to finance its imports. Such borrowings add to the foreign debt and increase the vulnerability of relying on foreign creditors. In the mid-1990s, America's overseas obligations could reach $1 trillion, requiring interest payments of $80 billion to $100 billion a year. In order to cut the growth of foreign debt and eventually reduce it, the United States will have to move from a deficit to a surplus on its current account (which includes both the trade balance and most of the interest on its foreign debt). It is difficult to estimate the precise numbers, because future G.N.P. growth rates will have a large bearing on U.S. import levels. But an educated projection, based on past patterns and an extrapolation of projections by both the

International Monetary Fund and the Organization for Economic Co-operation and Development in Paris—both of which assume a U.S. recovery and hence an increase in imports—is that current account deficits in the mid-1990s could range between $50 billion and $100 billion. Assuming that the United States could produce a trade surplus in this amount (which would be a swing of over $100 billion from the deficit-ridden performance of the past few years), which nations would make room in their markets for U.S. products? Japan and Germany are sure to be among the major targets, but they themselves are supercompetitive.

The problem is even larger than that. First, a major portion of the deterioration in America's trade position has been in automobiles, which account for more than two-thirds of the trade deficit with Japan. Yet this is the area where the United States has had the most difficulty holding its own, with General Motors' North American operations accumulating losses of $500 million a month in 1991 and Chrysler selling off assets to survive. Trying to compensate for the competitive problems of Detroit by developing exports in other industries is an awesome challenge. There are no easy answers, and almost every alternative is confrontational. The usual tactics—supertough negotiations, retaliation, and pushing down the value of the dollar to make American products less expensive abroad —all have their own problems in terms of setting off a trade war, or in hurting the economy generally.

A second reason why America's deficit is such a big problem is that there has been a sea change in the nature of the barriers that interfere with trade these days. For most of this century, the problems have been tariffs and quotas—making imports more expensive or controlling their quantity. The result of trade negotiations since the 1950s, however, has been to reduce these obstacles to extremely low levels. Subsidies have also been a traditional problem, but even these are coming under control. Now we are left with much tougher barriers—so-called structural impediments—and here is where different kinds of economic systems butt up against one another. Structural barriers are policies like different regulatory systems for banking; different standards for health, safety, environmental protection; different rules for distributing products; different concepts of antitrust; different laws at national and state levels. For over forty years trade liberalization could proceed relatively easily because governments were negotiating the barriers at their borders. But now they are trying to reach deep into the domestic systems of one another. This promises to be a much different and more difficult challenge. There is no way to precisely quantify the trade-blocking impact of these truly domestic obstacles, but the World Bank has estimated that they have adversely affected between 25 percent to 40 percent of imports of the Western industrial nations and Japan over the past two decades.[1]

Nowhere is the agenda clearer than in Washington's latest effort to break down structural impediments in Japan. The political problems should be apparent by a quick description of what the United States is demanding.

• The United States wants Japan to overhaul its procedures for identifying and prosecuting antitrust violations. The assumption is that if the Japanese corporate sector were decartelized, foreigners could compete more effectively with Japanese firms on their own turf.

• America wants Japan to open up its distribution system so that U.S. firms would have a better chance to sell their products around the country.

• Washington is demanding that Tokyo lift restrictions on the locations of large retail department stores. Such restrictions were designed to protect small shops from competition. America wants to see more large stores, because they are the major importers.

• Japan is being pressed to reduce the cross-shareholdings of companies that have been closely tied together for generations and to grant more rights to shareholders in the running of corporations. The idea is to increase opportunities for foreign competition and takeovers.

• The United States wants Japan to spend more money on roads, ports, sewers, and parks in the 1990s. Washington is saying that Japanese people should have a better life with more leisure—all of which will make them buy more and save less. America has pressed Tokyo to specify the amount—$2.8 *trillion*—and the precise budgetary procedures it will use to raise the funds to achieve these ends.

• The United States wants Japan to reform many of the regulations governing the use of land and real estate. This, it is hoped, would also make Japanese big spenders. The American reasoning is that the price of land is too high; if it were cheaper, Japanese would live in bigger houses and they would buy more refrigerators and furniture. American proposals include changing various zoning ordinances and altering the way inheritance taxes are assessed.

Japan has agreed in principle to the thrust of many of the U.S. demands, although it insists that the extent of change and the timing are another matter. Thus far Tokyo has been restrained in demanding equal structural changes that the United States should make to rectify the trade imbalance; it has settled, instead, for fuzzy American commitments to reduce the budget, improve education, and so forth. But how long can such passivity last in the face of Japan's increasing power and ambition? This past year, for example, a widely distributed report from the Economic Planning Agency of the government admonished Washington to get its house in order—to reexamine its defense spending, to promote savings, to rein in spending.

The potential list of cultural and institutional differences that impede trade and investment among the Big Three is very long. Almost no issue is out-of-bounds: not tax systems, budget procedures, labor practices, educational standards, social welfare policies, health and safety regulations, or the cost of liability insurance. Japan even raised the possibility of curtailing the number of credit cards that Americans carry in order to reduce U.S. consumption.

Once this kind of negotiation gets going, it will not be just national laws, regulations, and customs that are on the table, but the whole set of U.S. state and local trade-distorting laws, of which there are many. For example, California, Texas, and Massachusetts have different laws concerning safety standards, packaging and labeling, transportation, environmental restrictions, banking, corporate takeovers. Putting these on the international agenda would open a true Pandora's box, leading to a level of trade conflict few dare to envision.

Pressures from Japan

Trade tensions are bad enough now, especially in light of the fact that in 1991 Japan's trade surplus with the world reversed its three-year decline and grew by nearly 50 percent. But the worst is yet to come. Indeed, there are pressures from Japan which promise to collide with America's relentless quest for new markets and the E.C.'s aspirations to develop world-class European firms. (It is customary to talk about the trade policy of the E.C. as a whole, rather than that of any one country such as Germany, since the E.C. coordinates all trade policy of its member countries.) The major new factor will stem from the results of Japan's massive investment program that has taken place over the past few years. Japanese companies have been plowing billions of dollars into new capacity, new products, new processes. In 1989 Japan invested 23.2 percent of its G.N.P. in plant and capital equipment while the United States invested 11.7 percent. In 1988, 1989, and 1990 Japan invested more in *absolute* terms than did America. About 30 percent of these enormous sums are going into techniques that improve productivity. Another 30 percent of capital investment is going to develop new products, and another 30 percent into new capacity.[2] At the same time, two other factors have contributed to Japan's increasing competitiveness. A strong yen has made Japanese products more expensive and caused manufacturers to redouble their efforts to keep down costs and to make their products more appealing. And labor shortages have resulted in large-scale automation plus more efficient use of the labor force, including advanced training.

Japan is investing not only in products but in new infrastructure. Improvements in communications and transport generally translate into higher levels of productivity, and the government and private sectors are committed to a massive program of upgrading and modernization of roads, ports, airports, state-of-the-art distribution facilities, and electric power. Neither America nor Germany can match this performance.

The result of all this will be that Japan will not only be positioned to capture more foreign markets, but that it will become even more difficult for foreign firms to break in. "As with interest rates, there is a compound effect," says Kenneth S. Courtis, one of the West's leading Japan watchers. "Each additional yen that Japan invests today is invested on an increasingly competitive base. America faces the reverse dynamics."[3] When the fruits of all this investment hit the market in the mid-1990s, a second wave of Japanese exports—in autos, advanced computers, telecommunications equipment, and other products—will set off new howls in the United States and Europe.

The course of the yen is another problem. For every nation there is a strong link between the value of its currency and its trade performance, and in the case of Japan it seems that no matter what the level of the yen is, the nation's trade surplus remains large. In the mid-1980s, America alleged that Japan's competitiveness was the result of a cheap yen. Then, beginning in 1985, the yen started to appreciate, eventually doubling its value relative to the dollar. But this revelation resulted in another source of tension: the strong yen has made manufacturing products in Japan very expensive. As a result, Japanese firms are moving offshore to produce in nations like Thailand or Malaysia where wage rates and other production costs are much lower. Then they export from these new locations. The true extent of Japan's penetration of Western markets, therefore, is not just evident in official statistics coming from Tokyo, but must also include sales from Bangkok, Jakarta, Kuala Lumpur, Taipei, and Seoul. The amounts are hard to estimate, but they are surely enormous.

Yet another set of pressures from Japan will come from the increased internationalization of Japanese companies. These global firms will be conducting a massive volume of trade among themselves. An increasing amount of Japanese imports will come from foreign subsidiaries of Japanese companies, just as occurs now when autos imported into Japan come from Nissan and Honda factories in Southeast Asia. Some estimates show that 70 percent of Japan's worldwide trade has a Japanese company at each end of the transaction, compared to 20 percent for the United States.[4] It is too early to tell what this system-within-a-system will do to the global trading order, but it certainly has the potential to produce yet another layer of political acrimony in economic relations among the Big Three.

All of this should be put in the context of Japan's low level of imports. The fact is that by some measures imports of manufactured goods into Japan have been growing at a more rapid rate than exports of manufacturers—but are growing from a much lower base. Between 1985 and 1990, for example, Japan's purchases from other countries grew from $24 billion to $90 billion, while its exports increased from $163 billion to $262 billion. The gaps therefore have remained very large, even without the new wave of competitive Japanese products on the horizon.[5] In addition, the composition of trade with Japan is a big problem for other countries. In general, America has exported commodities and raw materials to Japan while importing manufactured goods, although there is some evidence that the mix is changing. But even when the U.S. sells high-tech manufactures, all is not what it seems. For example, American computer exports to Japan in 1990 were up about 108 percent over the

1987 level, but Japanese computer exports to the United States grew by 150 percent in the same period.[6]

Finally, Japan has engendered great suspicion in America about manipulating the sales of high technology components to American firms. This has not become a cause célèbre yet, but it has the potential to become one. In 1990, for example, several U.S. companies were charging that Japanese firms were intentionally delaying the shipment of the latest chip-making equipment as well as parts for flat panel displays and lap top computers, all with the objective of retarding America's competitive position. The Defense Science Board cited examples of delays to defense contractors; the Senate Finance Committee and the General Accounting Office cited similar experiences. While Japanese firms hotly denied the allegations, the national security overtones are obvious.[7]

Pressures from Europe

Europe, too, will be creating new problems for global trade. In fact, aside from Great Britain, the European nations have always been comfortable with a strategic approach to trade in which government intervenes to shape the market. In the 1990s we are likely to see more of this.

Neither Western Europe generally, nor Germany in particular, are closed to imports in the way Japan has been. In Germany, for example, imports constitute nearly 23 percent of Germany's G.N.P., compared to 7 percent for Japan and 9 percent for the United States. However, several factors reinforce the view that the European Community could lean in a more protectionist direction.

First, although the E.C. has not yet turned into the trade fortress that Washington once worried about, these are still early days. The period since 1985, when the E.C. pledged itself to becoming a unified market, has been one of rapid economic growth for most of its members. In this environment it was easy for Western Europe to pledge that it would be fully open to the rest of the world. Now, however, the business boom has ended, and the growth prospects for the next few years are much more modest. As more men and women fail to find jobs, as governments come under pressure to make larger welfare payments, as more firms go bankrupt, the exuberance for open markets is sure to wane.

Aside from the economic climate, the future character of the E.C. is highly uncertain, despite agreements reached at the end of 1991 in which members committed themselves to the goals of a monetary, economic, and political union. Western Europe will increase its internal cohesion, but this doesn't tell us to what ends it will use its cohesion. If, for example, the E.C. has a common monetary policy dominated by Germany, there will be a strong preference for anti-inflation policies at the expense of growth—the historic German position. As a result, the European G.N.P. could increase more slowly than might otherwise be the case, thereby slowing American and Japanese exports.

There are also strong social democratic tendencies in most of the E.C. countries including two of the three most powerful—Germany and France. The E.C. has adopted a social charter that workers' organizations have already been pushing, which, when fully activated, could entail a level of worker participation in corporate decisions, such as plant reorganizations or the location of new investments, that would be extremely frustrating to American management and give a strong edge to European firms more accustomed to that environment.

Furthermore, the countries of continental Europe have a long history of cartelization and state intervention in their economies. It is quite likely that this tradition will be revived in the high-technology sectors, where the E.C. members are already worried about their competitive standing. Indeed, one of the main forces behind the E.C.'s 1992 vision was the hope that European high-technology firms would combine their strengths and compete effectively with their U.S. and Japanese rivals. But it hasn't worked out that way, and new efforts are a sure thing. An important arena is computers. Despite the fanfare surrounding several intergovernmental efforts to coordinate E.C. research, the big firms have all been losing money. Since the 1990s began, France's Bull required a massive capital injection from the state; Germany's Siemens had to buy its bankrupt rival, Nixdorf, and the combined entity was still in the red in 1991; and Holland's Philips laid off a third of its work force. In fact, the European firms lag behind their U.S. and Japanese rivals in innovation and efficiency, and their smaller size—in 1991 the combined sales of the top four European computer companies were just one-third of IBM's—constrain R&D expenditures and make catching up impossible without extraordinary new efforts. Indeed, throughout Europe the cries for "industrial regeneration" can be heard.

Another pressure that could reduce European openness is a backlash from intense Japanese penetration. Tokyo's trade surplus is mounting more rapidly with Western Europe than with any other area of the world. In 1990, for example, Japan ran an $18.5 billion surplus with the E.C., but in 1991 it rose to $30 billion. Tokyo has two strong motivations to keep up its strong export performance with Europe: it is anxious to diversify its trade away from heavy dependence on the United States, and it is intent on getting inside the E.C. in the event the Community turns more protectionist. From a European perspective, however, such lopsided trade may prove politically unacceptable. There is a strong likelihood that when it comes to Japan, the E.C. will tighten up on its efforts to demand that its firms receive the same kind of treatment in Japan as Japanese firms get in Europe. Such reciprocity is taken far more seriously in Europe than in the United States, and an effort to interpret the concept strictly could lead to a new set of contentious trade issues.

Europe also faces growing problems with America, which in recent years has been running a trade surplus with the E.C. as a whole. The trends are dramatic. In 1988, America's merchandise trade with the E.C. was $10 billion in the red. It turned slightly positive in 1989. But in 1990 it grew to a surplus of $15 billion. Confronted by pressures from both Japan and the United States, the E.C. could be looking for almost any policy to stop the bleeding.

Finally, the events in Eastern Europe and the former Soviet Union could force the E.C. to devote most of its commercial efforts to accommodating pressures from the East through special trade concessions, or through incorporation of Poland, Hungary, Czechoslovakia—even Ukraine—into the E.C. itself. Such deals could result in a flood of imports into Germany and other nations, making open trade with America and Japan that much more difficult.

The idea that Germany, in particular, could swing its weight toward a Europe-first policy is consistent with how its own trade has been evolving. When the E.C. was founded in 1958, 30 percent of (West) Germany's exports went to its member countries. By 1990, 53 percent of its exports stayed within the Community. If Scandinavia and Eastern Europe are included, then three quarters of all German trade is now on the Continent, while less than 10 percent is with the United States and less than 3 percent with Japan.[8]

There is also one unique factor that could reduce Germany's maneuverability to promote more open trade in the years ahead: the attitude of the former East Germans, who have had a half-century's tradition of heavily managed trade. Admittedly, their former system did not work well compared to that of the West. But conditions in the East are still grim, and it has yet to be demonstrated that Western capitalism will provide the jobs that East Germans need. In any event, under pressure they may very well have less enthusiasm for open trade than their colleagues in the western part of the nation, and their political resistance could well be felt in evolving policies.

The Special Challenge of High Technology

No aspect of trade will be more contentious in the 1990s than high technology. This sector is important not only because of the struggle in specific industries—such as aerospace or telecommunications—but because each of the Big Three sees its ability to compete in the high-technology arena as critical to the vitality of its industrial base and to its national security. "There is a growing conviction among some economists and political leaders that economic success in the 21st century will accrue to the nations that produce high technology products within their borders," wrote Bruce Stokes of *The National Journal*. "The spinoff economic benefits from manufacturing semi-conductors, high definition televisions and similar products may be so great . . . that few governments may be willing to let success or failure of their advanced industries be solely determined by the international marketplace."[9]

The race for supremacy in the high-technology industries is already distorting a good deal of liberal economic theory. In the past, the big exceptions to free market philosophy came when governments felt compelled to protect their dying industries like textiles or steel. In the future, there will be a new kind of protectionism, focussing not on "sunset" industries but on the "sunrise" sector—the businesses of the future.

There are three respectable ways to justify more government involvement in high technology industry, all of which governments are using now. One is to say that comparative advantage in this arena does not come naturally but has to be created. The costs of R&D, the development of firms with sufficient manufacturing capability, the need to coordinate efforts on a national scale—all this means that the Adam Smith model of free competition, based as it is on the ideal of small firms competing in an unregulated marketplace, is largely irrelevant in today's global high-tech sector. A second line of reasoning is that high-technology industry is simply too important to leave to the market alone, and that a major industrial nation simply cannot afford to be uncompetitive in computers. High-tech jobs pay better and lead to a higher standard of living, so the argument would go. Moreover, the beneficial spillover of the skills and knowledge from one high-tech industry to another, and to the economy in general, is enormous.

And the third reason for disregarding traditional free market theory is this: Japan has developed a certain approach to high technology that leaves America and Europe no choice but to respond *in kind.* Indeed, the Japanese model, characterized by close government-industry cooperation, strategic targeting of certain industries, sharing of risks among families of large firms, direct and indirect subsidies, and selected trade protection, has proved so successful that no one has come up with any better idea other than to try to copy it. Such replication may be an impossible task given the very different cultures in America and Europe. Nevertheless, Washington and Berlin will be pressing harder to compete in high technology, and the implications are, at a minimum, more public sector involvement in industry, more protectionism, more trade conflict.

In the United States there has been more debate than action, but it's hard to believe the nation will watch the rout of its high-technology industries without doing something radically different. As the nonpartisan, private sector Council on Competitiveness warned in 1991, "The U.S. position in many critical technologies is slipping and, in some cases, has been lost altogether. America pioneered such technologies as numerically controlled machine tools, robotics, optoelectronics, semiconductors, and memories only to lose leadership in them to foreign competitors. Moreover, in many critical technologies, ranging from leading-edge scientific equipment to precision bearings, trends are running against U.S. industry.[10]

Washington has been nibbling at the edges of policy changes—relaxation of certain antitrust prohibitions, tax credits for R&D, and support for selected government-industry consortiums like Sematech, whose mission is to build new capabilities in semiconductor manufacturing technology. But unless there are dramatic changes in approach, the likelihood is not for surrender to foreign competition but for a violent protectionist reaction to it.

Meanwhile, the European Community is frantic to arrest its decline in the high-tech arena, and to maintain at least a few corporate champions. The computer industry, as noted, is one area of concern. Another is the aerospace industry, where Airbus Industrie—a consortium of German, British, French, and Spanish companies—has been highly subsidized by governments for at least a decade. Airbus now has some 30 percent of the global market for commercial aircraft manufacture, and is aiming for 40 percent over the next few years—the extra 10 percent to come out of the U.S. share. Washington has challenged the legality of the subsidies in the GATT, but the process is taking years, the outcome is highly uncertain, and frustration is mounting in U.S. trade negotiations and within the American aerospace industry.

Breakdown of Cooperation: The Sad Saga of the Uruguay Round

In December 1990, a major effort to liberalize trade, conducted through a marathon negotiation that lasted four years, fell apart. The timing of the impasse was particularly significant, coming as it did when the Big Three were celebrating the end of the Cold War and the triumph of democracy and free markets. The issue which caused the breakdown was a dispute between the United States and Europe over opening trade in agriculture, a dispute that continued throughout 1991 and into 1992. At some point the negotiations are likely to be concluded, and, if history is any guide, they will be labelled a success regardless of the actual results. But the events of December 1990, together with the agonizing efforts to reach agreement over the following year, revealed the deep divisions among the Big Three.

The inability of the U.S. and the E.C. to settle on a reduction of subsidies to agricultural production and trade illustrates the kind of dispute that can arise between two powerful trading entities totally preoccupied with their own problems. At stake was far more than agricultural trade, for every other issue in the negotiations—from patent protection to freer trade in telecommunications—was put on hold pending progress on the farm question. In one corner was Washington, screaming for radical agricultural liberalization—the dismantling of export subsidies, and more open markets. In another was Germany, at first joining France in taking a highly protectionist stance, and later shifting its rhetoric but not using its influence to change Paris's position. Then there was Japan, staying in the background and hoping that no progress would be made so that its own agricultural protectionism would not be in the spotlight.

FOREIGN INVESTMENT

Foreign direct investment promises to be a new arena of conflict among nations in the mid-1990s and beyond, perhaps even overshadowing trade tensions. Companies are investing outside of their own countries at a pace that is far greater than the increase of international trade or the growth of national economies. From 1983 to 1988, direct investment across borders—that is, investment in plant, equipment, real estate (but not in stocks and bonds)—grew at an annual compound rate of 20 percent, while the comparable statistic for trade was 5 percent. Over the last decade, foreign direct investment grew four times faster than the G.N.P. of the major industrial nations. Some forecasts show that even under conservative assumptions, by 1995 the stock of foreign direct investment within the advanced industrialized world will be more than twice the level of 1988.[11]

Despite a temporary lull in 1991 and again in 1992, the Japanese dimension to this surge will be very large. Today, for example, the Japanese sell or produce abroad about 5 percent of their G.N.P., compared to 15 percent for the former West Germany and 20 percent for the United States. If Japan achieved roughly similar overseas positions of America and Germany in the 1990s, and if, as seems likely, its economy continues to grow at a steady pace and the yen continues to appreciate, then by the end of the decade Japanese companies could increase their presence abroad by four and a half times.[12]

German overseas investment has far less dramatic potential. However, German firms have been on an acquisition binge in Europe, and they have been much bigger players in the U.S. market than is generally recognized. In 1990, for example, German firms invested nearly $6 billion in America, adding to their ownership stock of U.S. companies, which includes major firms like A&P, RCA Records, the Bantam Doubleday Dell Publishing Group, and Fireman's Fund Insurance Companies.

Foreign investment encompasses all the issues—political, economic, cultural, emotional—inherent in one country's penetration of another. In the case of Japan's overseas investments, the problems have become particularly acute because of the sheer pace of penetration in so short a time, and the resulting visibility of Japanese activity. Since 1951, for example, Japan has registered some 57,400 cases of outward investment with authorities in Tokyo. However, two thirds of this has taken place since 1986.[13] Whereas a big fuss used to be made about the overwhelming presence of American investment abroad, it is now the United States that is complaining about the growing presence of foreign operations—particularly Japanese—on its territory. Because foreign investment heightens America's sense of vulnerability to outside forces, Washington is likely to deal with it in a far more aggressive way in the mid-1990s than it has thus far.

America's Reaction

What will the American government do? First, it is likely to condemn Japan and, to a much lesser extent, Germany for their lack of openness in letting American companies enter their countries, either de novo or especially via acquisition of existing firms. Although such mergers and takeovers are rare even among the firms within Japan and Germany, that argument will not distract Americans from the political issue of the absence of fairness—an idea that always raises America's indignation.

It may not count for much that relative to America's $6 trillion G.N.P., penetration by foreign investors is nowhere near a danger point. After all, foreign firms in America account for about only 4 percent of U.S. jobs and business output.[14] What will be much more significant is that key sectors of the U.S. economy—from autos to electronics—will have a heavy concentration of foreign ownership. Moreover, in its crusade over the fairness question, America can easily show that foreign penetration of Japan has been minuscule, and it will point to a host of Japanese policies and customs that do not augur well for change.

Washington will be able to show, as well, that although Germany has a much better record, it is the only major country in Western Europe where foreign investment was lower in the 1980s than the 1970s.[15] And despite the fact that Germany had the largest G.N.P. in Western Europe, its absolute level of incoming direct investment in the 1980s was far smaller than in England or France.[16] Moreover, the United States can point to a host of features in the German industrial structure that discourage new foreign investment. These include the heavy involvement of banks and labor unions in the management of German companies, which gives German interests overwhelming control over potential foreign investors, and high labor costs, high business taxes, and rigid employment requirements that discourage many new foreign investors from coming in.

But America may do much more than just condemn these practices. For example, it is very possible that it will harness the full energies of the government to clamp down. In the late 1980s, Washington established a government committee to review incoming investment, and in 1991 the committee's mandate was enshrined in legislation. This sounds like a modest step, but before that time Washington was so relaxed about foreign investment that it barely monitored what went on. Now, at least, the mechanism to exercise discretion and block or delay foreign efforts is in place.

Washington could force foreign investors to disclose much more financial information about their worldwide operations than they are used to doing. Such disclosure would be designed to make sure that foreign subsidiaries in the United States are paying their fair share of taxes in America—that they are not manipulating their books so as to show profits in lower tax jurisdictions abroad. In fact, the IRS has already begun investigating foreign banks' U.S. tax returns. In congressional hearings held in mid-1990, the IRS testified that foreign firms paid taxes on less than 1 percent of gross receipts in the United States. Sales by Japanese companies in the United States rose 50 percent in 1987 while reported taxable income dropped by two thirds.[17] More disclosure would also give Washington a better idea of who abroad is really controlling any foreign subsidiary in question, something about which Washington typically knows very little.

In another development, in 1990 the Justice Department began investigating whether the close relationship between Japanese automakers and Japanese manufacturers of auto parts, not in the United States but in their home country, puts American producers at an unfair competitive disadvantage. This examination extended the reach of American antitrust concerns in ways never before attempted. At the same time the Federal Trade Commission began investigating whether Nissan, Toyota, and Honda are giving preference to Japanese suppliers in the United States.

The United States is afraid of becoming an assembly plant for companies who keep the best jobs at home. As a result, it could demand that a certain percentage of that research be done on American soil using American citizens. In early 1992, for example, the city of Los Angeles was moving in this direction when it cancelled a $122 million contract with the Sumitomo Corporation to build railway cars for a new mass transit system. The reason was to give Southern California its own chance to build a new "made-in-America" industry.

The United States may redefine what kinds of foreign investments should be excluded, because of national security considerations, from Japan, Germany, and other allies. It is possible, for example, that various foreign investments in high-technology industries could be subject to new controls. This could mean that foreign companies would be denied access to big research projects financed by Washington, to technical data held by various agencies, or to certain types of university research. Such policies could, of course, lead to American firms being denied similar access abroad, just when overseas R&D is soaring.

Japan vs Germany

Disputes about foreign investment will not be just between America and Japan or America and Germany. As Japanese investment in Europe begins to increase, Germany and other European nations are sure to raise many of the same concerns voiced in the United States. As in trade, the balances are lopsided in favor of Japan. Between 1988 and 1990, for example, Japanese investment in Germany grew from $409 million to $1,242 million, whereas German investment in Japan went from $195 million to $259 million. [18]

An example of European distress over foreign investment is the E.C.'s attitude toward Japanese automobiles. In addition to exporting cars to the E.C., Toyota, Nissan, Honda, and Mitsubishi have been rushing to set up plants on European soil. The pressure on European manufacturers is severe. In 1991, therefore, the E.C. negotiated a "voluntary" restraint agreement with Japan. The objective was to hold down Japan's share of the E.C. market to 16 percent (Tokyo's share of the American market is about 30 percent). But the added precedent-setting element was the strong implication that limitations on Japanese penetration would apply even to Japanese firms that produce cars in Europe itself. In other words, the E.C. was saying, "We don't care whether you invest and produce here, and bring money and jobs; you're still Japanese and hence you should operate within an overall quota."

While both sides argued over the idea of a production quota in Europe, the handwriting is on the wall. Investment disputes will grow as Japanese production expands on the Continent. This is inevitable given the greater efficiency of Japan's manufacturing technology and projections of overcapacity in the European market. In 1990, for example, European auto production by Japanese factories totalled 151,000 cars. By 1995, it is expected to reach 654,000, and by the year 2000 over 1,200,000.[19] Moreover, with regard to Germany in particular, there will be big problems. The result of artificially limiting Japanese penetration of the European auto industry will be similar to what happened in the United States when Japan agreed to voluntarily limit its car exports to America. Constrained in the number of cars they can sell, Nissan and the others will want to make more profit on each vehicle. This means they will move to dominate the high-priced luxury market, a move that will result in a direct challenge to Daimler-Benz, BMW, and Porsche—important symbols of Germany's industrial success. The level of angst can be inferred by the views of Eberhard von Kuenheim, chairman of BMW. The Japanese, he said, "do not respect the rules of the market."[20]

Global Alliances

There is another aspect to the foreign investment issue that goes beyond the simple model of one company moving money from its own country to another. Many industrial alliances are being concluded between big companies of different nationalities—Toyota hooking up with General Motors to make cars in California, IBM linking up with Siemens of Germany, Mitsubishi Corporation tying up with Daimler-Benz. In the first instance, these combinations are a natural outcome of the overall increase in international commerce. It is tempting to look at them as new entities that will be able to deliver more and better products around the world at less cost. And to a great extent, that is true.

But from a more political perspective, these goliaths will cause problems for governments. It will not be long before politicians—American ones, at least—begin to think about the anticompetitive impact of such industrial power, and wonder whether America is not at a big disadvantage with these strategic alliances. After all, America does not see its companies as national champions; if traditional policies prevail, Washington will play no role in assisting U.S. firms to create big alliances or to dominate them. Tokyo and Berlin, however, will see things differently, because a Fujitsu or a Siemens is not just any bundle of financial assets to them—these are important pillars of their national communities, flagships of the state. The implication is not merely one of competitiveness; it is the political fallout from the perception that the rules of the game are stacked against the United States. Americans may begin to have serious reservations about the big global mergers taking place.

Considering all these issues, the mid-1990s will be a time when the foreign investment question will come to a boil. The disputes could take two forms. Individual cases could become very contentious, as happened when Japan's Fujitsu tried to buy Fairchild Industries a few years ago and was discouraged by a political outcry in Washington. Alternatively, America, with its penchant for legally binding rules, may well try to negotiate a broad set of international arrangements for foreign investors. The different perspectives between America and its major trading partners on issues like disclosure and antitrust, mergers and acquisitions would make such negotiations more conflict-ridden than anything we have seen in trade.

THE MOVEMENT OF PEOPLE

In the 1990s, a number of factors will propel the movement of people across borders: the economic pressures in the Third World, Eastern Europe, and the former Soviet Union; the acceleration of population growth in areas that cannot produce enough jobs; great uncertainties about political stability in many countries; the rapid development of communications and transport. America, Japan, and Germany will be under great pressure to admit more refugees and immigrants into their societies. As the three most prosperous nations in their respective regions, they will be poles of attraction for men, women, and families looking for food, shelter, education, and jobs. Moreover, the end of the Cold War gives added urgency to accommodating refugees and immigrants. After all, the West has long maintained that among its highest goals has been the human right to be free from political persecution and to emigrate.

As in trade or finance, the movement of people into the Big Three—or the barriers to their entrance—illustrates open versus closed societies and the conflicts that could arise from such differences. Foremost will be the question of relative responsibility: to the extent that any of the Big Three closes its borders, the others could experience an even greater crunch, with attendant costs of services, schooling, housing, and more immediate social tensions. Beyond costs, there is the potential for moral recriminations over the failure to accommodate refugees on humanitarian grounds. And there could be accusations that countries that do not accept their share of displaced people are contributing to the pressures in the countries from which they are fleeing, thereby leading to more political instability around the world. The movement of people, therefore, will become a surrogate for other issues among America, Japan, and Germany—fair burdensharing, human rights, maintenance of peace.

Rising Numbers of Refugees

The problems will be enormous. Even before the decade began, the growth of refugees worldwide was explosive. And over the next several years there is sure to be an acceleration of migration from East to West and from South to North. In 1970, for example, an estimated 2.5 million people sought asylum. A decade later, the number increased to 8.2 million. By 1990, not counting the fallout from the Gulf crisis, the total was 15 million.[21]

Looking ahead, three sources of new pressures are evident. First, the collapse of the Iron Curtain has removed the physical barrier between prosperous Western Europe and the impoverished eastern part of the continent. According to figures from the International Organization for Migration in Geneva, from the early 1970s to the first half of the 1980s, around 100,000 people moved from the Warsaw Pact countries to the West. By 1989 the figure was 1.3 million.[22] With growing unemployment in Poland, Czechoslovakia, Hungary, and the republics of the former Soviet Union, not to mention hunger, border conflicts, ethnic tensions, and persecution of minorities, the pressure is sure to mount. In early 1991 Soviet officials estimated that 1.5 to 2 million Soviet citizens were likely to move west over the next few years. Some U.N. agencies projected much higher numbers.[23] Whatever the case, the trend is clear.

Second, the Maghreb region of North Africa—including Algeria, Tunisia, Morocco—is becoming for Western Europe what Mexico is to the United States—a source of inexorable pressure to take in low-waged, unskilled workers, legally or not. Every year the population grows by 3 percent and the Maghreb work force increases by more than a million youths. Third, the population in the Big Three is aging, and the willingness of the natural population to do low-wage work is decreasing. In sheer economic terms, an influx of new workers seems natural. As a result, the marketplace in the advanced industrial societies is pulling in foreign workers. The case of Mexican, Caribbean, and Central American workers in the United States is well known, but another example is Japan, where the number of workers from Thailand, the Philippines, and Malaysia—virtually all illegal—is soaring.

Different Approaches

Each of the Big Three approaches the question of accepting foreign people much differently. America has historically been a melting pot. The United States was born as a nation of immigrants, and continues to be redefined and reshaped by them. It is a country psychologically attuned to immigration and relatively generous procedures for political asylum. One-quarter of Americans define themselves as Hispanic or nonwhite. In New York State, 40 percent of the elementary school children belong to an ethnic minority, and in California white students are already in the minority. Within thirty years, the Hispanic and nonwhite populations will have doubled, to almost 15 million, while the white population will remain steady.[24]

Despite fierce political debates, and despite occasional policies that seem inconsistent, there is no evidence that the nation will change its historical openness. Estimates indicate that immigrants were responsible for a third of America's population growth in the 1980s, and that more arrived during that time than in any decade since 1910–1920.[25] In a recent legislative overhaul of immigration legislation, moreover, the U.S. Congress provided for more generous levels, and a significant reduction in the scope and severity of restrictions, including a gutting of provisions that prevented immigration on grounds of ideology and sexual preference.

This is not to say that there will not be problems. In 1991 and 1992, for example, America was faced with a rapid influx of refugees from Haiti. Washington moved to send these refugees back to Haiti, claiming that they were not eligible for asylum. The reason was that Washington believed that the Haitians were coming to America for economic reasons, rather than fleeing political repression, and only the latter category would give them the legal right to sanctuary in the United States under current law. Beyond the highly publicized and controversial Haitian situation, California has been questioning the burden of immigration, especially on government services, and appears poised to legislate much tighter requirements for immigration into the state. While the broad sweep of American history is clear, so is the fact that new pressures are mounting.

Germany will be approaching the 1990s with a different history. While America has been a nation of immigration, Germany since the 1800s was one of *em*igration. In the late nineteenth century, when German industrialization took off, foreign labor was imported, but generally under restrictive conditions and with no contemplation of eventual citizenship. During World War II, the Nazi government used foreign workers in heinous ways, paralleling the character of the government itself. The entire German past, in fact, has been colored by the question of who is a German. Assimilation of foreigners was never a goal.

Since World War II, owing to its scarred history, Germany adopted the most liberal asylum policies of any West European nation. These were directed almost exclusively at people fleeing repression behind the Iron Curtain. Germany also used a system of "guest workers" as a way to import labor. These people were not considered immigrants, because they were invited on the assumption they would return home after a temporary stay. Guest workers were rarely naturalized, and their children, even if born in Germany, had no automatic citizenship rights. When it came to immigration per se, Germany had no policy except for people of German ancestry, all of whom are automatically entitled to citizenship. As Chancellor Kohl has characterized it, "This is not an immigration country." [26]

Germany faces severe problems now. There are over five million guest workers living in segregated conditions who do not want to leave. Germany has had a program of paying them to go home, but it has not worked. In addition, political asylum–seekers are increasing. In 1990, for example, some 200,000 refugees streamed into Germany, 50 percent of all people seeking asylum in Western Europe, and the numbers, once collected, were expected to have grown dramatically in 1991. Germany's situation is further aggravated by its membership in the European Community, where new laws allowing the movement of people within the E.C. could mean that immigrants or refugees going to France or Italy could eventually end up in Frankfurt, Hamburg, or other German cities.

Germany's response to the increased pressures to accept foreigners will test its political system and social conscience. In late 1991, all the major political parties were calling for a tightening of the laws relating to entry of people seeking to resettle in Germany. This reflected growing public fears that foreigners were taking jobs, housing, and subsidies away from German citizens. A poll taken in September 1991 revealed growing hostility to foreigners: 21 percent of Germans in the east and 35 percent of those in the western part of the country said they now have some sympathy for "radical rightist tendencies."[27] Violent youth gangs with neo-Nazi features terrorized foreign workers in a series of beatings, knife attacks, fire bombings, and other brutal tactics, evidencing a level of violent xenophobia that horrified many politicians. Tens of thousands of refugees were being rounded up in special centers, mostly for their own protection and to help the government speed up processing their applications. "Forty-six years after Adolf Hitler," said Cornelia Schmalz-Jacobsen, a leader of the centrist Liberal Party, "we are skating on very thin ice."[28]

Significantly, Germans are not alone in their concern about the influx of foreigners. Throughout Western Europe, from France to Sweden, antiforeign policies are gathering momentum, and tougher controls on migrants are being considered. This could give comfort to German extremists, letting them believe not only that they are right, but that no one should single them out for xenophobic policies.

Japan is more closed to the influx of people from abroad than Germany. Tokyo has historically excluded almost all refugees and all immigrants not of Japanese descent. There is a strong belief that foreigners will disrupt the uniquely, close-knit Japanese society, which identifies itself as one of homogeneity, harmony, and consensus. Any ethnic Japanese is welcome, but members of other nationalities have been harshly treated, most notably the Koreans who have lived in Japan for generations and who have been denied citizenship and humiliated by procedures such as requirements for fingerprinting. A foreign national can become a Japanese citizen and be entitled to all civil rights enjoyed by Japanese only by denying his original ethnicity. Acceptance of refugees has been scant, too. While the United States had absorbed some 750,000 Indo-chinese refugees by early 1991, for example, and Canada and Australia had each taken about 130,000, Japan had resettled less than 7,000.

But pressures are mounting. The number of illegal unskilled workers arriving from neighboring Asian nations is growing and is now estimated between 100,000 and 200,000. The Justice Ministry acknowledges a 50 percent annual increase between 1989 and 1991. Charges of mistreatment are growing, as in the case of alleged exploitation of 42,000 Filipino women who entered Japan in 1990 as "entertainers."[29] In September 1991 the United Nations Commission on Human Rights was presented with a report by the World Council of Churches accusing Japan of being "a hotbed for discrimination and human rights violations against foreign workers.[30] Among the accusations were failures of employers to pay wages and lack of any labor protection such as injury insurance. In recent years Tokyo has proposed amending its laws to admit small numbers of skilled workers. The effort, by any international standard, is extremely modest.

In the coming world order, characterized as it will be by a focus on economic and social issues and the protection of human rights, the question of open borders for people will become increasingly high profile. The conflict among the Big Three will be less one of who is more moral, but that they will be approaching the refugee and immigration issue with vastly different traditions and inclinations. There will surely be more scenes like the Kurdish camps after the Gulf War, the anguished faces of Vietnamese refugees being forcefully repatriated from Hong Kong, the Albanian boat people desperate to gain entrance to Italy, the Haitians peering out from barbed wire fences of American internment camps. Under great pressure, America, Japan, and Germany will have to focus on how to deal with such human tragedies. They will have to work together to improve conditions in the nations from which these people are fleeing, including support for a variety of public and private institutions that can help. They will have to come to grips with the idea that in the post–Cold War era, political repression may be far less a problem than economic disintegration, and that people fleeing the latter deserve better than a new type of Iron Curtain. In addition, pressures generated by immigration and asylum seekers will increasingly drive other policies such as trade, investment, and foreign aid—all of which can be used to improve conditions in the countries people are leaving.

Finally, because of the human drama, including the certain media focus, the treatment of refugees and immigration will elicit great human emotion in the Big Three, both for and against open policies. In the 1990s, nothing may more influence the way people in one country view those in another than the way their governments respond to the plight of displaced people looking for security and opportunity.

In the end, national attitudes toward the movement of goods and services, capital, and people are linked. They reflect the character of a nation. They influence a country's worldview, including the roles and responsibilities that it is willing to undertake. Societies that are relatively open or closed have become that way over many generations, and these deep-rooted tendencies will have a major impact on how they relate to one another in an increasingly close-knit world.

CHAPTER VI

Dividing Up the World

Beyond the conflicts over economic policies lie the struggles over the way the world should be organized. These, too, reflect deep currents, including geopolitical circumstances, historic economic needs, and the way each society has seen itself for more than a century. How should the responsibilities for military defense and the world economy be divided up? How should emerging regional trade blocs be balanced with the requirements of global collaboration? What is the future of international organizations, including the International Monetary Fund, the U.N. Security Council, the Group of Seven major industrial nations? America, Germany, and Japan could well be at loggerheads over all these vital questions.

SHARING BURDENS

Military Responsibilities

Ever since Germany and Japan fully recovered from World War II, Washington has tried to persuade them to bear more of the costs of maintaining U.S. troops on their soil. Why, asked the Congress, should American taxpayers foot the entire bill for defending another nation? The emotional pitch of this debate varied depending on whether America was feeling economically strong or weak, and specifically on whether its balance of payments was positive or negative, but military burdensharing has been a consistent concern.

American pressure on Germany began to escalate in the 1960s. The Kennedy and Johnson administrations wanted to stem the drain of dollars from the U.S. to Europe. They identified one way to do this—get our European ally to share the costs of America's defense burden. Bonn and Washington did agree on a program in which Germany not only paid part of the cost of U.S. troops but also agreed to buy U.S. Treasury bonds at below-market rates, suspend conversion of U.S. dollars into gold, and purchase military equipment from American contractors. The agreement was constantly revised and renegotiated, however, and Washington was never satisfied. For well over two decades, Congress threatened to bring home its troops if Germany would not increase its contributions.

Beginning in the 1970s, similar pressure was exerted on Japan. Here, too, the arm twisting went beyond simply paying the bill for maintaining U.S. troops. By the 1980s, America was demanding contributions from Japan in the area of foreign aid, and Tokyo was pressed to use its wealth to help nations important to America's security interests such as Pakistan, Turkey, or Mexico. Washington also began to seek access to technology that Japan had begun to develop for civilian purposes, but that also had military applications—so called "dual-use" technology such as heat-resistant materials for use in aircraft.

Throughout the Cold War, Washington's pressures had several underlying themes. One was that the United States was spending twice as much of its G.N.P. for defense as were the Europeans, and six times more than the Japanese. In 1988, to take one year, NATO estimated that the U.S. allocated 6.1 percent of its G.N.P. to defense, Europe averaged 3.3 percent, and Japan spent a bit more than 1 percent.[1] Washington also complained that while it was spending some $150 billion to $200 billion to maintain its overseas forces, those nations who were being protected were not just getting off cheap, but were using their savings to build up their economies. "Many Americans," said a 1988 Congressional Report, "feel that we are competing 100 percent militarily with the Soviets and 100 percent economically with our defense allies."[2] Senator Sam Nunn (D-Ga.), chairman of the Senate Armed Services Committee, made a similar point. "Despite the shift in relative economic power to our allies," he said, "the cost of defense has remained disproportionately on American shoulders. Adjustments are long overdue."[3]

Although the burdensharing debate was highly emotional, it never came close to rupturing allied relationships. As long as the Soviet threat existed, America was reluctant to weaken its forward defenses. Successive administrations concluded that, after all, we were not only protecting Germany and Japan, but also ourselves. In addition, Americans felt a special responsibility for the defense of the free world, and we did not challenge the notion, left over from the horrors of the 1930s and 1940s, that German and Japanese armies should never again be allowed to march into foreign territory.

Just when these debates were becoming routine and losing their bite, Saddam Hussein invaded Kuwait. President Bush's reaction to the Iraqi threat was dramatic. He sent a massive contingent of American troops to Saudi Arabia; he brought together a diverse group of countries from the Middle East and Europe as a supporting allied coalition; he then skillfully encouraged the U.N. Security Council to give the allied intervention its approval. Finally, he asked Berlin and Tokyo, who were neither part of the coalition nor members of the Security Council, to provide a good deal of the financing for the military campaign.

When Japan and Germany were slow to respond, Americans were outraged. Suddenly the burdensharing question flared up again, unleashing a new level of American fury. Under the most severe diplomatic pressure, large financial contributions—over $10 billion from each nation—were eventually forthcoming. In the American view, however, the fact that this money was delivered with hesitations and delays was as significant as the amounts. Many Americans asked: how could these two countries, who had large armed forces, and who were even more dependent on Persian Gulf oil than the United States, even consider sitting out this war? Suddenly, almost no amount of money was enough. Americans began thinking that burdensharing for Germany and Japan should mean more than check writing—it should entail casualty sharing, too. For the first time in the postwar era, Americans began to seriously question why German and Japanese soldiers should not be exposed in international conflicts. Besides financial help, they wanted at least to see a token effort —transport planes, minesweepers, medics, *something*.

Berlin and Tokyo were shocked by the intensity of American anger. Each nation had totally misread U.S. sensitivities and expectations. But there was significant resistance among the German and Japanese citizenry about the war itself, and neither the Kohl nor Kaifu government wanted to move too far ahead of public opinion. In Japan, for example, a survey conducted by the *Nihon Keizai Shimbun* in November 1990 showed nearly 70 percent of the Japanese polled believed that the use of force in the Gulf was not justified under any circumstances.[4] Three months later, surveys showed that only a third of the people approved of Japan's making any financial contribution to the allied effort.[5] In addition, below the surface in Berlin and Tokyo—and not too far below it—was the feeling that it was time to challenge Washington's idea of burden-sharing. "If you want the Germans to carry more responsibility," said Foreign Minister Hans-Dietrich Genscher, "then you must also assure them a form of participation."[6] The identical sentiment was held in Tokyo, although officials were more reluctant to speak out. Both Germany and Japan had not been included in the decision to fight a war; now both felt they should at least be entitled to some time to think about their contributions. There were other common sentiments, too: that because of their history, neither Tokyo nor Berlin could be expected to move toward war without the utmost psychological reservation; that the war was mostly about oil and, despite their import dependence, neither country was prepared to fight over a commodity that would eventually find its way to the market anyway; that President Bush was making the war a typically American global crusade, a tradition that would no longer be enough to persuade Germany and Japan that they must blindly follow. Then, too, both Germany and Japan had "peace constitutions" deriving from the American Occupation; if asked to send troops abroad, they would need to make a change in the basic law, and that would take a long time.

And, of course, the brouhaha was about something else, too. As *Washington Post* columnist Jim Hoagland put it right after the defeat of Iraq, "Disputes brew in Washington, Bonn and Tokyo about how much the Gulf War cost and who should pay for it. These arguments are not really about money. They are about power in the new era. Germany and Japan can and should fulfill the monetary pledges they made to the coalition. Their new hesitations, which are rocking Congress, signal not miserliness but deep concern about what they will get for the billions they pay to finance a glorious American military victory."[7] As Japan and Germany dithered, large numbers of congressmen and senators, Democrats and Republicans, expressed their anguish. In September 1990, Senator John McCain (R-Ariz.), for example, described the emerging contributions of Japan and Germany as "contemptible tokenism." Senator John Kerry (D-Mass.) called them "almost an insult."[8]

The Gulf War revealed the anomaly of America's being the only military and political superpower, having to rely on its major trading partners and economic rivals to finance its mobilization. Underlying Washington's anguish was a growing sense of insecurity—that its allies were gaining ground in economic and technological leadership while America had to shoulder the old burdens that only depleted its energy and resources. America's debts and deficits began to explode in the 1980s, but it took Saddam Hussein to bring home the full national security implication, coined in the phrase "tin cup diplomacy." Some, like Congressman John D. Dingell (D-Mich.), introduced legislation that would impose prohibitive tariffs on goods imported from allies who pledged financial contributions to the war effort and failed to pay up in full. Others began to focus on the burdensharing question anew, talking about an automatic formula for future burdensharing commitments, with Tokyo and Bonn contributing 20 percent to 30 percent of future Gulf War–type military campaigns.

Fortunately, the war was short-lived, America could declare total victory, and U.S. casualties were minimal. Had it been otherwise, the relationship between Washington and its two allies could have been badly ruptured, so fundamental and so emotional had the burdensharing issue become. But Operation Desert Storm may have only hastened a showdown among the allies that would have come eventually. In the case of Germany, the old burdensharing arguments were bound to be lost in more complicated questions about whether American forces will remain in Europe at all, whether there will be a functioning NATO, and under what circumstances a U.S. administration and Congress would agree to risk American lives for problems that Europe itself could solve—such as intervention in civil wars in Eastern Europe or the former Soviet Union. For Japan, it would no longer have been possible to continue the paradox of Washington's spending an estimated $50 billion annually to protect the security of the Asian region that Japan was dominating economically. Wrote Japan scholar Kenneth Pyle, "An historian looking back on the 1980s might wonder why did the world's largest debtor nation continue to offer military security for the world's largest creditor nation? How was it that the United States continued to commit 50,000 military personnel to the defense of Japan at a time when Americans regarded Japan's economic power a greater threat than the power of any other country?"[9]

After the Gulf War, the Big Three put most military questions on the back burner, at least in terms of their emotional intensity. Arguments over Desert Storm were overtaken by new concerns about the breakdown of order in Eastern Europe and the crumbling Soviet Union. But conflict over military burdensharing is sure to resurface, especially since there is no agreement on such fundamental questions as: Is America willing to be the world's policeman? Should Germany and Japan remain only "civilian powers"? What are the criteria for military burdensharing in crisis situations?

Whatever Berlin and Tokyo do, it is doubtful that Washington will be pleased. Six months after the Gulf War, Germany and France discussed a joint military unit, to be the nucleus of an E.C. defense force. Washington might have appreciated that Western Europe was finally taking more responsibility for its own defense, except that it worried that its allies were becoming too independent and that America would lose its ability to influence European policy. In other words, Washington was looking for burdensharing *and* control. Meanwhile, Japan was struggling to pass a law to allow its troops to go overseas on U.N. peacekeeping missions. This, too, was a step in the right direction as far as the United States was concerned, but here Washington's concern was different—it was that Japan was doing too little. Prime Minister Kiichi Miyazawa, for example, explained to his parliament that under the proposed law, the U.N. secretary-general would not have the right to order Japanese peacekeeping forces to fire, nor would he be in a position to command them, nor would the U.N. commander be empowered to order Japanese soldiers to fire their weapons.[10] Even with these caveats, Japan failed to pass the new bill by year-end 1991.

As the nineties progress, moreover, America's future defense budgets will become entangled in the burdensharing issue. One of the key elements in Washington's decision to make large defense cuts will be whether other nations are ready to contribute forces and tactical weapons to prevent Iraqi-type conflicts. According to projections made by the Brookings Institution in Washington, such cooperative arrangements could save America some $800 billion over the next decade over current spending projections.[11] The problem is that the same geopolitical environment that will lead to America's wanting to spend less on defense will also discourage Europe and Japan from doing more.

Sharing Technology

In addition to traditional military burdensharing arguments, another dilemma has surfaced—how to share military-related technology? A prime example is the dispute that arose between America and Japan over the advanced jet fighter plane called the FSX. Here's what happened.

In 1988, after years of negotiation between Washington and Tokyo, the Bush administration agreed to jointly produce the FSX fighter with Japan, a $7 billion project. The agreement was contentious within the administration and Congress and also within the Japanese government. The American side feared that Japan would get a look at the latest American military technology (such as the source code for the aircraft's computer), that Japanese contractors would get too large a share of the manufacturing jobs, and that there would not be a compensating flow of technology in the other direction—from Japan to the United States. In Tokyo, there was resentment that there was co-production in the first place, since many Japanese wanted to develop their own plane and achieve an independent manufacturing capability.

Almost every issue in U.S.–Japanese relations surfaced in the FSX debate, including American anxieties that Japan is gaining superiority in computers, electronics, and other vital technologies. "Look, this is one area where we are still the best. There aren't that many left," said Senator Jeff Bingaman (D-N.M.) on a trip to Tokyo.[12] Others were pointing to the growing U.S. trade deficit and asking why Japan couldn't simply buy the planes off the U.S. shelf. "This is a trade issue we are talking about, not a military issue," said Senator Alan J. Dixon (D-Ill.). "The FSX agreement provides Japan entry into the high-tech aerospace industry."[13] Japanese officials complained that America was invoking national security interests when in fact it was trying to preserve economic advantage. Most disturbing to Tokyo was the tone of the debate in Washington, which revealed America as an increasingly insecure and distrustful ally.

The FSX agreement was eventually modified and completed, but the implications were far-reaching. On the one hand, Washington had tried to broaden its usual definition of national security to include economic competitiveness. On the other, Japan strengthened its determination to break free of the United States in the development and manufacture of high-technology military equipment, especially aircraft. There will be more such issues. In late 1991, for example, Japan had on the drawing boards plans to develop a light observation helicopter and a mid-range surface-to-air missile. American contractors were adamant about participating in these projects and were receiving strong support from Washington. But there were growing doubts in Tokyo about whether to let U.S. firms participate. It is only a matter of time, moreover, before European firms follow suit. As American troops depart, as NATO withers, as some type of European defense force is established, and as the E.C. begins to get a tighter grip on industrial policy, greater independence in military technology is inevitable.

Economic Burdensharing

Burdensharing can be applied to economic and social policy, too. The clearest example is the annual industrial nations' summit meetings. In one gathering after another, the United States has proposed policy measures that each country would take, the sum total being a set of recommendations for coordinated action. Typically, Japan and Germany were urged to grow faster; America would, in turn, reduce its budget deficits and make other changes such as cutting back on energy consumption, thereby lessening the pressure on world oil supplies and prices. This formula always sounded good but it rarely succeeded; each nation went its own way, and real burdensharing remained rhetorical at best.

The example of interest rate disputes between the United States and Germany is a good illustration of why economic burdensharing has not worked. On a general level, the officials in both nations had agreed that they should coordinate their financial policies, but exactly how this responsibility should be exercised had not been decided. Washington tried to get Germany to grow faster, so that its consumers would buy more American products. This, in turn, translated into pressing the Bundesbank to lower German interest rates. But the arm-twisting was futile. Germany has one overriding goal—the suppression of inflation. As a result, Germany manages its interest rates not with an eye on American exports or even on the fortunes of other European economies—it looks primarily at its economic conditions at home. If high rates are necessary to hold down inflation, that's what the Bundesbank will do, even if this means slower growth and higher unemployment in Germany itself.

German interest rate management reflects a distinct attitude about how a national economy works and how global coordination should be managed. Berlin believes that if every nation manages its own economy well, the international system will take care of itself. Keep inflation low and the rest follows—strong currencies, more growth, investment, and jobs. It is a much more single-minded approach than exists in the United States. Coming from the pivotal power in Europe, it speaks volumes for the difficulties of economic burdensharing.

The example of trying to coordinate interest rates is important for another reason: it demonstrates that much of economic burdensharing today is the attempt by one nation to reach deep into the domestic policy of another. At issue is not just whether a country will move in a certain direction but *how* it will move. In the 1980s, for example, President Reagan wanted to stimulate the U.S. economy. He chose to run large budget deficits. To control the potential inflationary impact, the Federal Reserve kept interest rates high. This might have been okay if America were a self-contained economy. But in an interdependent world, this particular mix of fiscal and monetary policy caused great anxieties abroad. Europe, for example, complained that high U.S. interest rates caused capital from Germany, France, and others to move out of Europe and into the United States, thereby depriving the Continent of much needed investment. This forced individual European nations to raise their own interest rates to keep their money at home, with the unwanted impact of putting a damper on economic growth. They wanted Washington to pursue a more balanced mix of policies—less budget stimulus and lower interest rates.

Germany, too, is being told not just what to do but how to do it. As Berlin scrambles for the money to finance unification, for example, other nations are concerned that if it runs big budget deficits, it will have to borrow enormous sums in the markets. As a result its interest rates will be high and it will be doing what Reaganomics did—suck in capital that other nations need. America's preferred solution—and France's, Italy's, and the rest of the E.C.'s—is for Germany to raise taxes on its people, thereby keeping deficits in check. Once again, the mix of policy has become an international issue, with such disputes becoming intensely political questions not just for heads-of-state but also for politicians at all levels, not to mention their tax-paying constituents.

Looking to the next several years, Washington and Berlin will surely assign multiple responsibilities to Japan, all entailing deep-seated domestic change. It will become a matter of burdensharing that Japan continues to grow and that its consumers buy more foreign products. This will involve more deregulation, reductions in high personal income taxes, and more government spending. Whether or not such changes can be made will depend not just on whether Japan agrees in principle that they are, in fact, desirable policies, but also on the ability of the Japanese political system to implement such far-reaching changes.

Sharing Burdens for Environmental Protection

For as far into the future as can be seen, the agendas of Washington, Tokyo, and Berlin will be increasingly crowded with concerns about clean air, pure water, global warming, nuclear waste, and similar issues. To be sure, each of the Big Three is becoming more environmentally conscious. The problem among them is twofold. First, each faces a different set of constraints when dealing with these issues and places a different priority on them. Second, while each of the nations is taking a wide set of domestic measures—new legislation, new administrative regulations, new taxes, moral suasion—and while companies in each country are taking voluntary steps to pursue "green" policies, there is little cooperation among the key industrial nations to ensure that each is holding up its end, that the various national measures are compatible, and that the sum of the efforts is proportionate to the overall environmental problems, which by all accounts are becoming more severe daily.

Over the past two decades, international cooperation in the environmental arena has been heavily weighted toward attending large global conferences, and wrestling with guidelines, conventions, and targets. Now another contentious problem is arising: the relationship between environmental protection and trade. Not long ago, for example, the United States banned the importing of Mexican yellowfin tuna because it objected to the fishing methods that led to the killing of dolphins that swim above the tuna shoals. In another case, in 1990 Germany refused to import American beef containing certain hormones, and shortly afterward the E.C. shut out U.S. beef and pork on the grounds that conditions in American slaughterhouses posed a health risk to European consumers. In early 1992 the GATT criticized the agricultural policies of both the United States and the E.C., finding a relationship between protectionist policies, which result in overproduction, and the intensive use of chemical fertilizers. These kinds of issues are going to multiply.

California and other American states are leaning toward preventing the importing of vegetables sprayed with certain pesticides. The E.C. is putting environmental labels on products that pass certain tests, with implications for all manner of disputes about the nature of the tests, and the possibility of discriminating against foreign products. The fact that each nation will use different means to protect its environment will also be a source of trade friction. For example, American companies that have had to invest in environmental technology such as air scrubbers are now angling for special tariffs on products of foreign companies that have not had to make similar investments.

Environmental issues give Germany—the nation with the most passionate commitment to environmental causes—a righteousness it can press on others, much as America does with its crusade for human rights and free markets. It was in Germany that the first environmental political party (the Greens) gained momentum, and it is in Germany that there has been a long historical and emotional attachment to the forests, which are now being destroyed by carbon emissions. In a poll conducted in January 1991, 87 percent of West Germans and 82 percent of East Germans saw the environment as a top priority for government and industry, and the majority of Germans saw environmental damage as their chief fear for the year 2000.[14] In another survey in the spring of 1991, 17 percent of Germans polled said that environmental protection should be the government's number one priority, and 86 percent wanted Berlin to be doing more to further the goals of a "clean and green" country.[15]

Germany's domestic priorities have been carried into the international realm, reflected, for example, in the fact that it has pledged to reduce the level of greenhouse emissions by 25 percent to 30 percent by the year 2005, whereas most other nations are talking about stabilizing the level. "We must view the threat of climate change as a global challenge to all mankind," said Chancellor Kohl in Houston in July 1990.[16] Foreign Minister Hans-Dietrich Genscher went further saying, "There is an indissoluble link between our fundamental conception of global ecology and a political culture based on freedom."[17] Since reunification, moreover, Germany faces an enormous challenge in cleaning up the environmental degradation of its Eastern provinces—a colossal task that will not only be expensive but will surely heighten the awareness of the German population to every aspect of the global environmental agenda. It is possible that Germany may be pressed to foot the bill for Poland, Czechoslovakia, and Hungary, too, with a price tag estimated in the $200 billion range.[18]

Environmental policies in the United States and Japan have been moving at a slower pace than in Germany. America, with its wide open spaces, its dependence on the automobile, and its free market leanings, is reluctant to change its overall lifestyle. Relative to the other two countries, the United States pollutes more and is much less energy efficient, and thus would bear a greater burden in adjusting to prospective new standards and targets. There is also the question of budgets and priorities: U.S. coffers are thin, and more than Japan and Germany, it faces tough trade-offs between devoting funds to the environment or, say, education or crime control. As the 1990s began, government at federal, state, and local levels seemed to be deferring to environmental concerns when it came to opening new federal lands for drilling or permitting off-shore exploration. In his only major energy initiative, following the Gulf War, President Bush stressed production rather than conservation. Indeed, America has been the most recalcitrant of the major nations at various environmental conferences—demanding more scientific studies, refusing to adhere to mandatory limits in emissions of carbon dioxide, and refusing, except under enormous pressure, to contribute funds to international efforts, such as environmental assistance to the Third World. In early 1992, the U.S. administration was under particular pressure to revise its policies for an upcoming world conference, however. Reacting to new and convincing evidence that certain industrial chemicals were damaging the protective ozone layer, President Bush seemed poised to make some modest changes—reluctantly.

Japan's image is not good, either. Its reluctance to join international efforts to protect certain endangered wildlife, such as whales, and its exploitation of tropical forests in Southeast Asia have received particular attention. While Japanese firms operating within the nation have taken some far-reaching measures, on an international scale Tokyo has been closer to the conservative policies of Washington than to the fuller commitments of Berlin. Within Japan there are fierce debates between the government environmental agency, concerned with greener policies, and the Ministry of International Trade and Industry, more focussed on economic growth, but MITI is infinitely more powerful. Japan's views about environmental policies are conditioned by two factors that do not exist in

America or Germany. As an island nation, Japan has not yet been as affected by the pollution of neighboring countries. And Japan has far weaker consumer and environmental pressure groups.

German and Japanese Views of American Responsibilities

America's views about it allies' responsibilities often collide with their own views about themselves and the United States. Washington may complain about Berlin's policies, for example, but Germany would argue that its contribution to the world economy is enormous already. It believes that its primary global mission is the same as its domestic one: a sound national economy. Beyond that, Berlin believes its tangible support for Eastern Europe and the former Soviet Union is ample evidence of its willingness to contribute to global economic stability, and that it's time for others to do more. "The aid from the West must be as massive as the aid from Germany has been so far," said German Economics Minister Jurgen Mollemann.[19] "We Germans," said Chancellor Kohl after the 1991 abortive coup in the Soviet Union, "are already at the limit of our capacity."[20]

Japan, too, has a different view of burdensharing than does the United States. While Washington presses Tokyo to do more, the perspective of many Japanese is that Tokyo provided a crucial crutch for the debt-ridden U.S. economy in the 1980s. It helped to prop up the dollar when it appeared to be going into a tailspin, and provided massive investments, which allowed America to continue its defense buildup without raising interest rates. Japan also thought it deserved greater recognition for the role it played in stabilizing the world stock markets after the 1987 crash by encouraging its large financial institutions to keep buying even when others were expecting further declines. Tokyo is increasingly annoyed that it does not get more political credit for the large increases in foreign aid that it mounted in response to American demands.

Both Germany and Japan, moreover, share a particular view of the United States—that it's time for it to get its own house in order, to stop trying to shift economic burdens abroad. There is also rapidly growing impatience in Berlin and Tokyo for Washington's unilateral initiatives and arm-twisting. Germany and Japan believe the United States is dragging down the world economy in at least two areas: fiscal policy and energy. Berlin and Tokyo complain that huge budget deficits are sucking in capital from foreign countries that is vitally needed in the Third World or Eastern Europe. And they worry that Washington's unwillingness and seeming inability to curtail energy consumption puts upward pressure on world oil prices, and enhances the importance of the volatile Persian Gulf suppliers. No longer beholden to America for their security, and feeling they are doing their share in other areas, Germany and Japan are moving from the stage of being reluctant followers to just saying no.

Burdensharing in finance, energy, foreign aid, environmental protection, and a host of other issues will be discussed at virtually every important meeting of the Big Three, but the issues are made highly contentious because some of the most crucial assumptions are not agreed upon. In which areas should burdens be shared? How to decide who does what? What is the penalty for refusing to go along? No one has come close to answering these questions.

TRADE, CURRENCY, AND POLITICAL SUPERBLOCS

Alongside burdensharing is another set of developments dividing the Big Three— the rise of regional superblocs. Beginning in the mid-1980s, each of the Big Three has been building its own empire in its backyard. In some ways, it appears we are going back into time. The British had their commonwealth, the French their domain in West Africa and Indochina. America had its Monroe Doctrine warning others to stay out of this hemisphere. Germany and Japan went to monstrous extremes to develop their own empires in the 1940s.

Following World War II, one of Washington's major policy objectives was to break down tightly knit blocks, which were keeping alive an old, discredited political order and which America felt were obstacles to U.S. commerce overseas. The United States pushed to replace these closed colonial systems with a more universal, free trade concept. Thus America took special aim in the late 1940s at the British Empire, demanding that London dismantle the special economic preferences that existed between it and its far flung colonies. Thus, too, was born the International Monetary Fund and the General Agreement on Tariffs and Trade—global organizations designed with the American vision of one open, unified world economy.

Three superblocs are now emerging, one in North America, one in Europe, and one in East Asia. Their cumbersome names are appearing with increasing frequency—the North American Free Trade Area, composed of the United States, Canada, and Mexico; Europe 1992, comprising the twelve nations of the European Community; and the East Asia Economic Grouping (or one of its many variants), a concept describing the ever closer relationships of nations along the Asian rim. The blocs differ from those of the past in that they are not being forged by conquering armies or military threats. Nor are they organized along colonial lines. In each case, however, regional trade and financial ties are growing as are the political arrangements to manage them.

The New American Empire

An American Empire in the Western Hemisphere, dominated by the United States, has existed for some time. Since the early part of this century, the economies of Canada and Mexico have been closely linked to the United States, and America has always been the dominant importer and exporter in the region. The Federal Reserve has been, de facto, the central bank for the region between Ottawa and Mexico City, and the American dollar has been the hemispheric currency. The United States has been a haven for refugees from its southern border, as well as for undocumented workers.

In the last few years, this American Empire has become more important and more institutionalized. In the late 1980s the United States and Canada concluded a free trade agreement that will eventually lead to the dismantling of virtually all formal trade and investment barriers between them. The two nations are, in fact, merging into one market. Washington and Mexico are working on a similar type of arrangement, and eventually Mexico will become an extension of the U.S. manufacturing base. Ford engines, Whirlpool washing machines, Caterpillar forklifts are already being manufactured south of the Rio Grande, as are Sony components and Volkswagens destined for the United States. Companies like Zenith and the U.S. subsidiary of Hitachi have announced that they are moving various facilities to Mexico to produce for all of North America. The U.S.–Mexican agreement will deal with a variety of thorny issues—not just trade, but energy, immigration, narcotics control, and environmental protection. Oil in particular is likely to become a key link between the two nations, since America needs supplies from outside the

Persian Gulf and Mexico needs investment funds to expand exploration, development, and modernization of its refining facilities.

The North American Free Trade Area amounts to far more than the reduction of tariff schedules and the abolishment of quotas. The institutional framework is not as elaborate as in Europe, but is growing nevertheless in specific areas such as oversight of the automobile sector, regulation of environmental matters, and settlement of trade disputes. There is also a strong social dimension, such as the push from American labor unions for Mexico to upgrade the conditions and wages of its workers so that cheap products do not flood the U.S. market.

The German Empire

In the 1990s Germany will again be the pivot around which everything in Europe—West and East—revolves. The first dimension of its new empire will be the European Community, where the movement of nations to form a single group is most advanced. In the next few years a relatively unified market of some 320 million people will evolve and become the world's largest trading bloc. The E.C. has had common policies for trade and agriculture for many years. It has a highly developed institutional structure, which includes a Council of Ministers to perform executive functions, a standing Commission charged with administration, a European Parliament, and a European Court of Justice. By the end of 1992, it will have instituted more unified policies for financial services, transportation, business competition, internal travel. It is headed for a single central bank and a common currency. And it is aiming for much closer cooperation in foreign policy and defense.

Germany's role in the European Community has been a subject of great controversy. No one outside of Germany would be comfortable with German domination, and many within Germany would feel the same way. Some observers may object to the words, "German Empire," saying that no nation in Europe will stand out so clearly. But the trends are clear. Germany will control monetary policy, which means interest rates and economic growth. Germany will have the most to say about the biggest problem facing the E.C.—what to do about the nations to the East banging on the door to get in. Berlin will have blocking power on everything that counts—from trade policy to the establishment of a European defense force.

Germany's role in Eastern Europe and some of the republics of the old Soviet Union will be particularly critical in the years ahead. In the 1980s, the new German Empire would have been described as a more unified European Community composed of twelve or fourteen Western European countries. By the end of the 1990s, that empire will likely include Poland, Hungary, and Czechoslovakia. The inclusion of these Eastern regions will widen the E.C. and slow the integration process, since it will be impossible for so many nations of differing political traditions and economic prospects to harmonize economic, social, or security policies for many years. In this looser configuration, German influence will soar. Not only that, but by history and culture, Germany is best suited to help the Eastern countries merge with the West. In the past, German businessmen were as much at home in Prague and Budapest as they were in Paris and Rome. Germany today includes 16 million people in its own Eastern region, which for decades had close ties with the others behind the old Iron Curtain.

The republics of the former Soviet Union may or may not be part of the new German empire, but ties with several of the most important new countries will nevertheless be close. The perceived threat of a "Teutonic bloc," comprised of German links to Croatia, Hungary, the Baltics, and selected other republics has France, Denmark, and other Western European countries worried. And why not? Since Peter the Great, Russians have looked to Germany for help in technology and industrial management from firms like Krupp and Siemens, both of which helped Russia to industrialize. German and Russian aristocrats socialized in the spas and salons of Europe, and their cultural ties have outlasted two world wars, numerous betrayals, conspiracies, and ideological wars. Thousands of Germans migrated to Russia during the time of Catherine the Great. Marx, Engels, Tolstoy, Pasternak—they all reflected a combination of German and Russian experiences. And Germany and Russia have quietly been building closer ties for the last two decades.

Before the Soviet Union collapsed, moreover, Germany was its major trading partner in the West. Berlin had become the chief banker to Moscow, having extended tens of billions of dollars in trade credits, investment guarantees, and housing subsidies. As part of the reunification process, Chancellor Kohl agreed to bankroll Soviet troops in East Germany, and to fulfill all of East Germany's trade commitments to the U.S.S.R., Berlin and Moscow agreed to conclude a treaty to foster scientific, technological, and commercial cooperation. And when it came time to agree on the final provisions for German reunification in 1990, the deal was struck between President Gorbachev and Chancellor Kohl, with no other heads of state present. As the Soviet empire expired, Germany was poised to be its major source of support, and most likely the most influential Western nation in its survival. Now Russia, Ukraine, and other newly independent states could present tantalizing commercial outlets for German firms, who would have significant cultural advantages over their Japanese rivals, and, by virtue of their financial resources and proximity, advantages over most American companies, too.

The Japanese Empire

Before World War II, it was a central aim of Japan to create a "Greater East Asian Co-Prosperity Sphere," a grouping of countries in the region under Tokyo's domination. It has become a cliché to say that since the war Japan has achieved its goal without armies. Cliché or not, it's true.

The ties that bind the nations of East Asia today stem from the economic influence of Tokyo, which is very slowly overcoming the resentment and suspicion that many countries in the region still harbor toward Japan as a result of World War II. Unlike in Europe, there are few common institutions or policies in the region. Unlike in North America, there has been little momentum toward formal trade liberalization among the East Asian countries themselves. Nonetheless, integration is proceeding.

Japan's phenomenal growth is becoming a pole of attraction. Between 1985 and 1988 Japan's imports from the region increased over 200 percent, and by the end of the 1980s Japan's total trade with these countries exceeded that between the United States and Asia for the first time in the postwar era.[21] In that period, Japan's investment in the region grew about twenty-fold.[22] In 1980, to take one example, Japanese business invested $1.2 billion in East Asia; in 1989, it invested twice that much in Hong Kong alone.[23] Companies like Toyota and Canon are building plants throughout the area, coordinating production, assembly, and distribution facilities, using certain countries to specialize in distinct components and functions. Department store chains like Yaohan and Seibu are moving onto the continent in force, intent on dominating the retailing business.

Sumitomo Bank, Nomura Securities, and other Japanese financial institutions are dominating finance. The presence of Japanese firms on this scale on the East Asian landmass is hard to gauge, but the likelihood is that the impact will be underestimated. Once there is Japanese production, for example, there is a need for Japanese spare parts, Japanese quality standards, Japanese distribution channels. The impact is felt on non-Japanese companies that are compelled to mesh their operations into the Japanese system.

While the integration of the East Asian economy is spearheaded by Japanese companies, the hand of Tokyo's bureaucrats is not absent. The Japanese government and industry are working together with local groups to build roads, ports, and other essential infrastructure. Moreover, Japanese officials have a strategy for industrial development country-by-country. They have a guiding concept—for the kind of infrastructure each nation needs, the products it should produce, the development pattern it should follow. In their overall plan, for example, Thailand might concentrate on furniture and toys, Malaysia on sneakers and TVs, Indonesia on textiles and forest products. Tokyo's influence is exercised through aid for infrastructure, insured loans for joint ventures, selected preferences for imports in Japan, and "administrative blessing" to certain Japan multinationals to invest in particular areas. Specialized training centers have been established in each country.[24] The Bank of Japan began meetings with other central banks in the region to discuss common policy goals and to offer technical assistance.

Tokyo is trying to become more active on the political front, too, serving as a mediator in the Cambodian peace talks, and trying to bring about some reconciliation between South and North Korea. Even in the security arena, Japan has begun to assert itself. During the summer of 1991 the Japanese foreign minister proposed to other Asian countries an intensified dialogue on the region's political and security concerns, including Japan's future military role.

Japan's lack of a free market ideology, its pragmatic approach to government-business cooperation, and its willingness to consider deliberate industrial policy are big advantages in East Asia. Most of the nations in the region are comfortable with many elements of the Japanese philosophy of economic development. Lee Kuan Yew, Singapore's senior minister and a strong American ally, put it this way: He had little doubt, he said, "that a society with communitarian values where the interests of society take precedence over that of the individual suits [Asians] better than the individualism of America." [25]

The Japanese-Chinese relationship, which goes back over 2000 years, is especially important. Its recent manifestations are an important reflection of how the world is changing, and how Japan is likely to behave in the future. For three decades after 1945, Tokyo had no choice but to follow America's lead; until the presidency of Richard Nixon, that meant treating China as part of a monolithic communist enemy. When the United States suddenly changed course in the early 1970s, it did not even inform Japan, causing Tokyo severe embarrassment. Nevertheless, for the next fifteen years, Washington and Tokyo moved in lockstep and mounted extensive cooperation programs with the mainland. But in 1990 Tokyo did not ask the United States whether it could act unilaterally; it simply informed Washington that Japanese aid to China would resume. President Bush publicly admitted there was nothing he could do to stop it.

In July 1991 Japan went further when Prime Minister Kaifu became the first of the major heads of state to visit Beijing, giving the signal that relationships between Japan and China were fully normalized. He paved the way for large-scale aid, and he engaged the Chinese leadership in discussions of trade, arms sales, and human rights. The contrast between Japan's relations with China, on the one hand, and Washington's relations with Beijing, on the other, was stark, for at the same time the U.S. Congress—deeply concerned about China's unfair trade practices, its arms sales to Syria and Iran, its support for authoritarian regimes in Asia, and its human rights record—was debating whether the United States should impose trade penalties on China's imports into the United States. Various U.S. policymakers were implying that a major deterioration in U.S.–China ties, going well beyond trade sanctions, was possible.

There is controversy surrounding the true significance of the superblocs. Some economists cite statistics that trade between the various regions is growing as fast as trade within them; they therefore conclude that the blocs aren't really blocs at all. Another theory is that while trade and investment within the three regions are creating unprecedented economic ties in those areas, this development is but a stepping-stone to more extensive global economic integration. Others say that the political character of the three blocs is so different that it is a vast oversimplification to describe them as competing empires.

All this misses the essential point. It is not necessary to rake over the coals of history to recall that much of World War II was about the quest for regional power and influence by Germany and Japan, because no one is talking about renewed military confrontation among the Big Three. But in the 1990s and beyond, America, Japan, and Germany will be rivals on many different levels, and regional spheres will reinforce this competition. Downplaying the significance of these blocs amounts to a rosy view of the world that does not take full account of all the other forces in the post–Cold War era now being unleashed. Over a long period of time, the blocs may not be protectionist, but for the rest of this decade it is inevitable that American, German, and Japanese firms will be more concerned with deepening their economic ties in their backyards than they have in the past; and whatever past trade and investment data show now, it is certain that intraregional trends will accelerate. Mexico looms larger every day in America's future: immigration is soaring, imports from Mexico into the United States nearly tripled in the 1980s, and U.S. exports to Mexico doubled in the same period. E.C. cohesion is just gathering steam; there, too, intraregional business is responding positively to the dismantling of trade barriers and the prospect of a single currency. Japan's interest in East Asia is also growing more intense; booming economic conditions from Seoul to Jakarta and the threat of protectionism in the United States and Europe leave Tokyo little choice but to reorient its priorities toward Asia. The fact that the blocs are organized differently means that they reflect the Big Three's own distinct systems, and that it will be bloc-wide models of competing capitalism that increasingly will characterize trade and industrial relations in the years ahead.

The superblocs have potential to divide the world into three monetary zones, too—the dollar zone, the mark zone (or some other face-saving European name, like the ECU—European Currency Unit), and the yen zone. This would be a natural financial evolution, but one with enormous significance. America has derived great benefit from having the world's most powerful currency. It could print dollars with little discipline on the amounts, knowing that everyone would want to hold greenbacks. The United States could always borrow in its own currency and, therefore, not worry that exchange rate changes would make it more expensive to service our foreign debt. There have been political advantages, too; the dollar stood for more than money—it was the symbol of American strength. Whenever there was a crisis—a missile showdown, an oil embargo—the dollar increased in value because people saw it as a safe haven in a political storm.

As the use of the mark and yen expands in Europe and Asia, America can anticipate big changes. In the first instance, foreign investors will have more options; this means that they will buy and sell dollars with more confidence that there are other viable alternatives. This could lead to more currency instability. Another implication will be a greater need for Washington to follow sound economic policies in order to maintain global confidence in its currency, for when foreigners lose confidence in U.S. policies, it will be easier to exchange dollars for marks and yen. A third implication is the end of the dollar as a safe haven, with adverse political overtones for America.

Beyond that, Germany and Japan, by having the dominant currency in their regions, will gain influence. Other nations within the blocs will have to watch the Bundesbank and the Bank of Japan for changes in interest rates and the effect on mark and yen values. They will need to raise and lower their own rates in order to keep the links between their currencies and the mark or yen close; otherwise, their trade could be badly disrupted. Germany and Japan will therefore control everything from trade to the price of mortgages within their bloc.

Superblocs will also be disruptive because of the impact on the way each of the Big Three sees the world. Each will be compelled to devote time and energy to its respective region, thereby giving less attention to more global matters. President Bush devoted enormous political capital to get Congress to agree to the opening of trade negotiations with Mexico at a time when the Uruguay Round was collapsing. Germany is surely more preoccupied with events on the Continent than elsewhere; it declined, for example, to participate in Washington's high-priority effort to build up Latin America's private sector. Japan, weary about protectionist pressures in the United States and Europe, sees East Asia as a more congenial area for trade and investment. Blocs will also have military overtones, as the examples of a German-French initiative for a U.N. defense force, or the Japanese initiative for regional defense discussions clearly demonstrate.

A harmonious, borderless world? Not yet—by a long shot.

A THIRD GLOBAL BATTLEGROUND:
INTERNATIONAL INSTITUTIONS

The arguments over burdensharing and the regional tensions among the Big Three will be mirrored in international economic institutions. To the extent that the Big Three have divergent interests and pressures, these institutions will become battlegrounds rather than forums to solve problems.

These organizations were designed by the United States and Great Britain after the war to promote trade and investment around the globe and to prevent the kind of breakdown in international cooperation that occurred between the first and second world wars. By any measure, the International Monetary Fund, the World Bank, and the GATT played a major part in the general economic prosperity that materialized in the 1950s, 1960s, and 1970s.

Each of these institutions is now having a hard time adjusting to the demands of the 1990s. They are confused about their goals and missions. The IMF, for example, sees itself as a global monetary authority, policing the world's exchange rates, but in fact the Big Three do not include the IMF in their most important deliberations and the organization has in effect become a bank for the Third World, Eastern Europe, and the former Soviet republics. The World Bank has a murky focus and gigantic bureaucracy. The GATT is supposed to be the central institution dealing with world trade; however, most trade issues no longer fall under its jurisdiction, many of the more significant trade agreements are concluded without GATT participation, and regional trade blocs are undermining the idea of one global trade institution. The three institutions are under enormous pressure to handle an ever broader array of problems—from Latin American debt, to Eastern European stability, to environmental cleanup.

Yet the importance of well-functioning institutions that deal with global problems is going to grow dramatically. Common approaches to currencies, trade, investment, banking and capital markets, Third World development, environmental protection, telecommunications, narcotics traffic, and immigration are becoming crucial. One challenge is to articulate new rules for cooperation. A second is to find methods of enforcing them.

Throughout nearly all of the Cold War era, America could impose a consensus and see that it was implemented. The United States was able to dominate the international organizations and impose its own philosophy and foreign policy. In the mid-1990s and beyond, Germany and Japan will become obstacles to a continuation of this trend. They will have their own ideas about global economic management. They will have enhanced voting power in the economic and other international organizations deriving from their increasing financial contributions. And because of their growing influence in their geographical regions, they will also be able to muster support from neighboring countries. In fact, they will be looked to by their neighbors to uphold certain interests— Japan will de facto speak for Thailand, Malaysia and Singapore; Berlin will have the most to say about Poland, Czechoslovakia, Hungary, and others in the East.

In addition, the possibility of interventionism by international organizations has taken a gigantic leap. The sanctions against Iraq during the war and after, the sending of U.N. forces into Iraq to protect the Kurds, the invitation by Moscow for the IMF and others to advise on all manner of economic reforms—these may be just the beginning of the increased level of involvement in domestic affairs by international institutions that will occur. We may well see more intervention in border disputes and ethnic conflict, both of which are likely to rise significantly in the years ahead. We may see more intervention when it comes to human rights abuses, terrorism, control of nuclear weapons, and environmental abuses around the world. The different systems, drives, and objectives of the Big Three will make the process of trying to reach an international consensus on how to manage these delicate tasks highly divisive.

Conflicts among the Big Three will arise out of differing conceptions of what international institutions should do, how they should be organized and financed, and who should control them. The very notion that the United States alone can no longer call the shots will be increasingly disturbing to Washington. But as both Tokyo and Berlin are becoming more frustrated by the general gap between their economic power and their political influence, international institutions may well become one of the first arenas for self-assertion.

There will be conflicts over the level of financial contributions for international organizations. No one will deny that the capital requirements in Eastern Europe, the former Soviet Union, and the Third World will be huge, and it will become clear in the mid-1990s that private banks and private investors—burned in Latin America in the 1980s—are unlikely to take large commercial risks. This will put added burdens on public funds channelled through international institutions. But where will the money come from? America's coffers are bare and it will want others to take up the slack. When the U.N. General Assembly convened in the fall of 1991, for example, the United States was reported to be delinquent in paying dues of $344.5 million, over 30 percent of total arrears of all members. This did not include a further $173 million owed by Washington for past peacekeeping operations.[26] Germany is on the front line of the problems to its east, and, if it does not get its way, it may want to bypass international institutions in order to address problems that are imminent. Japan will be in the strongest position to ante up new funds, but it will object to doing so disproportionately, or without receiving some tangible benefits as a quid pro quo. The relationship between financial contributions and voting control will also be contentious. America's interest will be in decoupling the two so as to preserve its current clout, but Japan and Germany will want their new money matched by new veto powers.

There will be conflicts over priorities. America will want international efforts to concentrate on the awesome problems of Latin America and it will want a strong focus on all types of human rights, including free elections. Germany will look east, and it will want to focus on particular priorities such as political stability and environmental cleanup. Japan will be most concerned with Asian matters; like Germany, it will place economic and political stability highest on its list of priorities. For Tokyo, moreover, human rights could be much further down the agenda of concerns than it is for the other two.

There will be conflicts over philosophy. America will want institutions that dispense money directly to the private sector in recipient countries; Germany and Japan will have no such free market purity. America will push for faster deregulation; Japan and Germany will wish to proceed more slowly. Tokyo will promote a concept of development that emphasizes government-industry cooperation, a system that has worked remarkably well for Japan; this is an idea not likely to be welcomed in Washington.

Since the Berlin Wall came down, there has been ample foreshadowing of these kinds of struggles. The first new global institution to be set up after the Cold War was the European Bank for Reconstruction and Development, based both in London and Paris. West Europeans were anxious to create a new international bank to focus on Eastern Europe, but also to have more influence than they now have in the World Bank or IMF. During the establishment of the bank, Washington was at loggerheads with Germany and virtually all other sponsors in its insistence that the bank's lending go directly to private businesses rather than to government-owned entities. In 1990 and 1991, a similar dispute occurred in the context of new fund-raising for an affiliate of the World Bank, the International Finance Corporation, with America threatening to hold up its contribution until it was agreed that a larger portion of lending would go to the private sector in Latin America and Eastern Europe. The position of the United States was at odds with the less doctrinaire views of Germany, Japan, and others where the line between public and private interests is more blurred and government and business are accustomed to a higher level of cooperation.

Beyond these specific problems, there is even a bigger one—centrifugal political forces in the Big Three that undermine public support for international organizations in general. In America, support for multilateral institutions has never been particularly strong. It was its failure to join the League of Nations that irreparably weakened that organization. It was the U.S. Congress that torpedoed the proposed International Trade Organization in the late 1940s, leaving instead the much weaker GATT. Washington was able to muster enthusiasm for the IMF and other organizations so long as it was in control, so long as Congress could think of them as extensions of U.S. policy. In the 1990s, this will no longer be the case. In Germany the issue is whether the enormous tasks at home and elsewhere in Europe will leave any time for focussing on international organizations. As for Japan, if the enthusiasm of America and Europe for international organizations wanes, Tokyo will follow suit; while it uses the rhetoric of multilateral cooperation, it is quite comfortable with bilateral dealing.

The U.N. Security Council and the Group of Seven

A special problem relates to the U.N. Security Council. When the United Nations was founded in 1945, neither Germany nor Japan were permitted to be members. When Japan and the Federal Republic of

Germany joined the General Assembly, they were not included in the Security Council. During the Cold War, when the Security Council so frequently reflected U.S.–U.S.S.R. rivalries, the issue of membership was not a preoccupation of either Tokyo or Bonn.

Without Japan and Germany, however, the Security Council will have little legitimacy in the future. What does it mean to have the supreme body of the United Nations without the second and third most powerful and important nations? How can Japan's exclusion be justified when its financial contributions to the U.N. exceed those of Great Britain and France combined? Or Germany's exclusion when it will be the foreign nation that most determines the fate of the region from Poland to Siberia? How compelled will Tokyo and Berlin be to take on more responsibility for global peace when they are not at the table when the decisions are made? But changing the Council's composition is extremely difficult. It would require opening up the original U.N. charter and risking proposals for widespread changes that could lead to a decade of argument and paralysis in the U.N. itself. For example, there would be demands from developing nations like Brazil or India to get permanent Security Council seats, too. There may also be demands from the Third World to end the ability for any one Security Council member to have a firm veto over any of the Council's actions—something that would surely be objectionable to the United States.

In fact, it appears that the Security Council question may be eclipsed by the evolution of a new forum—the Group of Seven (or G-7) industrial nations: America, Germany, Japan, Great Britain, Canada, France, Italy, of which the Big Three constitute the pivotal inner club. These are the nations whose heads of state constitute the annual summits. When these gatherings began in the mid-1970s, their purpose was to deal with trade, currencies, energy shortages, and other economic issues. Gradually, however, the agendas have expanded to include nuclear nonproliferation, human rights, arms sales, stability in Eastern Europe and the former U.S.S.R.

For America, Germany, and Japan the shift of power to the G-7 has important implications. It is in this forum—which has no staff and no written procedures or rules—that the major decisions about global economic and social management will be made or avoided. It is from here that powerful economic carrots and sticks will be wielded to make other nations behave in certain ways. It is here that the Big Three will go head to head. Unlike in the U.N. Security Council, in the G-7 the legacies of World War II and the Pax Americana have been left behind, and the prominence of economic clout in global diplomacy is clearly revealed.

There are other issues that will test the Big Three, issues that cut across those that have just been discussed. Foremost among these are the potential strains that are likely to come with divergent policies toward the former Soviet Union.

If, as seems likely, the new republics continue their downward economic spiral, the questions of aid, debt relief, investment, trade, human rights, refugees, Western intervention in civil wars, etc., will be rolled together. Relationships among the Big Three could be seriously strained by arguments over who bears what responsibility, whose financial contributions are inadequate, and what policy demands to put on the Eastern nations. International agencies like the IMF and the World Bank could be the arenas in which many of these disagreements take place. If, as also seems highly possible, the economic strains in the former Soviet Union make the transition to true democracy and capitalism impossible, at least for the remainder of the 1990s, then relations among the Big Three would deteriorate even further. In this case, America could become disillusioned and hold back its assistance. Japan, never enthusiastic about aiding the former U.S.S.R., could find a convenient excuse to follow Washington. And Germany, having no choice but to deal with the crisis on its doorstep, would be left to fend for itself. Indeed, the magnitude of the disintegration of the former U.S.S.R. could be so great, and the implications so severe, that ties among the Big Three could be disrupted across the spectrum of all other issues.

CHAPTER VII

The Leadership Vacuum

Avoiding a "Cold Peace" will depend on whether the Big Three can overcome the forces that will be pushing them in separate directions. Collisions and chaos are inevitable unless someone takes control. This is the lesson of the period between the two world wars, when, as professor Charles P. Kindleberger has so eloquently written, British leadership of the international order had waned and no one, including the United States, stepped in to take over.[1] As a result, every major nation became absorbed with its own affairs, protectionism mushroomed, international lending slowed, and no one took responsibility for reining in centrifugal forces. Japan and Germany began their major military buildups, and England and America stood by and watched. It wasn't as if no one saw the dangers: disarmament meetings were held in the Pacific, and world economic conferences were convened to head off trade wars. But there was no nation in charge, and none to articulate a set of global rules or to enforce them.

It would be misleading to say that the 1990s will be just like the 1930s, or that the lessons of history require that one country, and one alone, now assume the mantle of leadership. The world has become more complicated: economic interdependence is growing, power is diffused, armies count for less and economic strength for more. But if leadership is to exist at all, at least one of the Big Three, and probably two, will have to take a broad and long-term view of their interests. Policies on trade and finance would have to take into consideration how other nations would be affected. Genuine compromises would have to be made on military burdensharing, global economic management, trade, sharing technology, coordinating refugee policies, protecting the environment— to take a few examples. A deliberate effort would be necessary to avoid clashes among regional blocs, and to strengthen the IMF, the U.N., and other international institutions. Will America, Japan, and Germany, alone or in some combination, rise to the occasion? If current trends continue, the odds are against it.

Optimists take heart from the assumption that the Big Three are not oblivious to the challenges they face. They say that these three nations remember the bitter lessons of past failures to work together and recognize the need for more collaboration in today's closer-knit world economy. They point to the endless conferences and negotiations that take place to deal with common problems—everything from clean air to unstable stock markets. Therefore, the argument goes, the Big Three will work things out among themselves, not perfectly, of course, but adequately.

Such optimism is understandable, but it is misleading. Leadership requires more than a sense of history, good intentions, or even a recognition of the problems ahead.

LEADERSHIP IN THE PAST

Historically, international leadership among nations has fallen into at least three patterns. The first is where one nation has single-handedly dominated large empires. Ancient Rome and Great Britain in the early 1900s both fit this mold; each exercised nearly unchallenged hegemony over a vast area. A second pattern is that of classic balance-of-power arrangements, in which three or four major countries of nearly equal strength work to preserve the status quo—Europe during the nineteenth century, for example, with France, Germany, Great Britain, Austria, and Russia among the balancers. And third, there has been a bipolar arrangement—the 1945–1988 period when America and the Soviet Union stood out among all other nations with their big armies, big economies, and distinct ideologies, and not only competed with each other but led opposing blocs of nations.

None of these models fits today's situation. Following the end of the Cold War, America has become the lone military and political superpower. But it rules no empire and is by no means in a position to exert its will on many crucial economic and social issues. The reason: in nonmilitary areas, it faces Japan and Germany, whose ability to pursue a different course, or at least to refuse to go along, is growing stronger.

A balance of power is also not an apt description for the 1990s. In the past such arrangements were designed to protect the *status quo* among the key countries, especially in the military realm. In the 1990s, however, many of the rivalries are economic. Given the nature of capitalist competition, it is nonsensical to think about maintaining the existing situation. Would we freeze trade and investment patterns just as they are?

There is today no bipolar standoff, either. Japan and Germany may be powerful rivals in global markets and in geographical regions—and they are likely to become even more so. But it is farfetched to believe, in the 1990s at least, that either nation would become a military rival to the United States.

History, therefore, is not a good guide for how leadership will unfold in the future. We have to look for something new. Will America emerge as a new type of first-among-equals, a broker, a mediator—a nation with enormous global influence by virtue of its financial and technological resources, its ideological attractiveness, its broad international involvement, its skillful diplomacy? Will Japan and Germany harness their economic dynamism, use their unique formulas for combining growth, social welfare, and competitiveness as a model for other nations, and emerge as new leaders? Or will there be a new type of collective arrangement—a Big Three directorate—that will provide the essential stewardship for the future?

It is unlikely that any of these models will emerge. We can anticipate a much messier situation, without clear patterns, alternating between order and confusion, and between cooperation and conflict. If current patterns prevail, the 1990s could well be notable for their lack of leadership. The New World Order will, in fact, be a world *without* order.

Qualities of a Leader

What would constitute the basics of leadership?

A true international leader should have influence on others by virtue of power—armies and weapons, financial clout, and highly competitive firms. Its military capability need not be overwhelming, but it has to be willing to deploy its troops, aircraft, ships, and missiles in order to enforce the rules of the system, as the United States did in reversing Saddam Hussein's aggression. Its economic power ought to be available to secure its own prosperity, as well as to exert a strong influence over global finance and trade.

A leader must have enough domestic flexibility to wield carrots and sticks. This requires that it have meaningful amounts of money to lend or invest around the world and not be too burdened by its own domestic problems—such as high inflation, a deteriorating currency, a poorly performing work force, or social unrest. A leader cannot be so vulnerable to the actions of others that it fears, say, trade retaliation or a cutoff of lending from abroad, thereby causing it to act too cautiously and defensively.

A leader must be more than rich, and it must dispense more than money. Its institutions and its society must be seen as having some relevance for other nations. The Persian Empire imposed rules on other countries and mediated disputes. Rome gave the Mediterranean a code of law. France once imparted its culture wide and far. Great Britain bequeathed a democratic philosophy.[2] America, in the first twenty-five years after World War II, led the way toward a liberal economic world order, where democracy, human rights, and free market principles were held up as ideals.

A leader must define its goals in broad terms. It must understand that it has a big enough stake in the rules of global politics and economics to pay the price of maintaining the overall system. In military terms, this means willingness to maintain significant forces and to intervene even when a nation's own territory is not threatened, as America did in Korea, Vietnam, and Iraq. In economic terms, paying the price means that a nation will keep its markets open even when others do not, so as to allow world trade to remain buoyant; that it will provide emergency loans to allow others nations to overcome temporary hardships and prevent a contraction of world trade; and that it will allow the national currency to circulate freely to finance trade and investment around the globe, even though this means giving up some control over national monetary policy. Between 1945 and the late 1960s, not only was America able to do all these things, but it saw its own national interest in doing them.

For one nation to be a leader, others must be followers. In some cases, they may have no choice, because they need either military protection or economic help. In other cases the incentive may be more positive—they may be attracted by the confidence that a leading nation exhibits, by the decisiveness of its policies, and by the kind of society it has developed at home. Of course, it is far more difficult to follow a country that is torn by internal political dissension. For example, America's global leadership position was undercut when the country was badly divided over the Vietnam War.

A leading nation needs clear objectives that its citizens and foreign followers can understand and in which they believe. In the postwar era, America had such a policy—"containing communism." As a theme, it was equated with support for individual free choice, free democratic elections, and free markets. Until the late 1960s, anticommunism justified a certain national loyalty that acted as a counterweight to America's strong individualist tendencies; it became the rationale for excellence in education and for massive defense-related R&D, for example, not to mention the underpinning for a national military conscription. Everyone —inside America and overseas—understood what was driving Washington's foreign policy. They may not have agreed with it, but they knew what we were doing, and why.

Over the last ten years, none of the Big Three—not even America—has been a real leader in the way the United States was during the years 1945–1965.

Throughout most of the 1980s, for example, America went its own way with Reaganomics. Here was a set of policies designed to boost U.S. growth without any afterthought about the long-term consequences to America itself or to the impact abroad. Taxes were lowered and spending on defense vastly increased, leaving America with large deficits and large debts. Unrestrained spending led to soaring imports and new protectionist pressures. Washington's answer was to relentlessly press Japan and Europe to open their markets and to threaten retaliation if they refused. At the same time, however, the United States took a series of actions to protect its own markets in steel, machine tools, automobiles, and semiconductors—making Reagan the most protectionist president since Herbert Hoover. America talked about strengthening the multilateral trading system, yet promoted new legislation for unilateral trade retaliation. It could not make up its mind whether the dollar was too high or too low and attempted to browbeat others to support the policy-of-the-month. It tried unsuccessfully to make Western Europe break natural gas contracts with the U.S.S.R., even as America abandoned any pretense of domestic energy policy and thereby contributed to the future likelihood of higher oil prices and supply disruptions. Washington steadfastly resisted recognizing the severity of the Latin American debt problem, and dragged its heels until the banking system itself was threatened.

Japan certainly played no leadership role. It focussed on its narrow self-interest, expanding exports and spreading its investments to foreign countries. It took no positive initiative on its own and acted only when American pressure became so intense that it had no choice except to give in. For example, when Washington demanded that Tokyo increase its foreign aid contributions, Japan did just that, called it the Nakasone Recycling Plan, and hoped America would get off its back for a while.

Germany also focussed on its own economy, building up its exports, expanding its investment position in Western Europe, and keeping inflation low. Only in the 1989–1990 period, in the midst of unification and the opening of Eastern Europe, did it become more energetic on the international stage, more actively supporting the consolidation of the European Community, and taking a leadership role in organizing economic relief for Eastern Europe.

In the past Japan and Germany shared some particular handicaps, all of which are still present. Both countries have been responsible for great tragedies in this century, and their crimes and actions are still remembered, particularly in their own respective regions. In Asia, almost no country is really comfortable with Japan's having a more influential role than it already has; in China, Korea, Singapore, Malaysia, and Indonesia in particular, the memory of Japanese wartime brutality lingers. In Europe, from London to Moscow there is great concern that Germany not follow too independent a course.

Neither Japan nor Germany has any history of peaceful and constructive leadership, even before World War II. And while both have demonstrated spectacular talents in recovering from wartime devastation and gaining economic superpower status, both had a free ride in being able to tap America's large markets and its technology, and neither had to shoulder the kind of defense burdens that the United States did.

Neither nation has the economic structure or political mindset to be a world leader. Their societies are too impenetrable to outside influence, too preoccupied with internal order. Japan and Germany are powerful engines of global trade and finance. But they do not see their responsibilities as going beyond the furtherance of their own prosperity, nor do they give any evidence of assuming responsibility for the maintenance of a broader global security or economic system.

In order to be global leaders, Japan and Germany would require clear visions of who they are and what they want to do. Identifying their purpose in the world was not a problem during the Cold War because each had a defined role under the American umbrella—they were to keep their troops at home and focus on economic policy, and they were to support American initiatives politically and financially. They understood the rules and flourished by following them. But now the old system is shattered, and both nations are going to be at bay for some time to come.

Amid all this, both Japan and Germany are not going to count on America to point the way as it once did. In the first place, they are becoming more assertive about their own interests, and, second, their calculation is that the United States is no longer prepared to play the powerful role it once did. For Tokyo and Berlin, therefore, there is an enormous vacuum to be filled in the absence of American dominance—but thus far there is no clear political and economic strategy from either, nor, given the depth of change and flux in each society, should we expect one for years to come.

Historically, both Japan and Germany have had awkward and abrasive foreign policies. They have often not understood the point of view of others, and they have chronically complained about being misunderstood themselves. It is hard to imagine Japan and Germany as leaders relating comfortably to diverse groups of nations, especially in crisis situations involving military matters or severe economic slumps.

Finally, it is unlikely that Japan and Germany would have much influence over one another. Going back in history, the era in which there was the most mutual respect was the late nineteenth century, when Germany made critical intellectual and cultural contributions to Japanese society. Until 1900, for example, German doctors accounted for most of the faculty of Japanese medical schools, German soldiers helped train the Imperial Forces, and German ideas about education, which emphasized national pride, discipline, and sacrifice, and which subordinated the individual to the national polity, infused the Japanese system.

But since then, the relationship has been rocky or distant. Germany opposed Japanese expansion before 1914. Japan fought against Germany in World War I. The Axis alliance in 1940 provided little benefit for either; the treaty may have provided mutual psychological support, but there was very little coordination of logistics or strategy. Throughout the Cold War, neither nation was particularly important to the other.

A closer look at each of the Big Three shows how each has a vastly different set of problems that will deeply affect its room for maneuver.

AMERICAN DISABILITIES

Compared to other nations, America possesses the broadest set of leadership resources—military, economic, scientific. More than Japan and Germany, it has ideological appeal, an international outlook, and a willingness to propose initiatives and muster global support for them. But this is a *comparative* judgment; it does not mean America's capacity for leadership is adequate to the needs of the next decade.

In the 1990s, like the 1980s, America is still sure to be called on whenever a major military crisis erupts. But its clout in the area of strategic defense will not carry over into other areas when the enemy no longer poses a direct threat to the nations whose cooperation America needs. In the Gulf War, for example, the United States safeguarded the oil supply of Japan and Germany. It put its own troops in jeopardy, and it revealed a level of technological weaponry that startled even its closest allies. But where did this get Washington? Following the victory, America pressed both Tokyo and Berlin to lower interest rates and promote growth around the world. At the same time, it made it clear in the Uruguay Round negotiations that the reduction of European and Japanese barriers to trade in agriculture is its top international economic priority. In both cases it could not make Tokyo or Berlin budge.

America's leadership position is increasingly tenuous, mainly for domestic reasons. Compared with those in Japan and Germany, America's challenges at home are overwhelming. They promise to preoccupy the administration, the Congress, and the voters for the rest of the decade—and possibly well into the next century.

In the golden age of U.S. power, the nation's economic and social problems were manageable. Until the 1960s, there was money for foreign policy and national defense, and there was money for building roads, expanding urban services, improving education; there were, in short, few painful trade-offs needed between guns and butter. Equally important, political leaders had the time and energy to put both sets of issues high up on their agendas. All this is unlikely now.

"[As] the new decade begins," said a team from Brookings Institution in 1990, "the proud achievements of the preceding four decades cannot obscure a growing sense that the United States is faltering, at home and abroad . . . Possessor of the largest and deepest capital stock in the world, its saving rate is lower than that of any other developed country . . . Beneficiary for decades of a system of free trade, it now quakes before economic competition . . . World pioneer of mass public education, its students now perform worse than those of virtually all other [industrial] countries. Underwriter of the world's most costly health care system, it leaves more than 31 million people uninsured . . . Richer than ever before, it has found no way to reduce the significant fraction of its population that is poor . . . Victor in the Cold War, its response to pleas from countries of Central America and Eastern Europe for help in rebuilding economies ravaged by central planners is to agonize over how to shift monies within an already shrunken foreign aid budget."[3]

America is not poor by any standards. But it is becoming enfeebled, psychologically and politically. There is growing agreement on the nature of America's disabilities, but no consensus on what to do about them.

Fiscal policy—one of the primary tools of any government to guide the economy—is out of control. The fact that the budget deficit continues to grow is probably less important in terms of America's predicament than the fact that politicians have, after years of debate, proved totally incapable of dealing with the problem. For most of the 1980s Washington showed the country and the world that it was incapable of governance. In blatant recognition that it had lost all control of the budget process—the vehicle for setting national priorities—Congress mandated automatic across-the-board cuts if certain targets were not met. Then, as the deadlines approached, it fudged the figures so that the cuts would not be imposed. It is not clear which was the sadder spectacle: Congress's abdication of responsibility or the fact that the American public became inured to the annual ritual of such scams.

As the 1990s began, the administration and Congress reached yet another budget accord. It too appeared to be an interim measure. The agreement provided no immediate penalty for missing targets, and it did not include the cost of the savings-and-loan bailout, nor the extra cost of social services in a recession. No sooner was the ink dry than projections for 1991 and beyond showed a continuation of staggering deficits, going well over $300 billion per year. By early 1992 the administration was projecting a fiscal 1992 deficit of $399.1 billion, which, at 6.8 percent of the G.N.P., would break the post-World War II record set in 1983. It was also estimating a $351.9 billion deficit for fiscal year 1993. In effect, all pretense of dealing with the budget deficits was abandoned.[4] This much is sure: the political system will be tied in knots for years to come as it struggles over taxes, entitlements, defense outlays, and the host of urgent problems requiring funding. These battles will not be confined just to the federal level, as financial shortfalls afflict state, local, and city governments too, causing widespread layoffs, severe cutbacks in social services, and slashing of investments for critical infrastructure projects.

Successive federal deficits are adding to the national debt, now exceeding $3.5 trillion and growing by $1 billion per day. Big borrowers are prisoners to events abroad. The real threat is not one of foreign lenders deliberately cutting off loans to the United States, but of cutting back their investments. It is already happening; as Japan and Germany begin to use more of their capital at home or in their respective geographical backyards, less money is coming to the United States. The problem was not so evident in 1990 or 1991 because the nation was in recession, and the need for capital was lower than it would have been in a growing economy. But if recovery is to be vigorous, massive new investments will be required, and the necessary funding will be more scarce and more expensive. Large fiscal deficits have also forced the government to forgo the pump-priming policies that have helped America to end past recessions. Instead, all the emphasis has been on lowering interest rates—with results that have been disappointing.

What kind of leader can be so tangibly beholden to foreign bankers and investors? What kind of leader can the United States be if it has none of the levers that nations normally have to manage the economy?

The weakness in the U.S. banking system is a serious disability. Banks have been failing at rates not seen since the 1930s. Taxpayers will be picking up the tab for the savings-and-loan fiasco for years to come, and there is a possibility that they will be subsidizing commercial bank bailouts, too. And the wobbly financial structure goes well beyond banks.

The insurance industry may become the next big financial debacle. Even the regulatory system for all financial services needs wholesale restructuring. "America has had credit woes before," said Wall Street economist Henry Kaufman, "but at no time since the 1930s have they been so oppressive or involved as wide a range of participants."[5]

The international competitive position of U.S. banks has been eroding dramatically. While U.S. financial institutions dominated global finance during the 1970s, by the end of the 1980s no American banks were in the world's top ten, ranked by assets. But size is not the only important indicator. American institutions were retreating from global lending and refocussing their activities at home. One institution after another pulled back from overseas activities, to the point where only two or three could be said to be truly international firms. Meanwhile, foreign banks were gaining market share in the United States.

In a world governed so much by the movement of money, what kind of leader will the United States be with hobbled financial institutions?

Central to the America economy is new investment. If the United States is not to become even more reliant on money from abroad, the rate of domestic savings will have to increase. But the trend has been entirely the other way, no matter how it is measured. Throughout the entire postwar period America has been saving a smaller percentage of its national income than Europe or Japan. Savings rates in the 1980s, moreover, have been lower than in any comparable period in our history. Between 1980 and 1987, for example, net saving in America was 3.7 percent of G.N.P., compared to 9.1 percent in Western Europe and 17.6 percent in Japan.[6] Since 1987, moreover, the U.S. earned the distinction of having invested less in plant and equipment as a share of real Gross National Product than any major industrial economy. Public investment declined, too; as a percentage of G.N.P., in the 1980s it was half of what it was in the 1970s and a third of what it was in the 1960s. In the last half of the 1980s, moreover, America's investment in public infrastructure averaged about 1.5 percent of G.N.P., compared with 5.0 percent in Japan and 2.3 percent in Germany. The impact of these trends can be seen in a number of areas. It shows in the nation's infrastructure, where 40 percent of the nation's 200,000 bridges are structurally deficient or obsolete, with an estimated repair bill of some $51 billion; and where 62 percent of the highways need repair, with a projected cost running into hundreds of billions.[7]

Can a nation that fails so miserably to save and invest for its future be a global leader?

A great deal has been written about the erosion of the U.S. manufacturing base. Scores of books and studies, all by highly respected authors or groups, some in the private sector and some in the government, have been sounding near identical alarms.[8] Virtually all of them dwell on the same case studies—declining domestic market share in machine tools, steel, automobiles, computers, copiers, semiconductors. The more technical treatments point to dramatic erosions in such American high-technology businesses as robotics, advanced materials like ceramics, integrated-circuit fabrication and test equipment, fiber optics, printed circuit boards, electronic display materials, high-fuel economy engines, medical equipment. Some of these studies have examined American industry from the bottom up, beginning with the shop floor, the laboratory, the board room, the class room. Others have focussed on comparisons with other nations. Whatever the methodology, the conclusions and recommendations are broadly similar—that a wide range of policy deficiencies are contributing to America's problems. These include lack of coherent government policies, government-industry-labor antagonism, poor savings and investment, short-term financial horizons, inadequate work force training, second-rate secondary education, too little nondefense R & D, and outdated antitrust policies. In fact, discussion of the weakening industrial and technological infrastructure of the United States has become almost a preoccupation in America. But virtually no new measures have been taken to address the well-recognized problems.

Can a country that cavalierly watches the deterioration of its industrial and technological base be a world leader?

Energy is another chronic problem for America. In 1991, on the heels of the Gulf War, the administration proposed a new energy policy. The thrust was to increase domestic production. Curbing demand was not a priority even though imports as a percentage of domestic consumption had risen from 31 percent in 1985 to 50 percent in 1990, even though oil was a major reason for sending 500,000 troops to Saudi Arabia, and even though all experts agreed that American dependence on Persian Gulf supplies was sure to intensify. Japan and Germany were paying about four times the price of gasoline as Americans, but neither the administration nor Congress was prepared to consider higher gasoline taxes. The United States seemed headed for a fourth energy crisis later in the 1990s.

Does a nation that has failed to heed the warnings of three energy crises in the last two decades—crises which have adversely affected every aspect of our lives—have what it takes to lead other nations in the future?

In light of America's inability to gain control of its economic fate, perhaps it comes as no surprise that it has put its hand out for help abroad, and not just for legitimate burdensharing. When Bank of America was teetering in the late 1980s, a group of Japanese lenders made an emergency loan. When Manufacturer's Hanover started to weaken, Dia-Ichi Kangyo Bank came to the rescue. In early 1990, California, New York, West Virginia, Alaska, Arkansas, Mississippi, and Louisiana applied for low-interest loans from the Japanese Export-Import Bank—an institution that normally extends credit to Third World countries. When Washington became enthusiastic about building a gigantic superconducting supercollider, top officials first asked Japan for $2.6 billion to help. As the 1990s began, the U.S. Commerce Department and Japan's Ministry of International Trade and Industry proposed a scheme whereby Japan would help revive the American machine-tool industry by training U.S. engineers, transferring technology to the United States, and increasing its imports. More recently Japanese automobile companies have been offering to help American suppliers survive with intensive courses in new manufacturing methods. Virtually all leading U.S. microchip producers and all major steel manufacturers need Japanese partners. As 1992 began, administration officials were hinting that the U.S. recession was in part due to Japanese trade barriers, and Prime Minister Kiichi Miyazawa was issuing a New Year's plea for Japan to summon compassion and help General Motors. Maybe this is merely evidence of the increasing internationalization of the U.S. economy. But it has the ring of something more ominous.

More serious than all these problems is the deterioration of America's social fabric. Despite President Bush's vision of a kinder and gentler America, the United States is turning into a harsher and meaner country. From the standpoint of America's ability to lead, the implication is that the socioeconomic model that was so attractive to the rest of the world is coming apart. Once people in other countries admired what the United States stood for. Can this still be said?

America has become an exceptionally violent society, with one person murdered every twenty-five minutes in 1988. In 1990 the U.S. homicide rate was increasing across the nation at a rate of 10 percent to 50 percent over the previous year—attributed to drug disputes, deadlier weapons, and young people starting out life with criminal behavior. The murder rate was set to break all records with a rate of 10.5 per 100,000, just about ten times the rate in Japan and Germany.[9] In the 1980s, American expenditures for criminal justice increased four times faster than the budget for education, and twice as fast as money spent on health and hospitals. Between 1970 and 1990 the number of Americans behind bars tripled, as the United States became a country that imprisons a larger share of its population than any other nation.[10] In addition, a new arms race is now in the making. This time, however, it is not with another country, but between urban police departments and American criminals. It involves not pistols and handguns but semiautomatic weapons.[11]

The education system is in a shambles, despite recent publicity about improving national standards. While U.S. colleges and universities are still held in exceptionally high regard around the world, the high school dropout rate is running at 25 percent overall (far higher among blacks and Hispanics), with no vocational training as backup. Over 50 percent of dropouts are unemployed or receiving welfare; they account for 60 percent of prison inmates and 87 percent of pregnant teenagers. An estimated 13 percent of seventeen-year-old Americans cannot read, write, add, or subtract, and functional illiteracy in the adult population is much higher than that.[12] (In 1992 the Speaker of the House in Japan created a furor in the United States by saying that 30 percent of American workers could not read. He was not so far off target.) Compared to students in Europe and Japan, Americans rank near the bottom in almost every category of problem-solving and literacy. The crisis promises to get worse as jobs in the future will require even more advanced skills and as more than half of new entrants into the labor force come from minorities and immigrants—the groups who are already falling behind. In late 1991 the administration presented America's first national report card on how the secondary education system is progressing. Among the results: by the year 2000 there is virtually no chance of meeting the goals set just a few years ago. The National Association of Manufacturers added another depressing note: in the 1990s, it said, some 30 million workers already in the work force will require "massive" retraining to keep pace with changing job requirements. [13]

Another component of leadership is the confidence of the population, which depends in large part on its standard of living. Admittedly, the definition of what constitutes poverty has been changing, but the trend is unambiguous. The United States had one in seven people living below the poverty line in 1970, one in six in the 1980s, one in five in 1990, and a projected one in four by the year 2000. In 1991, the Census Bureau estimated that 2.1 million more Americans were living in poverty in 1990 than in 1989. [14]

A particularly striking problem concerns American youth. One in five American children now lives in poverty, a startling increase from the 1980s, and estimates show that 25 percent to 30 percent of all children may need some form of public welfare assistance before the age of 17. [15] Meanwhile the incidence of teenage pregnancy among the poor is soaring—with implications for family structures and individual health that could be staggering. All this comes on top of the fact that America is ranked twentieth in the world when it comes to infant mortality, with a black baby having a better chance of surviving its first year in Trinidad or Jamaica than in Washington, D.C. "Never before has one generation of American children been less healthy, less cared for, or less prepared for life than their parents were at the same age," said a national commission in 1990. [16]

Combining these problems, it is no wonder that America's productivity —the output per worker—has been declining, too. This may be the single most important component in the nation's ability to enhance its living standards and compete in the world economy. The picture is bleak. In the 1950s and 1960s, the average annual increase in worker productivity was 2.8 percent. Since 1970 it has been 1.2 percent, less than half that of the boom years and about half of the average rate of the 1900–1970 period. A survey conducted by the U.S. Department of Labor in early 1992 showed, not surprisingly, that since the 1960s U.S. per capita productivity in manufacturing was growing significantly more slowly than in Japan and Germany. [17]

Beyond all this lies the slow erosion of most Americans' hopes. The 1980s were a decade in which the average family income stagnated. It was the first decade since the 1930s in which large numbers of Americans suffered serious declines in living standards. [18] It was a time when the rich became richer and the poor poorer, reversing thirty years of growing equality. In 1990 and 1991, many of these trends seemed to worsen under prolonged recession.

What is emerging in America is an intensely polarized society. Against the backdrop of declining economic prospects for a large number of people, the issues of what the government should do, of who should pay for essential services, and of regional, class, racial, and even generational antagonisms are likely to become explosive. If current trends persist, America could find itself torn by dissension, and totally preoccupied with internal divisions. How could a nation under these strains be an effective international leader?

There is, in fact, a real danger that America's economic and social debilitation and its increasing vulnerability to outside events will result in a mood in favor of lessening its global involvement. The pressures are there, as is the force of history. "Americans," said George Kennan, the former U.S. diplomat and a noted scholar, "seem to oscillate between fleeing from the rest of the world and embracing it with too ardent a passion. An absolute national morality is inspired either to withdraw from 'alien things' or to transform them; it cannot live in comfort constantly by their side." [19]

Indeed, as America entered the 1990s, calls for the president to address the domestic agenda grew increasingly loud almost two years before the presidential campaign. Said *Time* magazine in naming President Bush man of the year in 1990, "His domestic policy, to the extent that he has one, has been to leave things alone until he could no longer avoid taking action. That strategy of deliberate drift burdens the nation with a host of problems that have become worse over the past decade: drugs, homeless-ness, racial hostility, education, environment. In sharp contrast to his foreign policy performance, Bush affected domestic events decidedly for the worse." [20] Months later William G. Hyland, editor of *Foreign Affairs* and an important member of the traditional foreign policy establishment, indicated how the tension between foreign and domestic priorities might have to be resolved. He wrote: "America needs to start selectively disen-gaging abroad to save resources and seize the unparalleled opportunity to put its house in order. The enemy is not at the gate, but it may already be inside." [21]

JAPAN'S HANDICAPS

Whereas America's handicaps are primarily a result of festering economic and social problems, Japan's shortcomings relate more to the structure of government and to the nation's historical mindset.

No one can accuse Japanese officials of not recognizing the need to play more of a leadership role. "It is now an invalid idea that Japan is responsible only for itself," said Vice Foreign Minister Takakazu Kuriyama about the Gulf conflict.[22] But rhetoric aside, can Japan be a true leader? Can it be more than an economic power attempting to satisfy its narrowly defined domestic interests? Can it even come close to playing the role that Great Britain and then the United States did during various periods of this century? The answer is a certain "no."

Historically, Japan has been a follower. In the late nineteenth century it built a modern industrial state after Europe and America first plowed the way. In the early twentieth century it became an imperial power seeking colonies, again aping the pattern in the west. After World War I, Japan had a brief fling with democracy and internationalism when those movements were in vogue elsewhere. In the 1930s, it was attracted to the kind of authoritarian fascism that was sweeping Germany and Italy, and although it was behaving aggressively, it had picked European role models to emulate.

In the postwar era, Japan has been a follower, too. Its foreign policy has been driven by goals such as access to markets and natural resources. It has also been characterized by an overwhelming wish to stay close to the United States, the only nation that has come close to being a trusted ally. "Waiting for demands from the Americans and then responding to them . . . is the single basic theme running through Japan's postwar foreign relations," said Atsuyuki Sassa, a former cabinet official in charge of security affairs.[23]

In addition to being a follower, Japan has a political structure that is badly suited for international leadership. Since 1955 one party—the Liberal Democratic Party (LDP)—has been in power continuously. While this has given Japan some important policy stability, the LDP's unique political structure makes the pursuit of broad international policy almost inconceivable.

The starting point for understanding Japan's political process is the fact that each electoral district can elect several representatives. Members of the same party run against each other for national office by appealing to small local interest groups. The implication is that politicians themselves tend to be interested only in the most parochial issues. Beyond that, the LDP is organized into powerful factions, each competing with one another. As a result, the party is highly fragmented, and what moves politics is not national (or international) issues so much as intraparty rivalries. The prime minister is chosen not because his party won, because it always wins. Nor is he chosen because of his views on issues, because the elections are not about issues. Instead he is selected in the "back room" as a result of a deal among competing factions of the LDP. He is, most literally, the compromise candidate, the result of a delicate political balance among factions. Were he to take positions that upset the balance, he would be unlikely to remain in office for more than his two-year term. There is, therefore, no strong executive.

Real power is mostly in the ministries, which are staffed by highly professional bureaucrats. Each ministry alone is adept at running its own business, but international policies frequently call for policy coordination among MITI, the Ministry of Finance, the Ministry of Foreign Affairs, and others. This is often a slow and painful process, for a consensus among the different interests has to be formed. The sheer effort involved makes it more likely that the government will be more efficient reacting to another country's demands and policy initiatives than in making far reaching proposals of its own. Moreover, while the civil servants are excellent at pursuing concrete goals—reaching a target for G.N.P. growth or foreign aid, implementing an energy policy, encouraging companies to invest in a specific project—they are not equipped to change the overall direction of policy. This has never been their mission.

The Japanese culture is also constraining. The homogeneity of the Japanese population contributes to the unease in dealing with the diversity of peoples abroad. This impedes the kind of communication with other nations that is normally taken for granted in the West. Many Japanese believe that their culture does not have international relevance, that it cannot be fully understood by non-Japanese, and that foreign influence would only weaken Japanese society and should therefore be tightly controlled. The immigration question, discussed before, is a good case in point.

The Japanese approach to policy problems is extremely pragmatic. It is hard to discern a consistent set of philosophical values, except for the primacy placed on cohesion at the level of family, village, company, or nation. The Japanese preference is to solve every problem on a case-by-case basis, reshuffling whatever rules or precedents might exist to fit the particular situation. "There are no examples in our history of Japan standing up for one value against another," said a senior official in the Foreign Ministry in late 1990.[24] "Unlike Americans," said another Japanese diplomat, "Japanese do not associate their identity with any faith or convictions."[25] This way of thinking makes Japan particularly unsuited for leadership in the 1990s, when political, economic, and social values —from free elections to self-determination to human rights—will be very high on the global agenda.

Like the United States, Japan in the 1990s will be preoccupied with its own agenda, with little time or energy to look after managing the global system the way America once did.

In the first place, Japan will have to focus on the chronic problem of political scandal at the highest level of government. The fact is that administration after administration is now preoccupied with defending itself against charges of bribery and corruption, a pattern that makes the passage of essential legislation impossible, let alone the earning of any stature or respect on the international scene. It seems that no sooner does a new prime minister take over than he is embroiled in intense domestic controversy about whether his tenure will last beyond a few months. It is a pattern befitting not even a poor African nation, let alone a superpower on whom the world is depending.

Japan also will be grappling with domestic problems that pose threats to its tightly knit society. These are far less severe than the strains in America, but potentially explosive in the Japanese context. For example, the rapid increase in Japanese national wealth has enriched some of the population, but in general it has not trickled down. Living standards have lagged well behind other major industrialized nations, from basic plumbing to health care to parks. Tensions are appearing in a society that prides itself on being totally middle class.

Another set of pressures is coming from the deregulation of the Japanese financial system. It used to be that the Ministry of Finance had total control over who received loans and at what price, thereby giving it tight rein on the pattern of economic development in Japan. But in the late 1980s, liberalizing of financial regulations began. Not only were interest rates responding to market forces, but Japanese companies now had the ability to borrow money from outside the country if they could get better terms; similarly, investors could take advantage of profitable foreign opportunities. Although there have yet to be the kinds of disruptions that have taken place in the U.S. financial system, problems are mounting. As in the United States, banks are under pressure to build their capital base; the profitability of securities firms has been plummeting; regulators are struggling to keep up with changes in the marketplace; and scandals are erupting in every corner of the system. If history is any guide, the skillful Japanese bureaucracy, together with the overlapping ties between government agencies and financial institutions, will prevent a U.S.–style crisis. But in the mid-1900s Japan will be preoccupied with restructuring its financial system to an extent not seen since the U.S. military Occupation. This in turn could translate into a hesitant and erratic global performance on the part of the world's major international lender.

All aspects of Japan's foreign relationships are in flux, too. Change itself is always unsettling, especially for Japan. But the agony is made worse by the fact that Japan has, by its own standards, prospered under its old system. Major departures are made only with great reluctance; why, after all, change a winning strategy unless absolutely forced to do so?

For most of the postwar period, Japan has had but one friend and one ally—the United States. It has had virtually no ties to Europe. It took no active role in international organizations and its nationals held almost no prominent positions, with the few exceptions of the World Health Organization, the Asian Development Bank, and very recently, the U.N. Commission on Refugees. Then, in the mid-1980s, this all began to change. Relations with the United States, while still overwhelmingly predominant, started to experience deep strains. Investments in Europe began to grow. Japanese visibility in global forums took on new significance.

The growing prominence of Japan in world affairs coincided with pressures on Tokyo to change the way it behaves. Today, Tokyo is besieged from all sides. With America, there are constant tensions with regard to trade, but, as noted, Washington is going much further and demanding fundamental changes in the way Japan does business generally—in its approach to saving and investment, in the tight relationship among Japanese companies, in the retail distribution system, in the way antimonopoly laws are applied. In addition, the United States is pressuring Tokyo to increase its efforts to provide finance to the Third World countries, to Eastern Europe, to the republics of the former Soviet Union, and to international financial institutions. On the defense front, Japan is being asked to take added responsibility for its own security, and to participate in international peacekeeping forces. "Your 'checkbook diplomacy,' like our 'dollar diplomacy' of an earlier era, is clearly too narrow," Secretary of State James A. Baker 3d told a group in Japan. "Japan should step forward as a leader confronting global issues."[26] The list of demands made by European nations is not as extensive but it is growing. One European trade mission after another is travelling to Japan to pound the table for a better trade balance, and the E.C. is squarely behind the United States in pressing Japan on such matters as more liberal banking regulations and more aid to Eastern Europe and the former Soviet Union.

The upshot is that Tokyo is very much on the defensive, reeling from having to respond to one set of outside pressures after another. Yet Japan continues to see the international arena in traditional terms. There is Japan, and then there is the rest of the world. When many Japanese talk about making a contribution to peace or to economic progress abroad, it's often as though they were not part of the broader global system but doing a good deed to avoid heavy criticism from foreigners, particularly the United States. Needless to say, this is hardly the position of a country that will be a leader on the international stage.

None of this should rule out Japanese assertiveness in a few selected areas, as in East Asia where *regional* clout is not the same as global leadership.

There is, in fact, no evidence at all that Japan *wants* the burden or responsibility of maintaining order or initiating change; there is no suggestion that it wants any constraints on its traditional pursuit of its narrow self-interest. One Japanese official after another repeats the same message: they would prefer to see a strong United States in the lead, and would like Japan to be an important partner who is consulted regularly. "We want to be the best number-two country in history," said Koichi Kato, chief cabinet secretary and former defense minister.[27]

GERMAN LEADERSHIP?

In contrast to Japan, post–World War II Germany has had a string of worldly leaders—Konrad Adenauer, Ludwig Ehrhard, Willy Brandt,

Helmut Schmidt, Helmut Kohl—and has forged much deeper international ties. Germany has enjoyed an intense relationship not only with the United States, as did Japan, but also with France, Great Britain, Italy, Belgium, Holland, Spain, Portugal, and others. It has been active in multilateral organizations, and Germans have served as the Secretary General of NATO, Executive Director of the World Bank's International Finance Corporation, Executive Director of the International Energy Agency, and as Minister for Industrial Affairs in the European Community.

At the same time, however, Germany has maintained a low profile, hiding behind NATO and the E.C. Before the collapse of the Berlin Wall, few would even have raised the issue of global leadership for Germany, for West Germany was de facto half a sovereign state, host to hundreds of thousands of foreign troops, fearful of an East-West confrontation on its soil, as self-absorbed as any major industrial nation.

Indeed, any discussion about leadership would have had a hollow ring right up until the 1990s. West German politics was fragmented and Chancellor Kohl's popularity was plummeting. A small number of right wing politicians had been elected in Berlin and in the state of Hesse. There was growing alarm that their nationalist, antiforeign movement might be the start of something larger. On the left, the Green party was opposing Germany's centrist policies. There was talk of a "rainbow coalition," which many believed would be a recipe for stalemate in German domestic politics, and a major problem for German maneuverability on the global scene.

In the excitement and momentum of reunification, the environment changed dramatically. The fringe parties seem to have hunkered down or disappeared. Chancellor Kohl became a powerful leader. "We should not just look at our own problems," he said, evidencing his new statesman's role. "We are at the center of Europe. Everything we do affects the rest of Europe, and therefore the world."[28] It sounded good, but what did it mean?

Any reading of Germany's leadership potential over the next several years must take account of several basic problems.

Despite being a nation that produced some of the world's great poets, writers, musicians, and scientists, Germany never had a philosophy to impart that had attraction for its neighbors. Germany never had a broad mission, or a cause that was not totally self-centered. Whereas seventeenth century England gave the world the universal ideal of human liberty, and eighteenth century France championed the power of reason in human affairs, Germany projected mostly state power and self-glorification.

The German political system is not well suited for leadership. The parties are composed mostly of state officials, bureaucrats, teachers; they have become insular and sluggish. This situation suited the Cold War, since international initiatives were not expected from Germany during that time, and the focus was intentionally internal. But can the system change, and, if so, how long would it take?

Germany's exceptionally strong federalist system contributes to insularity. Elections at the local level are often determined by parties' stands on national issues. As a result, national party positions rarely stray from the grass roots. This ensures democratic accountability, but also gives extraordinary weight to narrowly focussed concerns. With the addition of new *Länder* from the East, preoccupied as they are with massive unemployment, environmental problems, and refugees, German federalism is sure to become more cumbersome and more centered on domestic concerns.

The emergence of charismatic chancellors is a possibility, of course, much more so than in Japan. But for good historical reasons Germany's neighbors, and many Germans themselves, fear domestic politics that revolve around powerful personalities.

There is a unique feature to Germany's situation—it is enmeshed in the decision making of the European Community. In time Germany will no doubt dominate the coordination process in Brussels, but for now the sheer bureaucratic machinery of the multinational government will reduce Berlin's maneuverability. From the German standpoint, policy making and implementation will become ever more complicated as the smallest decisions will have to pass muster at the local, state, federal, and E.C. level of government. At the same time, the E.C. gives Germany a built-in excuse not to do something it does not want to do, or to pass the blame for unpopular international actions on the need for an internal European consensus.

There is another special aspect to Germany's situation that might prevent it from leadership. "Germany is a country whose people have been taught that their fathers and grandfathers committed the worst crimes known to mankind, that their ancestors habitually dragged the world into ruinous conflict," wrote Marc Fisher of *The Washington Post.* "The recurrent metaphor is the sheltered child who must not face the real world." [29] The psychosis is likely to translate into a defensive type of activism—that is, Germany will be assertive only when its basic interests seem threatened, as with instability on its eastern borders.

Just as in America and Japan, domestic preoccupations will be awesome in Germany. "West Germany's economy has been such a sleek and steady juggernaut for the last decade," wrote Richard E. Smith in *The International Herald Tribune,* "that many experts doubted that even unification would faze it much. They were wrong." [30] Indeed, almost every aspect of West German life is likely to be affected: labor, housing supply, education, relations among social classes. The enormous costs of rebuilding East Germany—some estimates have put total reconstruction costs at between $600 billion and $1 trillion over the decade of the 1990s —are sure to affect every aspect of German life. This includes interest rates, taxes, social harmony. [31]

Problems are growing. In the summer of 1991, McKinsey & Co. warned that "the problems of East Germany will pull West Germany into a downward spiral." [32] Germany's Council of Economic Advisors reported at the end of 1991 that unemployment could increase by over 30 percent in 1992. [33] Without subsidies, said German Labor Minister Norbert Blum, the total of 1 million jobless in the former East Germany would be 3 million higher. In its 1991 report, the normally staid and cautious OECD described the eastern region's economy as experiencing a "virtual collapse of production and employment." [34] In addition, the social strains of uneven economic conditions between the old West and East Germany could become politically paralyzing, creating internal divisions not seen in Germany in the postwar years. Between July 1990 and February 1991, for example, East German industrial production fell by 43 percent while West German output rose by over 8 percent. Unemployment in the East soared between July 1990 and May 1991 and declined in the West. [35]

It is now clear that much of the investment in the eastern portion of the country will come from government and not private funds. This raises the specter of higher budget deficits or higher taxes, or both. Pressure on Berlin is fierce to pay former East German workers on the scale of the old West Germany, even though such payments are not justified by labor productivity. This creates a vicious spiral, consisting of inflation, a reluctance of private business to invest, more government subsidies, higher taxes, and slower growth. It is not a recipe for economic progress or social harmony.

The pressures of reunification are coming on top of other vulnerabilities: an influx of refugees from elsewhere in Eastern Europe, and increasing trade competition from Japan and the rest of East Asia. In addition, the last half of the 1980s was good to Germany because of the strong growth of its export markets. To a great extent, this masked problems that Germany worried about before the boom and that are still below the surface—rigid labor laws, high corporate taxes, and technological innovation that is focussed on a narrowing base of industries, for example. These underlying pressures worry many German leaders, and are apt to make them less secure than other nations think they should be.

Germany's foreign relations are likely to be dominated by three sets of issues, all of which reinforce its exclusive focus on the European continent. First, there is the management of more rapid integration in Western Europe, especially monetary and political union. As the strongest member of the European Community, Germany has been cast front and center in the unprecedented debates about whether to give up control over national currencies in favor of just one European currency, and whether to cede political authority over questions of foreign policy and national security in favor of some as yet undefined supranational substitute. These issues are fundamental to German society. It is as if America were being asked at one time to share control over the dollar, pool national security decisions, harmonize banking and security laws, and revamp its social security and labor legislation so that all these policies were more or less the same as those of its major trading partners.

The second preoccupation will be Eastern Europe. Berlin knows it will bear the brunt of the cost for bailout and reconstruction. In a bleak 1990 year-end assessment, Morgan Stanley & Co. estimated that the region would require an investment of between $270 billion and $370 billion over the next five years to prevent economic and political chaos.[36] A year later, the United Nations Commission on Europe issued an even more somber report, citing a continuous plunge in economic production for the region, with a decline of 25 percent over the past three years.[37] Unlike the United States or Japan, Germany will not be able to turn its back on this situation. Berlin will have to do all it can to keep the region relatively stable—including bilateral economic treaties, large financial and technical assistance, pressing the E.C. for more aid and trade concessions for the East. What is clear is that it cannot afford to fail.

A third problem is the former Soviet Union. Here the situation is so out of control that no numbers are worth much to illustrate the depth of problems. For starters, there is inflation exceeding 300 percent, no credible currency, substantial shortages of food, fuel, and consumer goods, a broken-down distribution system, and a decline of production on the order of 15 percent per year. With simultaneous revolutions taking place in the political and economic spheres, and given the size and complexity of the economic entity, there is no precedent for the crisis that is unfolding—not Japan or Germany after the war, not Mexico or Chile at the height of the debt crisis in the 1980s.[38] More than any other nation, Germany will be the initial haven for Soviet refugees, and Germany will suffer most from debt defaults and from economic reverberations that occur in Eastern Europe as chaos in the former U.S.S.R. spills over to Czechoslovakia, Hungary, and Poland. The instabilities in the republics will become a monstrous and continuous problem for Germany's leaders.

Germany's regional focus, as opposed to its global outlook, has emerged clearly in the different approaches it took in the Gulf and Yugoslavia crises. In the first case, it did not want involvement. In the second, it defied everyone—the United States, Great Britain, France, the U.N. secretary-general—and took the lead in recognizing the breakaway republics. We can expect more of a close-to-home focus. "Germany is carrying more than its fair share of the burden for the establishment of a peaceful, peacefully evolving world," said Foreign Minister Hans-Dietrich Genscher shortly after the Gulf War ended.[39] Referring to the mounting burdens on German taxpayers, Otto Lambsdorff, leader of the Free Democratic Party, which is part of the ruling coalition, put it this way: "We have reached the end of the rope."[40]

COLLECTIVE LEADERSHIP?

Is there an alternative to the way that global leadership has been exercised in the past? Instead of one dominant power, could there be a kind of collective leadership, a Big Three directorate?

Shared leadership seems appropriate for a period in which no nation has a monopoly of power and in which so many problems must be addressed cooperatively. And because America, Japan, and Germany are long-time allies, it would seem that while collective management might not be perfect, it should not be impossible and it might well work in selected instances. But the need for collective leadership does not mean that it will happen. There are several reasons that make a joint effort unlikely to succeed—at least to the extent necessary to overcome many of the problems on the horizon.

Setting aside the platitudes about cooperation, the interests of the Big Three are in many critical instances not the same. It is one thing to say, for example, that everyone has an interest in currency stability, but which nation is going to strengthen its currency and which is going to accept devaluation in order to get the relationships right? It is one thing to acknowledge the need to protect the environment, but what to do if common targets have a vastly differential impact on each country?

Even more fundamentally, the Big Three are fierce economic competitors. They will be competing for the same markets, including their internal markets. They will be competing for capital. They will be trying to dominate the same high-technology industries. They will be doing all this starting from different economic bases, and using different models of capitalism. Economists might pontificate about how everyone gains from more trade and investment, and over some period of time perhaps they are right. But in the next several years politicians and most of the citizens in the Big Three are apt to see such fierce and all-encompassing competition in terms of winners and losers.

There is also the vexing issue of different military capabilities coming on top of economic competition. Even if troops and missiles count for less than they did in the Cold War, they will not be irrelevant, and defense issues will add to the tensions inherent in collective global management. It is inevitable that America will try to offset its competitive economic problems with political muscle; and it is inevitable that such attempts will work on occasion, creating great resentment in Japan and Germany, leading to backlash and resistance.

In order to have a really collaborative management system, moreover, each nation must be willing to make relatively proportionate contributions. In the 1990s this is unlikely to happen. America, as President Bush has said, may have "more will than wallet." Japan has the reverse situation, especially as its financial surpluses continue to build up. Given the task in the East, Germany may be short on both accounts, at least outside of its own backyard. The different situations, in other words, are too complex to balance effectively. Efforts to impose collective management could add tension rather than reduce it.

Finally, there is no precedent for nations sharing leadership. Historically, national egos and drives are too strong. When responsibility is shared, no one really has it. And there is constant instability when there are more than two leaders: some are always siding with others, creating suspicions and alliances. Here is a sampling of what could well happen:

Washington and Berlin vs Tokyo. An American-European "gang up" against Japan could easily arise as Tokyo resists calls to open its economy as wide and as fast as others are demanding. America and Europe have not so far put concerted pressure on Japan except at the most general, rhetorical level. Now they may well coordinate their strategies.

In addition, some of the big European companies engaged in high-technology industries will have a strong interest in forming alliances with U.S. firms to protect themselves from Japanese competition. Such possibilities multiply as the full results of Japan's extraordinary investments in manufacturing and distribution come on stream in the mid-1990s. Europeans will, of course, conclude alliances with Japanese firms, too. But for cultural reasons, and because of much longer standing ties, their preference is sure to be for American companies.

How will U.S. firms react? It is hard to say, given the substantial reliance already on Japan. But as the dependence of American firms on their Japanese partners grows, a new type of diversification may become a high priority. IBM's tie-up with Siemens, for example, gives it another source of memory chips and reduces its reliance on firms like Hitachi or Toshiba who are not only rivals in the chip-making arena, but who compete in the finished computer and electronics sector.

Washington and Tokyo vs Berlin. America will be watching Germany's stated commitment to a European Community that remains open to international trade and investment. But if the E.C. drags its feet, Washington will try to put enormous pressure on Berlin. It would certainly be joined by Tokyo, which is already nervous about Europe's potential protectionism.

As the penetration of Japanese industry into the United States continues, another kind of problem is likely to arise with Europe. America will be exporting products of Japanese companies that are fully incorporated in America and staffed by U.S. workers. For example, the United States is once again becoming an exporter of cars. They are not Buicks or

Mercuries but Hondas and Toyotas. America will become an exporter of Japanese fax machines and laser printers, made by firms like Canon and Ricoh. Any European reaction against such Japanese-American hybrids would create a firestorm in Washington.

From a European perspective, moreover, there are two great sources of suspicion concerning the U.S.–Japan relationship. The first is that the interdependence of the two countries is unstoppable, and will push them ever closer together. Europeans can point to the large number of Japanese takeovers of American firms, and the many U.S.–Japanese joint ventures and strategic alliances. The second E.C. concern is the possibility of a variety of special bilateral trade deals between Washington and Tokyo that could exclude Europe. Further down the road, many Europeans worry that the United States and Japan intend to exclusively dominate the dynamic Pacific Basin.

Tokyo and Berlin vs Washington. Japan and Germany have been the principal financial backers to Uncle Sam (although Germany's role has temporarily diminished while unification absorbs so much funding). In the future, the two may have a thing or two to tell Washington about its economic policies, as any banker would. They could attack budget deficits and neglect of the dollar; they could critique domestic social problems like the education system. In the past, they have been reluctant to act in unison, but in the future they might. The logic of a concerted Tokyo-Berlin effort is that alone, neither country would be as comfortable confronting the United States as they would acting together.

In the past few years strategic alliances between German and Japanese firms have begun to emerge for the first time in generations. Daimler-Benz and Mitsubishi Corporation concluded a broad-ranging agreement to cooperate in aerospace and automotive production. Matsushita Electric Industrial Company and Siemens are coordinating strategies for producing and distributing personal computers in the European market. C. Itoh & Co. and Klockner-Werke have agreed to a wide-ranging pact in the steel, machinery, and chemicals businesses. The combination of engineering skills, attention to quality, and access to capital that these corporate link-ups entail represent a potentially new and awesome force in the world economy—a force directly competitive with American industry.

※   ※   ※

In the end, there will be specific cases in which the Big Three will collectively decide how to handle a problem, and pursue a common course. A major economic debacle like the 1987 stockmarket crash, or a collapse of one economy like Poland's, could summon such efforts. But looking over the broader challenges we should not be fooled: there is no substitute for one or two countries that not only are willing to take charge but are in strong, credible position to do so.

For now there are no great candidates. In the panoply of challenges in the 1990s, this may be the biggest problem of all. The world is never static, however, and it is possible that someone could emerge as a result of changes in policy and attitude that do not seem probable now. Were that someone to appear it would have to be the United States, since the handicaps to Japan and Germany's potential global leadership run too deep. As we have seen, the obstacles facing America itself are exceptionally difficult. But this should not stop us from asking what should be done to overcome them.

CHAPTER VIII

America in the American Mind

With the end of the Cold War the familiar guideposts of American foreign policy have disappeared. All of our underlying premises about political alliances, about war and peace, about military and economic leadership, about ground rules for trade and investment—all of these were based on the existence of U.S.–Soviet competition. That international order has now disintegrated, and almost none of the old assumptions can be taken for granted.

Of course, despite the dramatic events of the past few years, there will be a continuation of some basic themes in American foreign policy. We will still be uncomfortable with any nation rising to disproportionate power in Asia or Europe—especially Japan and Germany. We will still want the world to embrace the ideas of Thomas Jefferson and Adam Smith. We will have an abiding interest in a global economy that is open to our grain, our telecommunications equipment, and our banks. We will worry about threats to our national security from terrorism and nuclear proliferation. We will try to protect American citizens and companies who are mistreated abroad, and we will also protest human rights abuses of non-Americans. But the international setting will be radically different from what we have known, and effective policies will require a vastly changed American mindset.

Finding new bearings at home and abroad will be America's greatest challenge as we approach the new century. It is not merely a question of defining what we must do, but of reexamining who we are. Incremental changes will not suffice. It will not be enough just to pull ourselves out of this recession, or to make some moves toward a better health care system, or to transfer funds from the defense budget to social programs —important as all this is. We need no less than a revolution in the way we see ourselves and our involvement in the world.

We must move quickly to come to grips with ourselves and the changing world order, for time is not on our side. Relative to Japan and Germany, our economic prospects are poor and our political influence is waning. Their economic underpinnings—trends in investment, productivity, market share in high technology, education, and training— are stronger. Their banks and industry are in better shape. Their social problems are far less severe than ours. At the same time, a leadership vacuum has arisen as the roles of both Washington and Moscow radically change, and as regional economic blocs, led by Germany and Japan, emerge to challenge our long held vision of a unified global economy managed according to American precepts, and underpinned by American firms, American banks, and the American dollar. It is very possible that these different trajectories among the Big Three will stretch established political and economic ties toward their breaking point; that, at least, is what history teaches us about what happens when power shifts so dramatically among nations. The real danger is a repeat of the 1920s and 1930s when fragmentation and disorder reigned, when no single country took up the leadership challenge, and when competition and confrontation overwhelmed the ability of nations to work together.

Thus far America has barely made a start in the reorientation that must come. We are preoccupied with daily events, and polarized over issues such as abortion, gun control, or affirmative action. Our media does its political analysis on the basis of soundbites, and our politicians plan their strategies accordingly. The sex lives of our officials get more attention than the dramatic fraying of America's social fabric. Neglected altogether is solving the long-term problems that are crucial to our future—the issues of physical infrastructure, of education and job training for our citizens, of technological competition, of rising poverty, and of rising income inequalities. Also given short shrift are our relationships to Japan and Germany, which cannot be divorced from the so-called domestic issues. The big question is whether America will drift along, or whether it can summon the will and energy to confront the new realities.

DEFINING THE PROBLEM

It is critical that we define our challenge correctly. We should begin by agreeing what the problem is *not*. It is not that the United States lacks the wherewithal to compete successfully with other nations; no one seriously denies America's awesome physical resources, the vitality of its people, the innovative nature of its financial markets, the potential strength of a diversified six-trillion-dollar economy. It is not that we are oblivious of our competitive problems; aside from the massive increase in the number of foreign products we use, there is a consensus among most experts that America is losing ground in several key industries such as the auto and consumer electronics industries, and also about those industries in which we need to be competitive—for example, software, communications equipment, precision machinery, advanced materials, aerospace, biotechnology. The problem is not that Japan and Germany have achieved their successes by cheating on the rules; few would make this charge against Germany, and even Japan's infractions of generally accepted trade law are a minor problem compared to the fact that its economic system is structured much differently than ours. And it is not that Japan and Germany owe America anything for past generosity and are failing to pay up; it is high time we put the past behind us. All of these charges might be convenient excuses but they miss the point: America is on the wrong course, not marginally, but fundamentally. Simply put, the problem is within ourselves; it is the failure to come to grips as individuals and as a nation with the world as it is evolving. We have failed to diagnose our problem correctly and to recognize the enormous distance we must now travel to reinvigorate our society.

The greatest source of American strength has always been the American Dream: economic growth, equal opportunity, upward mobility. It was this dream, and its substantial realization, that repeatedly has given this nation its vitality, its confidence, and its strength. It was this dream that enabled us to emerge victorious in 1945, to shepherd Japan and Germany through decades of physical and political rehabilitation, to help much of the Third World grow, and to lead the West and most of East Asia in the battle against communism. Unless there is a national determination to redress the entire span of domestic policies that have gone astray and destroyed this dream—from fiscal depravity to the stagnation of middle-class incomes, from the deterioration of our public schools to a scandalous health care system, from our failure to make long-term investments to our growing urban battle zones—unless we can turn these trends around, the prospect is for a slow ebbing of our cherished way of life, not to mention U.S. power and influence in the world.

The fact is, we are badly equipped to make the necessary changes. Too much of our self-identity is based on outmoded precepts. Too much of our thinking, our talent, our resources are still geared to military conflict. And too much of our economic policy is aimed at satisfying short-term consumption. In the new era, wrote global strategist Edward N. Luttwak, "Patient investment capital is displacing firepower, the development of civilian products is displacing military innovation, and the penetration of foreign markets is displacing military garrisons on foreign soil."[1] Equally true is that the education gap separating America from Japan and Germany is as serious as military imbalances would be in a war; that the problems of American social fragmentation are as damaging to our global economic goals as faulty weapons would be in battle.

CHANGING OUR VIEW OF OURSELVES

How should we change? Americans have been imbued with a sense that progress is inevitable—that everything will always get better. We have always been confident that the combination of our rich natural resources, our expansive territory, and our relatively hands-off government would ensure that our incomes and our opportunities would grow. We took it for granted that our children would be better educated than we were, that they would have a greater range of choice about what they would do, and certainly that they would be more secure—physically, financially, and psychologically. "We were always about becoming, not being; about the prospects for the future, not about the inheritance of the past," wrote Lewis H. Lapham, editor of *Harper's.*[2]

None of these assumptions is valid any longer. Progress is no longer a birthright for Americans. Whether measured by economic growth, productivity, median real family income, elimination of poverty—in fact measured by nearly anything other than the income of the very rich— the train has slowed dramatically. Our expectations about its destination are lowered every day, as we sense that our ability to compete is stagnating or declining, and that even more difficult competitive challenges are still ahead.[3] As our yawning budget gaps at federal, state, and county levels show, the claims on our nation's resources outstrip supply, and we are increasingly resigned to do with less. We have become inured to living with more pressure, more uncertainty, more firms that cannot meet foreign competition, more deteriorating roads and bridges, more reports about the failings of our public schools, more crime, more homeless people. As Washington tries to make ends meet we are getting accustomed to borrowing from ourselves and our children, not to mention from Tokyo and Berlin.[4] There is no law that says that such conditions cannot be reversed, but there is no reason to believe they will be under current policies. It is up to us to stop accepting the inevitability of further deterioration.

Another outmoded aspect of our self-image has been the American identity with the frontier and with the rugged individualism it connoted. When the frontier meant expanding across the continental United States, or even across the Pacific Ocean, the lore and lessons were important motivating factors for the American population. When, after World War II, the frontier was the extension of American power and influence to every corner of the free world, or when it meant exploration of outer space, that, too, held real meaning for our lives. But the plethora of economic and social problems requires that we redefine what the most important frontier is today—not the president's goal of reaching Mars, and not the bailout of the former Soviet republics. The frontier to be conquered is the challenge of improving our lives at home, including educating our young and pulling them out of poverty; applying our scientific know-how to combat cancer and AIDS; translating our inventions into commercially useful technology; coming to grips with ethnic and racial polarization. These challenges are not new in themselves, but today they need to be addressed with the priority and the intensity of effort that Americans have historically accorded to their most important national missions.

We need to reevaluate the universalism of our values—to tone down our penchant for carrying the "American message" abroad, for using our "city upon the hill" as the example for mankind. Throughout our history, we have alternated between vigorous promotion of our way of life abroad, and being a passive example for others to emulate. For all of the Cold War period, we have chosen the more pro-active course. The time has again come to work on our own institutions before becoming enthusiastic exporters. It's not that we should avoid promoting our values abroad forever. But how can we offer the American model to others when it is so tarnished at home?

Part of America's outdated self-image is still related to the memory of the Pax Americana, the era of omnipotence for the twenty years following World War II. It was a time of unparalleled prosperity, when foreign economic competition was virtually unknown, when the dollar was king, when we could afford unrestrained consumption because we were still investing in the future, when military prowess was all-important and the military-industrial complex itself could pump out funds to stimulate the economy in periods of economic slump. These were very special years in the American experience, to be fondly remembered, even cherished. But they were, looking back, a transition period between the total collapse of Japan and Germany and their revival to a place in the world commensurate with their energy, talents, and historical ambitions. We need to find a way to put these years and what they represented behind us, without at the same time becoming so disillusioned or so self-defeatist that we fail to appreciate our enormous potential for the future.

SEEING OURSELVES IN THE WORLD

When it comes to viewing ourselves in a new global context, we will have to focus not just on what appear—mistakenly—to be purely domestic concerns but also on Tokyo and Berlin. For the past forty-five years we have measured ourselves against the Soviet Union; for the next generations the new yardsticks will be Japan and Germany. Indeed, we should be prepared for the fact that the next phase of history will see a return of these two nations as central actors on the world stage, with the American role much altered from what it has been.

Our confrontation with the Soviets catered to our penchant for seeing things in black and white. There was the free world and the communist bloc, the good guys and bad. These were all-or-nothing propositions. In the coming decades the categories will be far more ambiguous. Japan and Germany will be our friends in many areas, of course, but they will also be our fiercest challengers. Our political leaders will have to describe the new world order in ways that go beyond the familiar analogy of cowboys and Indians. This is no small task, given the simplicities to which we have been accustomed. The risk of papering over our differences with Japan and Germany is that resentment in the United States will only build, Americans will not be properly mobilized, and eventually an extreme backlash will ensue. But there is also a risk in labelling Tokyo and Berlin as enemies. This would breed resentment abroad and create a feeling in those nations that we are their antagonist, thereby ruining any chance of close collaboration on the matters that count most to us. We must find a middle ground, and articulating what it is will be the true test of our president, his advisors, and the congressional leadership.

Learning how to live in a more complicated world means, among other things, putting aside the false choice between active engagement in the world and an attempt to reduce our participation. The issue we face is not foreign policy versus domestic policy, but how to achieve the right balance. Given the growth of trade, investment, currency exchange, foreign debt, technological links, and global transportation and communications systems, we cannot disengage from the world; America cannot "come home." Interdependence is an irrevocable reality, whether measured by the 10 percent of sales of manufactured goods sold in the United States by foreign companies, the 20 percent of loans that Americans get from foreign banks, the 30 percent of U.S. Treasury bonds and notes bought by foreign purchasers, or the chronic U.S. trade deficits. The only issue is *how* we manage this interaction. How high should we allow our foreign debt to go before we rein in our budget deficits? What sorts of technology should we try to keep in American hands in the interest of independence and national security? What sorts of rules will be needed to create a fairer environment for foreign investment in the United States and overseas? Questions like these will have to be American preoccupations, and dealing with them requires *increasing* foreign policy activism, not reducing it—albeit with a thrust much different from that of the postwar years.

Too often the debate in America is between those who say that we should be more like our competitors and those who argue we should try to make them more like us. Part of a realistic American view of Japan and Germany would consist of steering a fine line between maintaining our own traditions and learning from their successes. No one should advocate that America abandon its historic emphasis on individualism, but no one should deny that there are features of Japanese and German societies that we could usefully adopt.

On the most fundamental level, some of these features include learning from the way they integrate competitive economic considerations with their foreign policy, and the emphasis they have put on the development of their human resources. There are also practical lessons for America in Japan and Germany's cooperative working arrangements between government, business, and labor; their fiscal incentives for encouraging savings; their programs to reduce widescale poverty and attendant social problems; their education and training systems; their advanced manufacturing techniques. We should be neither so proud nor so arrogant as to avoid admitting that in these arenas we have often fallen short of our two most important allies and rivals.

We need to understand not only that power in this more complicated world will rest on economic strength and social cohesion, but also that it will be *relative* to Tokyo and Berlin. Our inflation rate, our investment patterns, our cost of capital, our literacy indices—all these have little meaning unless compared to our major rivals, day in and day out. "When we consider how we measure national power," said Yale professor Paul Kennedy, America's foremost historical chronicler of the rise and fall of nations, "it is important what is happening to others, to other societies, to other people, to other companies. Outside this country is as important as what is happening to us." [5]

We need to acknowledge that the very basis of American dominance in the world is ending. Talk about our being the sole remaining superpower has a hollow ring, because even if it's true, it camouflages our serious predicament and exaggerates our real capabilities. This is not just a problem of psychology or of failed policies. The collapse of communism means the end of the requirement for America to militarily protect Japan and Germany, with the end of all the leverage this once implied. By the end of the century, moreover, the three principal trading regions of the world—North America, Western Europe, and East Asia—will be approximately the same size in terms of economic activity. There is no longer a political or economic basis for U.S. domination and in the future we will have to practice international politics among relative equals, something that we have rarely had to do in the past half century. [6]

For example, America will have to become more adept at playing one power off against another, of siding with Japan against Germany or vice versa, of becoming part of a coalition of other nations against Berlin and Tokyo together. Also, we will have to anticipate the unthinkable—that either Japan or Germany, or both, could exercise real leverage over us—as creditors, as suppliers of vital technology, as hard-to-please partners in endeavors that Washington finds exceptionally important. This kind of concerted intervention into American affairs has not yet happened, but as we become less dominant in the arenas that count most, it well might. Creditor interests often do not coincide with those of debtors; regional powers could have different security concerns than a nation that has interests across the Atlantic, the Pacific, the Rio Grande, and the Middle East. Our challenge will be to try to avoid any kind of gang up against us, to be sure. But we will also need to put such pressure in the perspective of the new configuration of politics, including the fact that on many occasions the United States will ally with either Japan or Germany against the other.

During the Cold War, we connected every crisis to our rivalry with the Soviet Union. The Greek Civil War, the Korean War, the Cuban Missile Crisis, Vietnam, Nicaragua, and Afghanistan were all seen as part of a global struggle against communism. Now, of course, we need not think this way any longer. For the first time in over four decades, America has the luxury of allowing most local disputes to be handled in the neighborhood where they occur, and to let them run their course without the commitment of American money or troops. Washington can thereby devote more time and resources to problems at home. This is not a prescription for noninvolvement; we should not sit idle if nuclear weapons are involved, or if our vital energy supplies are threatened, or if our citizens are being mistreated. Nor does this mean withdrawing from the world; America has many tools it can use to exert pressure short of military involvement, including economic carrots and sticks and greater use of the U.N. and other multilateral organizations. In the years ahead we will have to fine tune our diplomacy in these areas, but by whatever means, in the end we must continue to press Japan and Germany to take on more responsibilities, even though it will definitely mean that they will have a larger voice in global decision making. What's wrong, after all, with asking them to take on more of the burden for order in their respective backyards? Why should they have the luxury of devoting all their attention and resources solely to the economic and social issues that are at the foundation of national strength and influence?

It is certainly not in the U.S. interest to deliberately encourage Japanese or German separation from American policies. But we should not be under the illusion that we have very much leverage in any event. Without a common enemy, America's best chance of keeping these countries reasonably aligned with us depends on the success of two efforts. The first is to build strength at home. This will give us the instruments of power—competitive products, a strong currency, resources for foreign aid—that give us influence. It will also give us another weapon: a society that others want to emulate, and a reason for Tokyo and Berlin to want what we want and, therefore, to pursue policies that are broadly similar to ours. The second requirement is to build up our effectiveness in international organizations, many of which can have a restraining impact on Japan and Germany. Multilateral diplomacy will be far more difficult for Washington in the absence of being able to dominate as it once did. But Tokyo and Berlin are highly sensitive to world opinion and fear isolation. And virtually all nations in the world are concerned with the potential of Japan and Germany to go their own ways. America, therefore, has a significant opportunity to build strong coalitions that support its goals among nations like Great Britain, France, Canada, Brazil, India, Indonesia, and many others who wield influence on the world stage.

THINKING ABOUT FOREIGN POLICY AND DOMESTIC POLICY AS ONE

Part of the challenge facing America is to look at the relationship between foreign and domestic policy in a new light. In a world dominated by military competition, it was possible to separate trade, interest rates, and educational achievement, for example—where the roots of policy were clearly domestic—from strategic forces, missile deployment, and military alliances that were traditional foreign policy issues. But there are many reasons why such differentiation between domestic and foreign policies no longer makes sense. We can no longer say, "politics stops at the water's edge."

The need to integrate foreign and domestic policy grows out of dramatic changes in the world over the past few decades. In the heyday of American power, we saw ourselves as a self-contained economy for which most of the requirements could be satisfied within our borders. It was not that we ignored the rest of the world, but in our minds we felt no critical dependence on it. We all know that this situation is no longer true, but few of us appreciate how dramatically different America's needs now are.

In the first place, we now require the cooperation of other nations in order to achieve an extremely broad array of policy objectives. With imports growing at nearly 8 percent annually over the past five years—more than twice the rate of economic growth in the United States over the same period—there is no need to belabor our growing reliance on foreign products for every aspect of our lives or the fact that the economy relies on imports to provide much-needed competition for American firms. There is probably no need to belabor the fact that exports, once a luxury, have been growing at over 9 percent annually and have become a critical stimulus to America's growth—especially at a time when fiscal policy is paralyzed and a weak financial system seems unable to make full use of ever lower interest rates. We all know, moreover, that large chunks of America's fiscal deficits are financed abroad. Beyond traditional trade and finance, however, is the requirement to get foreign help in enforcing American laws relating to banking and securities fraud, drug interdiction, antitrust prosecution; beyond that is the need to harmonize the capital requirements for banks acting globally and to devise compatible rules for environmental protection.

The second reason why domestic policy and international policy must be meshed together, however, is that the foreign policy agenda is so dominated by issues rooted in policies at home—trade, investment, currencies, technological cooperation. There is no way America can wield real clout in these areas unless it has a highly skilled and adaptable work force, manufacturing firms that are globally competitive, a healthy banking system, and a confident population with the will to invest in the future rather than hunker down and try merely to hang on to the bounties of the past. We have already seen how far away from these conditions America has drifted in the last two decades.

In a world where foreign and domestic policy merge, there should no longer be two disconnected communities of policymakers, one that worries about national security and another that preoccupies itself with trade, investment, housing, health care. Both groups will be dealing with America's strategic interests in the world and both will have to work in tandem. Those who have traditionally made foreign policy are going to have to think in terms of trade-offs between aid for the former Soviet Union and funding for domestic R&D, to take one example. Those who support automatic social security entitlements for everyone will have to consider the alternative possibilities for, say, helping Mexico to stop the flow of drugs and illegal immigrants to the north. Because they are so crucial to economic and social policy, governors and mayors—heretofore foreign policy dilettantes—will need to be organized and educated for a more coherent approach to America's international policies. Business leaders will need to increase their involvement in policymaking, possessing as they do so much information and so many resources critical to the nation's position in the world. "While the world remains a dangerous place requiring us to maintain military strength," said Peter G. Peterson, chairman of the Council on Foreign Relations, "our failure to invest in productive capacity, R&D, and infrastructure; the crisis in American education; the exploding underclass, and other domestic problems may have greater *direct* impact on the United States as a free society than threats from abroad . . . Moreover, continued failure to address these domestic priorities may entail a progressive loss both of political will and economic capacity to take actions abroad that promote our real national security interests."[7]

When foreign and domestic policy are one and the same, economics has to be seen in strategic terms. Adam Smith's invisible hand, as both means and end, is not enough. As long as the American leadership is totally preoccupied with whether this fiscal quarter is better than next, whether IBM's short-term prospects are good or bad, whether the next year's federal deficit will be a little higher or a little lower, there is no hope for the fundamental economic and social reforms that will recognize the real connection between the domestic agenda and national security. The United States has to have real, long-term fiscal targets and credible policies to back them; we have to decide which manufacturing technologies to preserve in American hands and do whatever is necessary to achieve self-sufficiency in those areas; we have to set education targets backed by political commitments and adequate funding; we have to sever our dangerous dependence on Persian Gulf oil with tough-minded policies at home—to take just a few examples.

It is no longer enough to think about the link between domestic and foreign affairs as if we were merely putting together two strands of policy that needed connecting. At times in American history, domestic and foreign policy were aligned—such as when America acquired territory on its continent to satisfy the needs of an expanding population, or when various presidents tried to open foreign markets to help the expansion of American business. But the requirement now is fundamentally different.

It is not to follow the same domestic course we are on and project that abroad. It's not the same as during the 1950s, when we could assume that others should follow the American way. It is to change the basic course of much of our domestic policy in order to deal with the world that is evolving. It is to redefine our goals and reconstruct our institutions in light of changes in the nature of global competition and in the altered distribution of power.

Of course, the connection between domestic and foreign policy can be easily abused, too. A good example was President Bush's trip to Tokyo in January 1992. As the visit began, administration officials were blaming Japan for America's recession and the president was telling the nation that his mission was "jobs, jobs, jobs." In an effort to show that he had America's domestic commercial interests at heart, he then proceeded to take with him the whining chief executives of America's ailing automobile companies. There were many problems with this approach, but one was that it was undisguised foreign scapegoating for made-in-America problems, from bad economic policies to uncompetitive cars. Such linking of domestic and foreign policy may have been the recommendation of political consultants in an election year, but is a shameful prototype for what American policy must not be in the future.

A NEW SENSE OF COMMUNITY

America will be successful in linking foreign and domestic policy only if it can restore some sense of community values. In a world where nations are competing primarily in the economic realm, there is a great need for a high level of social cohesion. Competitiveness will depend in great part on the ability of government and business and labor to work as a team, and the various classes and races of society to avoid confrontation at the expense of productivity. That some strong sense of community spirit exists in America, waiting to be tapped, is evident from the response to the Gulf War. After the defeat of Saddam Hussein, wrote columnist George F. Will, "Clearly this nation, though steeped in the severe individualism of the frontier notion of freedom, has a yearning for the community feeling that comes from collective undertakings . . . The question is whether any enterprise other than war can tap that yearning."[8]

An enhanced sense of community would require, first, a new approach to politics at the national level, one that is designed to solve well-known problems rather than to polarize the electorate. We are all getting tired of a political system that continues to pit rich against poor, white against black, city against suburb, young against old, and we now crave leaders in the White House and Congress whose agenda is to try to solve our problems, rather than inflame them. "Because of the particular myopias of left and right, American politics came to be mired in a series of narrow ideological battles at a time when much larger issues were at stake," author E. J. Dionne, Jr., wrote of the 1980s. "While Americans battled over the Religious Right, Japanese and German industrialists won ever larger shares of the American market. While left and right argued about racial quotas, the average take-home pay of all Americans stagnated. While Michael Dukakis and George Bush discussed Willie Horton and the Pledge of Allegiance, the savings and loan industry moved inexorably toward collapse . . . But America's restive middle class is weary of a politics of confrontation that seems to have so little to do with the challenge the nation faces to its standard of living and with its uncertainty about the role it will play in a world without communism."[9]

A sense of community would entail a renewed spirit of nationalism, one different from the kind we have known. For the last fifty years, American nationalism was aimed first at Japan and Germany in World War II and then at the Soviet Union. For many years, it could be seen in the pride of military victory in Europe and Asia, or the glow of scientific achievements in the space program. Most recently, national spirit swelled after Saddam Hussein was ousted from Kuwait.

What we have not had, however, is a brand of *economic* nationalism that aims at the challenge of the world marketplace—the kind of nationalism historically evident in Japan and Germany and likely to grow stronger in both countries as global competition gets increasingly fierce. The reasons are obvious: for most of the Cold War period, we were able to dominate without much effort, and historically, competitiveness was a private matter for companies and individuals, not the domain of public policy. Economic nationalism and heightened sense of community are two sides of the same coin, however, and America needs to devise a formula that is aggressive but not protectionist. This is a tall order, and a delicate one, too. Given America's chronic trade deficits and the continued pressures from Europe, Japan, and elsewhere in Asia, it is inevitable that some protectionism will characterize the U.S. landscape for years to come. The critical question is what else happens at the same time. Will the training of American workers be enhanced and accelerated, or will the skills of the U.S. labor force fall further behind our competitors? Will there be programs to plough funds back into plant modernization, or will profits be used to compensate executives regardless of performance, or to repurchase a company's shares to pump up short-term stock quotations? Protectionism is acceptable if it is tied to real change in the performance of those firms being shielded, and if it is selective, temporary, and transitional; in fact, this is not protectionism as we used to think of it but a realistic way to manage trade in an era when it is expanding very quickly and causing many disruptions in people's lives. But any attempt to permanently shut out competition, or to merely appease a politically potent special interest group, would be damaging to America —directly through higher prices and more broadly through the undermining of the world trading system on which we depend.

OTHER ELEMENTS OF NEW THINKING

In the spirit of economic nationalism, America's perception of what makes economies strong must change. We have to acknowledge that international competition is not simply a matter of individual companies slugging it out in the global arena. That may have been true years ago, and we may wish it were true now, but the fact is that *countries* are competing and that governments in Japan, Germany, and elsewhere work far more effectively than Washington to enhance national economic strength. This is not a question of socialism or statism—this is a matter of other kinds of capitalism which work exceedingly well. The imperative for America is not to ape someone else's system, but neither is it to blindly follow our own antigovernment ideology that no longer serves our interests. The revolution of thinking that must sweep across this country should include the realization that the sum of private interests does not necessarily constitute the public interest. How the government interacts with business, workers, and schools, and how it sees its responsibility for rebuilding America's total infrastructure, including human productivity, is critical. "A nation that lags behind in providing infrastructure," wrote economist Robert Heilbroner, "cannot count on the pressures or avenues of the market to bring economic performance up to that of more successful countries . . . All this applies with special force to the U.S., which lags in the strength and flexibility of the public foundation in which its private economy works." [10]

We must recognize, in fact, that we have entered a new industrial revolution in which the competitive advantages are not the same as they were in the last one hundred years. Starting in the late nineteenth century, for example, America was wonderfully equipped for the onset of the emerging industrial model—standardized mass production. We had a big continental commercial market without the disruptions of class, religious, and political antagonisms that plagued other societies. We had a continuous supply of new immigrant labor that could be trained for repetitive production requiring low technological skills. We had a management philosophy that said that one worker was interchangable with another, just like standardized parts on an assembly line, and that one supplier was the same as another except for the price of its services. In the old model, management and labor were natural antagonists; the white collar executives felt that the workers were easily replaced and labor felt it should band together to get minimal benefits from the company. Government was important, of course, but outside the defense-related industries, hardly anyone thought of Washington as a partner.

Unfortunately for America, the game has now changed. The production systems for the future are the kinds of cooperative capitalism practiced by Japan and Germany, replete with respect for a highly skilled, highly motivated work force, dedicated suppliers who have a stake in reliability and innovation, and a government that shares the cost of highly risky R&D. To be sure, American industry has been changing in this direction, but not fast enough. Indeed, as consumers demand products with increasing degrees of sophistication and reliability, and as the industries of the future head deeper into microelectronics, biotechnology, and the like, the needs of industry are moving toward even higher skills, closer ties between producers and suppliers, and more harmonious relations between business and labor, and between firms and their governments.

Another major American shortcoming is the emerging tendency to see the solution to all our problems as one of cutting back and downsizing. In the fiscal arena, for example, spending reductions at every level of government are beginning to bite into essential social services that are part of any compact between the government and its less fortunate citizens. Moreover, in the sterile debate over how to spend the peace dividend that emerges from a leaner defense budget, many are advocating that savings not be redirected to other programs but be applied instead to reducing the large budget deficits. No one can deny the pressing need to restore some fiscal balance, but there is a *greater* need to make investments to turn around the country's downward trajectory. In practice, of course, there will have to be both spending cuts and new investment, but we must make the complex trade-offs in the right proportion.

Much of the private sector also seems bent on cutting back to make up for the excesses of the 1980s. The euphemism for what so many firms are doing is "restructuring," a word that often gives a short-term lift to a company's stock. In just a few months at the end of 1991 and the beginning of 1992, restructuring plans were announced by some of America's finest firms: General Motors said it would lay off 74,000 people, and IBM announced it would cut 20,000 from its payrolls. Others were following suit, such as United Technologies with 13,900 jobs, Bethlehem with 6,500, Allied-Signal with 5,000, Tenneco with 4,000. Again, everyone can agree that bloated operations need to shape up, but this is not the total picture. Will such downsizing be accompanied by new investment to make these firms competitive? What will be the cumulative impact of so many cuts on the national environment—on consumer demand, consumer confidence, and the fabric of our communities?

America's policy toward the dollar is a third example of a mentality of downsizing. Since the mid-1980s Washington has seen an ever weaker dollar as one answer to the country's competitive problems. A dollar that is lower in value relative to the mark and the yen, so the argument goes, creates less expensive American products in world markets and causes us to slow our purchases of imports, which become more expensive. This may be good textbook economics, but no one should be fooled about what is really happening. A lower dollar means a lower standard of living in America—simply put, we get paid less for our products and, because we are so dependent on imports, rather than forgo them, we pay more for cars, robots, or computer screens from abroad. In addition, we might take a look at Japan and Germany and ask why they favor strong currencies and do so well by them. At least one reason is that in today's world economy, a strong currency is associated with nations that understand the requirement for providing higher wages and higher living standards for their populations. They understand that if you produce products with leading-edge technologies and unsurpassed quality you don't have to make price competition your primary marketing strategy, as you might have had to do during the days of mass production of undifferentiated washing machines or televisions. America is behaving more like South Korea or Argentina—where the comparative advantages are low-tech computers or soybeans, where price competition is everything—than like its two leading rivals. Just as in the preoccupation with budget cuts and employment layoffs, reliance on a weak dollar means constricting America's future, not expanding it. Whatever else the consequences, social struggles over the division of a smaller pie will be one of them.

Finally, there is a need to reevaluate our traditional approaches to various international commercial policies, trade being the best example. American foreign policy is heading toward confrontation with scores of countries over trade, but the framework for our thinking is sorely outdated. In slapping tariffs and quotas on foreign products, in screaming about unfair practices by foreign companies and countries, in looking for new ways to "buy American"—in all these matters we have in our minds the same assumptions that Adam Smith made in the eighteenth century. That is a world in which small firms compete freely with one another around the globe, a world in which companies and the products they make have distinct nationalities, and in which comparative advantage derives from natural resources or the size of a market. While not all of this is irrelevant to modern trade theory, surely a good deal is. We know that big conglomerates dominate a good deal of global trade and that entry by new participants is unlikely given the high costs; we know that an increasing amount of global trade does not take place between companies of different nationalities but within the same multinational company located in several nations; we know that it's hard to tell whether a made-in-the-USA Mazda is any less American than a Pontiac assembled from imported parts; we wonder why, if natural resources constitute comparative advantage, Japan, Germany, Taiwan, or South Korea have done so well despite the fact that they import nearly all of their raw materials.

We also have in our minds that the trading interests of the United States are the same as the interests of firms that have American names and are headquartered in the United States. But as more U.S. companies manufacture abroad to sell abroad (as IBM in Singapore sells to IBM in Japan, for example), or as more American firms in the United States import their parts from abroad merely to assemble the finished product in the U.S. (as Smith Corona does), thereby adding to the trade deficit, we must wonder whether Washington's current obsession on protecting the interests of American firms is the right one.

The main point is this: trade policy, like every other aspect of American foreign policy, requires a fundamental reevaluation, in this case going well beyond merely tightening up existing laws, demanding that others reduce their trade surpluses according to rigid formulas, and threatening gunboat-type retaliation.

NEW INSTITUTIONS

In the aftermath of World War II, America created new institutions to deal with the world order it saw coming. These included the National Security Council, the Department of Defense, and the Central Intelligence Agency. It is time for another burst of such innovation, this time to meet a different set of challenges.

We can begin with a notion of what the president is supposed to do. We need a leader who is not afraid to talk about the country's deep-seated problems, as opposed to promoting a misleading optimism. We need someone who can help us redefine the relationship between public and private interests away from the destructive antagonism that now exists and toward a greater overlap of interests. We need someone who underscores the primacy of strong domestic policies to our lives at home and our position in the world, not someone who seems to subcontract the management of education, or health, or banking to his advisors; but someone who, at the same time, understands the connection between these goals and our foreign policy. And we need someone with the guts to express outrage about behavior that weakens our society domestically and internationally—the spectacle of top corporate executives who earn multimillion-dollar bonuses while their firms buckle under foreign competition; the people who undercut our financial markets with illegal behavior; the laws that allow anyone to buy a firearm and terrorize our communities; the health-care system that leaves large segments of the population uninsured and living in fear of being bankrupted by medical bills. There is no substitute for a president who uses the power of his office to summon a change from within the American population.

Next, we need new institutional structures that are designed to force leaders to make the tough decisions that Americans have been avoiding for so long—on taxes, spending, automatic entitlements for retirees in upper-income brackets; on health care, education, infrastructure repair; on energy development and protection of the environment; and on a host of other decisions that have been sidestepped by administrations and Congresses over the past decade.

One possibility would be to reorganize the National Security Council, now devoted almost entirely to traditional foreign policy concerns. The NSC's membership is dominated by the Departments of Defense and State. It could now be enlarged to include departments essential to economic and social policy—including the Treasury Department, the Labor Department, the Department of Education, the Department of Commerce—not only because many of the issues they deal with have become questions of national security, but also because we need a central policy mechanism for making trade-offs and balancing priorities. Right now the closest such institutions are the Office of Management and Budget, and the president and his immediate staff. Neither is adequate. O.M.B. is more focussed on fiscal results than on overall policy. And the job of reconciling domestic and foreign resources and priorities is surely too big for one person and a small staff. Beyond broadening the mandate of the NSC, moreover, Washington should consider ways to bring in business leaders whose direct experience with financial markets or the development of technology often outstrips whatever knowledge exists in the government. It should be possible, for example, to create an NSC subcommittee structure with private sector participants appointed for a finite term. Here would be a type of public-private overlap that Japan and Germany have already marshalled, each in its own way.

Illustrative of the kinds of questions that a reconstituted NSC should consider are these:

What can we do to improve education and training for the American work force, without which we are sure to become a second-rate power? In the past this might have been an issue for the departments of Education and Labor, although they probably would not have cooperated well on the project. But in light of what is at stake for the nation's well-being, it is essential to bring into the picture the Department of Commerce and the Department of Defense, among others: Commerce to analyze global competitive factors, Defense to take into account not just national-security needs but the thousands of employees under its jurisdiction, including huge numbers with advanced skills.

A second issue for a new NSC is savings and investment. For all the talk, our government needs to take a consolidated, long-term view about this crucial issue. Beyond marginalia such as initiatives to change Individual Retirement Accounts or the limited benefits of fiddling with the tax on capital gains, lie the big questions about massive investment needs that this nation has no hope of fulfilling if current policies prevail—while, as we have seen, our major competitors face no such constraints.

A third example for the NSC agenda is the handling of cutbacks in the defense budget—how much to pare, how fast, and how to allocate the savings. This is the biggest variable in fiscal policy. The decisions are also crucial to communities around the nation who are suffering from the closing of military bases and the drying up of defense contracts. Beyond this are other questions such as the retraining and reemployment of the enormous reservoir of scientific talent now employed by the military-industrial complex. It is not satisfactory to leave such crucial issues to the Department of Defense alone, nor to allow the outcome to be determined only by the combination of Darwinian markets, turf battles among congressional committees, and short-term politics—as is happening now. In the end, the transition process will be messy, of course, but surely the administration ought to set the parameters of debate with some strategic plans. Where better to tackle such a problem than a reconstituted NSC?

There is also a need to rethink the division of responsibility between the federal government and the states. The lines have become blurred on a host of economic and social issues, creating confusion, buck passing, and great ineffectiveness. Moreover, in the years to come, the administration and Congress will become more rather than less preoccupied with keeping America strong and competitive in a complex world; they will need the help of the states to focus on issues for which they will, quite simply, not have enough time or expertise. Likewise, the states and local governments are not going to have the wherewithal to handle the more international pressures that they will be under. How to redraw the lines is worthy of a major national debate, and one must take place. The changes would go to the very heart of our political system, and the stakes couldn't be larger.

A new division of responsibilities between federal and state governments would have to deal with such issues as who has lead responsibility for boosting nondefense research and development, who is to retrain the American work force, who is to provide the health care that is essential to the well-being and, therefore, the productivity of so many Americans. It would also have to deal with the funding mechanisms to match these responsibilities. Admittedly, the debate over federalism is as old as the nation and will, we hope, never end. But we've never had the debate in the context of new global pressures and challenges—and now it's time.[11]

There is a need to re-evaluate the best use of our human resources in the international arena. Between the spring and fall of 1991, Secretary of State Baker made at least eight trips to the Middle East to get key parties to the negotiating table. In Geneva, meanwhile, the Uruguay Round of trade negotiations, in progress for at least four years and repeatedly identified by President Bush and other world leaders as the number one international economic priority, was languishing. Could this have possibly been the right set of priorities for America's most accomplished negotiator?

In the future, moreover, no one person can handle all of the multilateral negotiations in which the United States will have a vital interest, especially since the issues—trade, finance, environment, refugees—will require as much harmonizing of domestic interests as achieving breakthroughs abroad. In previous eras, American presidents made good use of high level emissaries from the private sector—Cyrus Vance and Sol Linowitz, for example. For the past ten years there has been very little of this. Private citizens can and should be enlisted in the public cause to a far greater extent than has been the case in recent years.

Beyond recruiting existing talent, there is the need to develop people with the requisite skills to conduct national policy for the 1990s and beyond—people who can operate on both the domestic and foreign policy fronts. In today's world, for example, trade experts have to understand not only tariffs and quotas but also the deep-seated institutional and cultural traits among countries that constitute the new barriers to global commerce. They have to understand the connection between trade and environmental protection, or trade and the movement of refugees. In the past, banking regulators were almost exclusively focussed on their home turf; now they have to worry about international capital standards, not to mention the different systems of national regulation that impinge on considerations of competition and banking stability. In public health, officials and sociologists concerned with narcotics addiction could devote their time to local problems; today and tomorrow they'll have to apply their expertise along the U.S.–Mexican border or even in countries like Peru, where the links between supply and U.S. demand are strong. All this is in great contrast to the days when generals and nuclear strategists could dominate American foreign policy, and the other disciplines were seen as significant only on the home front. But training people to operate in this complex world will require more than acknowledging the need; it means a sea change in our educational system. [12]

Congress, too, should do more than debate the changes that the Executive Branch should make. Its fragmented committee system on issues like trade, technology, and financial reform is more than inefficient—it is paralyzing. Congress could recreate groups in the image of the old Joint Committee on Atomic Energy, which was formed in the 1950s to oversee a critical national interest that cut across the jurisdiction of many committees; why not a Joint Congressional Committee on National Security Affairs to parallel the revamped NSC, sharing its new emphasis on domestic economic and social affairs?

And institutional changes should not be confined to the federal government, of course. We need change throughout our system—in state governments, where coordination between business, education, and research holds great promise; in business associations, where more than holding out an open palm to the government is essential; in labor unions, where new ideas about improving the efficiency of the work force, as opposed to efforts to ensure their jobs and their benefits, are in short supply.

We need, as well, to think about institutions that create a sense of national community in the face of so many forces of fragmentation. Throughout a good part of the Cold War, compulsory military service performed part of this function. Conscription brought together young men from every part of the country, and from every conceivable background, including race, religion, and family income. President John F. Kennedy's Peace Corps became both a practical and an idealistic variant on the theme. Could we not recreate mandatory national service, now for young men *and* women, aimed at improving economic and social conditions both at home and abroad? There is more than enough to do

—be it a stint in the armed forces, teaching in impoverished areas, serving in the police, assisting the elderly, supporting day care centers.

Washington should also consider issuing a national report card that measures America against Japan and Germany in various ways: trade, savings and investment, education, poverty. These statistics already exist, of course, but they have not become part of the American psyche in the way that is appropriate for the fierce competition we face. Such a report card could be issued as part of each year's presidential state-of-the-union speech. It could be the focus of debate as Congress opens its annual sessions. It could be the subject of media attention and public response.

A report card may sound like a gimmick, but it should be seen in the context of the need for a presidential administration to educate Americans about the realities we face. Today, Washington's efforts in this regard are appalling. In the early 1970s the Nixon administration published a series of annual reports entitled "International Economic Report of the President." It was an easily readable document, containing charts of U.S. performance and that of our competitors. But the effort was not sustained and nowadays the government's publications on these matters are either too narrowly focussed, too technical, or too politically slanted to provide American citizens with the alternatives they need. An enhanced government effort to provide such information would not substitute for analysis from many private sources, but alone among the Big Three our federal government has abdicated the role of even trying to set a framework for understanding its nation's competitive position in the world.

Among the new requirements is a major effort to build a domestic consensus about America's new global position. Thus far we have the president's speeches that include reams of rhetoric about the New World Order. But we are at the same kind of watershed that existed in 1945, when the world lay in ruins, or in 1947 when it was clear that a bipolar Cold War was emerging. Where are the high-level commissions asked by the president and Congress to muster the options? Where are the heated congressional debates about America's role in the world? If the present course prevails, the decisions on military posture will hinge more on budgetary politics than on any reasoned defense strategy; the question of aid to Russia and the other former Soviet republics will be decided in arm-twisting sessions at the Group of Seven summits rather than through a hard-nosed analysis of whether it will make a real difference, or through serious considerations of what the resource trade-offs are. The future of American trade policy will be in the hands of special interest groups rather than policymakers thinking about long-term strategy; the focus on education and training will have but a tangential relationship to foreign policy and national security. The need for a greater degree of public involvement is more crucial than ever now that foreign affairs have such a direct impact in our lives. It is often said that America needs a bipartisan foreign policy, the implication being that political differences should be reserved for domestic issues. The days of such two-track possibilities are over. If there's no consensus at home, there will be none when it comes to our policy abroad. It is a much different ball game from the days when foreign policy could be driven by an elite club in the White House, State Department, and Pentagon, and when foreign and domestic questions could be separated.

Beyond institution building at home, we will have to give greater weight to the structure and purpose of existing global organizations. Today's institutional framework does not look a lot different from what existed in the late 1940s and early 1950s; it now needs not only new blood but major modification. Multilateral structures for peacekeeping, for the environment, for refugees, for international investment, for human rights are all sadly inadequate. It is in America's interest to take the lead in promoting such organizations, and American inventiveness is called for in designing them, too. There ought to be a way to keep from having to scrounge around for peacekeeping forces every time a crisis occurs; why not have standing, preassigned units in various nations, including Japan and Germany, that can be called up by the U.N. secretary general? On environmental matters, where new scientific evidence arises every day, a way must be found to design international treaties that are flexible enough to accommodate constant change in the level of knowledge. There are no agreed-on rules for global investment—no standards for mergers and acquisitions, takeovers, antitrust, rules for local hiring, financial disclosure—and they are badly needed. When it comes to human rights, the day should be long past when individuals and ethnic groups who feel they are oppressed can appeal only to the very governments that are the oppressors. Why not a U.N. Court for Human Rights to whom private groups could bring their cases? Whatever is done, it is in the American interest to do it *now*, when U.S. clout vis-à-vis Japan and Germany is greater than it may be by the late 1990s.

These proposals are merely illustrative, but they suggest how inert we have been. Taking some initiative now would serve several purposes: it would focus on rebalancing and integrating resources and priorities between domestic and foreign affairs; it would help us to make trade-offs and choices; it would help us compete in the global economy; it would help get the most out of Tokyo and Berlin while constraining centrifugal forces among the Big Three. It would give America an activist international policy that does not rely only on military might or enormous financial resources.

There has, as yet, been no one event to jar the American people into the broad self-reevaluation that I am suggesting is now critical. But whether or not we want to admit it, the crisis in our society is now full-blown. We can measure ourselves against what we as a nation once were. We can measure ourselves against what Japan and Germany are becoming. Whatever the yardstick, the conclusion is the same: for America, the New World Order must begin not in the Gulf or the GATT, not in our response to the plight of Eastern Europe or Russia, not in NATO. It must begin with a realistic assessment of who we are and the role we are capable of playing in a global order that has changed radically.

It was just about a century ago that America first saw the rise of Japan and Germany. There was concern then not just about the ascendance of new military powers but also about the challenge to our way of life. "I preach to you," said Theodore Roosevelt in 1899, "that our country calls not for the life of ease but for the life of strenuous endeavor. The twentieth century looms before us big with the fate of many nations. If we stand idly by . . . if we shrink from the hard contest . . . then the bolder and stronger peoples will pass us."[13] Today the challenge is no less. At the turn of the last century, our forefathers rose to the occasion. Will we?

NOTES

1. Challenging Old Assumptions

1. Fred Bergsten, "The World's Economy after the Cold War," *Foreign Affairs* Vol. 69, No. 3 (Summer 1990): p. 111.
2. John Tagliabue, "Defying Its Allies, Germany Insists on Recognizing 2 Yugoslav States," *The New York Times* 15 December 1991: p. A1.
3. "Asian News: Goh Asks Japan to Win Asian Trust to Play Bigger Role," *Kyodo News Service* 2 May 1991: p. 2; "Germans Ready To Pay More for Gulf, President Says," *Reuters* 24 January 1991: p. 1; and, David Marsh, "Germany Unites: Economic Strength Proves Irresistible—Stronger Bonds Weld Germany's Disparate States Together Once More," *The Financial Times* 2 October 1990: p. 6.
4. Leonard Silk, "Deep Divisions at Summit Talks," *The New York Times* 13 July 1990: p. D2.
5. R. W. Apple, Jr., "A New Balance of Power," *The New York Times* 12 July 1990: p. A1.
6. David Marsh, "Today's Germans: Peaceable, Fearful—and Green," *The Financial Times* 4 January 1991: p. 2.
7. "Chancellor of Angst," *The Economist* 6 April 1991: p. 11.
8. Andrew Rosenthal, "U.S. to Give Up Short-Range Nuclear Arms," *The New York Times* 28 September 1991: p. A1.
9. Hobart Rowen, "Japan and Germany Must Take Bigger Military, Policy-Making Roles in World Affairs," *The Washington Post* 3 March 1991: p. H1; Yusuke Kashiwagi, address, Japan Society, New York, 11 July 1991.
10. Quentin Peel, "Kohl Reveals Vision of European Defense Identity," *The Financial Times* 7 November 1991: p. 3.

11. Stanley Hoffman, "The Case for Leadership," *Foreign Policy* No. 81 (Winter 1990–1991): p. 35.

12. Paul Blustein, "Japan Grows Uneasy on Eve of Bush Visit," *The International Herald Tribune* 26 December 1991: p. 7.

13. Zbigniew Brzezinski, "Selective Global Commitment," *Foreign Affairs* Vol. 70, No. 4 (Fall 1991): p. 1.

2. Germany and Japan in the American Mind

1. David Halberstam, *The Next Century* (New York: Morrow, 1991) p. 60.

2. Golo Mann, *The History of Germany Since 1789*, trans. Marian Jackson (New York: Praeger, 1968) p. 65.

3. John Rohl and Nicolaus Sombart, eds., *Kaiser Wilhelm II—New Interpretations: The Corfu Papers* (Cambridge, New York: Cambridge University Press, 1982) p. 31.

4. Michael Balfour, *West Germany: A Contemporary History* (London: Croom Helm, 1982) pp. 112–113. Also, in Richard Mayne, *The Recovery of Europe: From Devastation to Unity* (New York: Harper & Row, 1971) p. 29.

5. Hans W. Gatzke, *Germany and the United States: A "Special Relationship?"* (Cambridge, MA: Harvard University Press, 1980) p. 173.

6. Gatzke p. 166.

7. Arthur F. Burns, *The United States and Germany* (New York: Council on Foreign Relations, 1986) p. 5.

8. Geoffrey H. Hartman, ed., *Bitburg in Moral and Political Perspective* (Bloomington, IN: Indiana University Press, 1986) pp. 174–178.

9. Burns p. 15.

10. Harold R. Isaacs, *Scratches on Our Mind: American Images of China and India* (New York: The John Dey Company, 1958) p. 37.

11. William Manchester, *American Caesar* (New York: Dell Publishing Co., 1978) pp. 318–19.

12. Townsend Harris, *The Complete Journal of Townsend Harris* (New York: Japan Society, 1930) p. 435, in footnote 519 citing *The Intercourse between the United States and Japan* (Baltimore: Johns Hopkins University Press, 1891) p. 46, no author is given.

13. William L. Neumann, *America Encounters Japan: From Perry to MacArthur* (Baltimore: Johns Hopkins University Press, 1963) p. 11.

14. Neumann p. 24.

15. Dee Brown, *The Year of the Century: 1876* (New York: Scribner's, 1966) pp. 298–99.

16. Neumann p. 66.
17. Sheila K. Johnson, *The Japanese through American Eyes* (Stanford, CA: Stanford University Press, 1988) p. 1.
18. Harris pp. 362–263.
19. Neumann p. 30.
20. Neumann pp. 217, 220.
21. Johnson p. 10.
22. Ruth Benedict, *The Chrysanthemum and the Sword* (Boston: Houghton Mifflin, 1946) p. 2.
23. Neumann p. 129.
24. Neumann p. 221.
25. John Hersey, *Into the Valley: A Skirmish of the Marines* (New York: Knopf, 1943) p. 55.
26. Clayton R. Koppes and Gregory D. Black, *Hollywood Goes to War* (New York: Free Press, 1987) p. 254.
27. Isaacs p. 406.

3. Different Historical Legacies

1. Alexis de Tocqueville, *Democracy in America* (New York: Dell, 1956) p. 39.
2. Frances FitzGerald, *Fire in the Lake: The Vietnamese and the Americans in Vietnam* (Boston: Atlantic-Little Brown, 1972) p. 8.
3. Gordon S. Wood, *The Creation of the American Republic 1776–1787* (New York: Norton, 1969) pp. 67–70.
4. James Oliver Robertson, *American Myth, American Reality* (New York: Hill & Wang, 1980) p. 73.
5. Frederick Jackson Turner, *The Frontier in American History* (New York: Henry Holt & Company, 1948) p. 37.
6. Robertson p. 123.
7. Thomas K. McGraw, "Business & Government: The Origins of the Adversary Relationship," *California Management Review* Vol. 26, No. 2 (Winter 1984) p. 43.
8. David Vogel, "Why Businessmen Distrust Their State: The Political Consciousness of American Executives," *British Journal of Political Science* Vol. 8 (1978) p. 45.
9. Robert B. Reich, *The Work of a Nation* (New York: Knopf, 1991) p. 19.
10. David Calleo, *The German Problem Reconsidered: Germany and the World Order, 1870 to the Present* (New York: Cambridge University Press, 1978) p. 4.
11. Turner p. 3.

12. H. W. Koch, A History of Prussia (New York: Dorset Press, 1978) p. 240.

13. J. P. Mayer, Max Weber and German Politics (London: Faber & Faber, 1956) p. 78.

14. Calleo p. 62.

15. Ralf Dahrendorf, Society and Democracy in Germany (New York: Norton, 1967) p. 36.

16. Harold James, A German Identity 1770–1990 (New York: Routledge, 1989) p. 84, citing H. Hauserr, Germany's Commercial Grip on the World (London, 1917) p. 210.

17. James p. 140.

18. Hans W. Gatzke, Germany and the United States: A "Special Relationship?" (Cambridge, MA: Harvard University Press, 1980) pp. 195–196.

19. Andrew Shonfield, Modern Capitalism; The Changing Balance of Public and Private Power (New York, Oxford: Oxford University Press, 1965) p. 240.

20. Ralf Dahrendorf, Reflections on the Revolution in Europe (New York: Times Books, 1990) p. 129.

21. Robert Bellah, Tokugawa Religion: The Cultural Roots of Modern Japan (1957; New York: Free Press, 1985) pp. 109, 114.

22. Byron K. Marshall, Capitalism and Nationalism in Pre-War Japan: The Ideology of the Business Elite, 1868–1941 (Stanford, CA: Stanford University Press, 1967) p. 30.

23. William Miles Fletcher III, The Japanese Business Community and National Trade Policy, 1920–1942 (Chapel Hill, NC: University of North Carolina Press, 1989) pp. 21–22.

24. Chalmers Johnson, MITI and the Japanese Miracle: The Growth of Industrial Policy 1925–1975 (Stanford, CA: Stanford University Press, 1982) p. 109. I am particularly indebted to Professor Johnson on whose book this section draws heavily.

25. Fletcher pp. 110–111.

26. This is a recurring theme in Chalmers Johnson's book.

27. Marshall p. 35.

28. Johnson pp. 158–164.

29. Johnson p. 113.

30. Johnson p. 305.

4. Different Kinds of Capitalism

1. Andrew Shonfield, Modern Capitalism: The Changing Balance of Public and Private Power (New York, Oxford: Oxford University Press, 1965) p. 319.

2. "Bonn Is Urged to Sell Assets to Finance Union," *The International Herald Tribune* 3 October 1990: p. 11.
3. Kenneth S. Courtis, address, "Perspective on the Japanese Keiretsu," The National Advisory Board on Science and Technology Symposium, Toronto, 1–2 March 1990.
4. Peter J. Katzenstein, *Policy and Politics in West Germany: The Growth of a Semisovereign State* (Philadelphia: Temple University Press, 1987) p. 88.
5. Edward J. Lincoln, *Japan's Unequal Trade* (Washington, D.C.: The Brookings Institution, 1990) p. 19.
6. Lincoln, pp. 39–60.
7. *Special Report: International Survey of the Taxation of Personal Saving and Savings Rates* (Washington, D.C.: American Council for Capital Formation, August 1990) p. 1.
8. "Business Taxes, Capital Costs, & Competitiveness," (Washington, D.C.: American Council for Capital Formation, July 1990) p. 34.
9. For a thoughtful, more extensive discussion, see Michael T. Jacobs, *Short-Term America: The Causes and Cures of Our Business Myopia* (Boston: Harvard Business School Press, 1991).
10. Jacobs p. 12.
11. Richard J. Samuels, "Cooperation and Conflict in Science and Technology," *The JAMA Forum, Tokyo* Vol. 8, No. 7, December 1989, p. 7.

5. *Open vs Closed Societies*

1. World Bank Development Report 1991, Washington, D.C., p. 104.
2. Kenneth S. Courtis, interview, "Strategic Challenge," *The JAMA Forum*, Vol. 9 No. 1, January 1991, pp. 19–20.
3. Kenneth S. Courtis, address, "Japan's World Role in the 1990s," The North American Institute, Vancouver, 14 July 1990.
4. Nigel Holloway, "Reluctant Converts," *Far Eastern Economic Review* 11 October 1990: p. 72.
5. "Economic Survey of Japan," *OECD*, Paris, 1991: p. 171.
6. Kevin L. Kearns, "Behind Those Shrinking Trade Deficit Numbers," *The Wall Street Journal* 25 July 1991: p. A9.
7. G. Pascal Zachery, "U.S. Probes Japanese Companies on Charges of Withholding Parts," *The Wall Street Journal* 16 January 1991: p. B4.
8. Susan Stern, *Meet United Germany* (Frankfurt, Germany: The *Frankfurt Allgemeine Zeitung* GMBH Information Services, 1991) pp. 187–190.
9. Bruce Stokes, *The Inevitability of Managed Trade* (New York: The Japan Society, 1990) p. 2.
10. *Gaining New Ground: Technology Priorities for America's Future*, High-

lights (Washington, D.C.: Council on Competitiveness, 1991) p. 1. The Council on Competitiveness is a nonpartisan, private sector group, not to be confused with the administration's council under Vice President Quayle.

11. DeAnne Julius, *Global Companies and Public Policies: The Growing Challenge of Foreign Direct Investment* (London: Royal Institute of International Affairs, 1990) p. 6.

12. Courtis, "Japan's World Role."

13. Keikichi Honda (Director of Research, Bank of Tokyo), "Investment is Investment is Investment, but Japan Must Still Prove Itself Abroad," *Japan Economic Journal* 10 November 1990: p. 8.

14. *Economic Report of the President* (Washington, D.C.: U.S. Government Printing Office, 1991) p. 261.

15. Julius p. 44.

16. DeAnne Julius, *Foreign Direct Investment: The Neglected Twin of Trade* (Washington, D.C.: Group of Thirty, 1991) charts, as summarized in *IMF Survey* 15 July 1991: p. 218.

17. Hilary Stout, "Lawmakers Seeking Revenue Sources, To Study Taxes Paid by Foreign Firms' U.S. Subsidiaries," *The Wall Street Journal* 10 July 1990: p. A18.

18. Takashi Masuko, "Japan Firms Expanding E.C. Base in Germany," *Nekkie Weekly* 21: December 1991 p. 1.

19. Diana T. Kuryiko, "European Transplants Take Firm Root," *The International Herald Tribune* 10 December 1991: p. 20.

20. Reuters, "BMW Warns of Trouble over Japan Car Trade," *The International Herald Tribune* 5 November 1991: p. 13.

21. Jurek Martin, "A Chance to Rectify Past Omissions," *The Financial Times* 19 December 1990: p. 19.

22. Bimal Ghosh, "The Exodus That Could Explode," *The Financial Times* 23 January 1991: p. 13.

23. Paul Lewis, "As Soviet Borders Open, the West Braces for an Economic Exodus," *The New York Times* 10 February 1991, sec. 4: p. 4.

24. William A. Henry III, "Beyond the Melting Pot," *Time* 9 April 1991: p. 28.

25. "Ellis Island Revisited," *The Economist*, 26 October 1991, American Survey: p. 11. Also in Arthur M. Schlesinger, *The Disuniting of America: Reflections on a Multicultural Society* (Knoxville, TN: Whittle Direct Books, 1991) p. 70.

26. Marc Fisher, "On the Border: A Quiet Watch," *The International Herald Tribune* 23 September 1991: p. 1.

27. Stephen Kinzer, "A Wave of Attacks on Foreigners Stirs Shock in Germany," *The New York Times* 1 October 1991: p. A1.

28. Kinzer.

29. Maria Lux Y. Gabuioro, "Filipino 'Hepatitis' Victim Was Murdered, Officials Say," *The Nikkei Weekly* 26 October 1991: p. 2.

30. Gwen Robinson, "Japan Faces Charges of Foreign Workers' Abuse," *The Nikkei Weekly* 14 September 1991: p. 1.

6. Dividing Up the World

1. Christopher Coker, ed., *Shifting into Neutral?: Burden Sharing in the Western Alliance* (London: Brassey's [UK], 1990) p. 13.

2. Coker p. 14.

3. Sam Nunn, "Our Allies Have to Do More," *The New York Times* 10 July 1988, sec. 4: p. 31.

4. *Discord or Dialogue: The United States and Japan in 1991* (Washington, D.C.: The Reischauer Center at The Paul H. Nitze School of Advanced International Studies, The Johns Hopkins University, 1991) p. 20.

5. Tatou Takahama, address, "Japanese Policy Making: The Case of the Gulf Crisis," The Japan Society of New York, 6 May 1991.

6. Timothy Aeppel and Frederick Kempe, "German Official Backs Mideast Marshall Plan," *The Wall Street Journal* 1 March 1991: p. A5.

7. Jim Hoagland, "For Bush, a Delicate Time with Germany and Japan," *The International Herald Tribune* 22 March 1991: p. 4.

8. R. W. Apple, "Bonn and Tokyo Are Criticized for Not Bearing More of Gulf Cost," *The New York Times* 13 September 1990: p. A1.

9. Kenneth Pyle, Edward J. Lincoln, and Chalmers Johnson, "Japan and the World: Considerations for U.S. Policy Makers," analysis, (Seattle, WA: The National Bureau of Asian and Soviet Research, November, 1991) p. 2.

10. Reuters, "Maybe Yes, Maybe No," *The International Herald Tribune* 21 November 1991: p. 3.

11. Leonard Silk, "Getting the Benefit of Military Cuts," *The New York Times* 26 September 1991: p. D2.

12. David E. Sanger, "The Technology the U.S. Doesn't Want Japan to Have," *The New York Times* 2 April 1989, sec. 4: p. 3.

13. Stuart Aeurbach, "Senators Step Up Attack on FSX Deal with Japan," *The Washington Post* 11 May 1989: p. A5.

14. David Marsh, "Today's Germans: Peaceable, Fearful—and Green," *The Financial Times* 4 January 1991: p. 2.

15. *German Brief*, The *Frankfurt Allgemeine Zeitung* GMBH Information Services, 9–16 April 1991: p. 1.

16. Roberto Suro, "Europeans Accuse the U.S. of Balking on Plans to Combat Global Warming," *The New York Times* 10 July 1990: p. A10.

17. Hans-Dietrich Genscher, "The Mentality of the Nation State Has Been Consigned to the Past," *The European* 11–13 October 1991: p.II.
18. Joseph Stanislaw and Daniel Yergin, "Don't Let an Energy Crisis Shut Off Eastern Europe," *The International Herald Tribune* 27 June 1990: p.6.
19. "Germans Urge Talks on Soviets," *The New York Times* 24 August 1991: p.A9.
20. Quentin Peel, "Kohl Warns Soviet Union Must Retain Unified Policies," *The Financial Times* 5 September 1991: p.1.
21. "Asia's Emerging Standard Bearer," *The Economist* 21 July 1991: p.30.
22. "Japan's Direct Investment in East Asia," Global Investment Research Group, Deutsche Bank Capital Markets Research, December 1991, Chart.
23. Patrick L. Smith, "Japan in East Asia: A Boom Pays Off," *The International Herald Tribune* 30 May 1990: p.1.
24. Bernard Wysocki, Jr., "In Asia, the Japanese Hope to 'Coordinate' What Nations Produce," *The Wall Street Journal* 20 August 1990: p.A1.
25. Michael Richardson, "As West Pushes for Democracy, Asia Leans Towards Japan," *The International Herald Tribune* 9 November 1991: p.1.
26. Edward Mortimer, "New Boss for Fitter UN," *The Financial Times* 18 October 1991: p.22.

7. The Leadership Vacuum

1. Charles P. Kindleberger, *The World in Depression* (Berkeley, CA: University of California Press, 1973) p.292.
2. Robert Gilpin, *War and Change in World Politics* (London, New York: Cambridge University Press, 1981) p.36.
3. Henry J. Aaron, ed., *Setting National Priorities: Policy for the Nineties* (Washington, D.C.: The Brookings Institution, 1990) p.1.
4. Robert Pear, " '90 Pact Failing to Curb Deficit, Lawmakers Say," *The New York Times* 4 November 1991: p.A1; Steven Mufson, "Bush's Budget Abandons Deficit Reduction Hopes," *International Herald Tribune* February 1–2, 1992: p.7.
5. Martin Dixon, "Hang-Over from a Decade Long Party," *The Financial Times* 28 December 1990: p.9.
6. B. Douglas Bernheim, *The Vanishing Nest Egg: Reflections on Saving in America* (New York: Twentieth Century Fund, 1991) pp.1–11.
7. "Annual Report," *The Bank for International Settlements* (Basle, Switzerland: 1991) p.31; Thomas S. Foley, address, "After the Persian Gulf War: American Politics and Policies in the 1990s," Dichley Foundation Lecture, Dichley, England, 5 July 1991, O.E.C.D. Economic Survey of Japan, 1991: p.49.

8. A sampling includes: *The Next American Frontier* by Robert B. Reich (New York: Times Books, 1983); *The Reckoning* by David Halberstam (New York: Morrow, 1986); *Manufacturing Matters: The Myth of the Post-Industrial Economy* by Stephen S. Cohen and John Zysman (New York: Basic Books, 1987); *Trading Places* by Clyde V. Prestowitz, Jr. (New York: Basic Books, 1988); and *Made In America: Regaining the Productive Edge* by Michael L. Dertouzos, Richard K. Lester, and Robert M. Solow (Cambridge MA: MIT Press, 1989). There have been countless commission reports, such as the "President's Commission on Industrial Competitiveness" (1985); the National Governors Association's report, "Making America Work" (1987); and the "Cuomo Commission on Trade and Competitiveness" (1988). Agencies of the executive branch and Congress have chimed in, including a series of devastating industry reports from the National Science Foundation, and loud warnings from the Defense Science Board and the Congressional Office of Technology Assessment—the latter's latest report being "Competing Economies: America, Europe and the Pacific Rim" (1991).

9. Michael de Courcy Hinds, "Number of Killings Soars in Big Cities across U.S.," *The New York Times* 18 July 1990: p.A1; and A.P., "U.S. Headed for a Homicide Record, Senators Say," *The New York Times* 1 August 1990: p.B3.

10. Fox Butterfield, "U.S. Expands Its Lead in the Rate of Imprisonment," *The New York Times* 11 February 1992: p.A16.

11. Andrew H. Malcolm, "Many Police Forces Rearm to Counter Criminals' Guns," *The New York Times* 4 September 1990: p.A12.

12. Byron N. Kunisawa, "A Nation in Crisis: The Dropout Dilemma," *National Education Association Today* January 1988: p.61; The Congress of the United States, *The 1990 Joint Economic Committee Report* (Washington, D.C.: U.S. Government Printing Office, 1990), p.6; and Ezra Bowen, "Losing the War of Letters," *Time* 5 May 1986: p.68.

13. Jerry J. Jasinowski, *America's Work Force in the 1990s*, National Association of Manufacturers, Washington, D.C., March 1990: p.7.

14. Jason DeParle, "Poverty Rate Rose Sharply Last Year As Income Slipped," *The New York Times* 27 September 1991: p.A1.

15. Sylvia Ann Hewlett, *When the Bough Breaks: The Cost of Neglecting Our Children* (New York: Basic Books, 1991) p.12; Foley address.

16. Hewlett pp.11–12.

17. Paul Krugman, *The Age of Diminished Expectations* (Cambridge, MA: MIT Press, 1990) p.12. "Japan Is Near Passing U.S. in Productivity," *International Herald Tribune*, Associated Press, 20 January 1992: p.9.

18. Krugman pp.12, 19, 20, 22.

19. Louis Hartz, *The Liberal Tradition in America* (New York: Harcourt Brace Jovanovich, 1955) p. 286. Hartz is paraphrasing Kennan.

20. George J. Church, "The Tale of Two Bushes," *Time* 7 January 1991: p. 20.

21. William G. Hyland, "It's Time for Americans to Turn Inward," *The International Herald Tribune* 20 May 1991: p. 6.

22. Hisao Takagi and Yuko Inoue, "Japan and the U.S.: New Balance Sought," *Japan Economic Journal* 29 December 1990: p. 1.

23. Robert Delfs, "Carrying the Can," *Far Eastern Economic Review* 18 July 1991: p. 18.

24. Steven R. Weisman, "Japanese Leaders See Support for U.S. Stand in the Gulf Ebbing," *The New York Times* 11 December 1990: p. A17.

25. Kazuo Ogura, Op-Ed, "Japan and America: Pride and Prejudice," *The New York Times* 24 November 1991, sec. 4: p. 17.

26. Thomas L. Friedman, "Baker Asks Japan to Broaden Role," *The New York Times* 12 November 1991: p. A1.

27. Russell Watson, with Bill Powell and Richard Thomas, "Coming to Terms with Japan," *Newsweek* 25 November 1991: p. 47.

28. David Marsh, "Year of Victory for Modest Statesman," *The Financial Times* 30 December 1990: p. 6.

29. Marc Fisher, "In Germany, Mid-East War Opens a Bonn-Washington Gulf," *The International Herald Tribune* 29 January 1991: p. 1.

30. Richard E. Smith, "Economy Feels Strain as Price of Unity Mounts: Without a World Recovery, Bonn Fears a Slowdown," *The International Herald Tribune* 10 April 1991: p. 11.

31. Ferdinand Protzman, "Fight Looms over Bonn's Plans to Finance Unity," *The New York Times* 11 December 1990: p. D8.

32. "United, but Still Divided," *German Brief, Frankfurt Allgemeine Zeitung* GMBH Information Services, 7 June 1991: p. 1.

33. Quentin Peel, "Wise Men Criticize Bonn for Failure to Curb Spending," *The Financial Times* 15 November 1991: p. 1.

34. "Economic Survey of Germany," *OECD*, Paris 1991: p. 11.

35. Martin Wolf, "A Nation Unified, and Yet Apart," *The Financial Times* 1 July 1991: p. 16.

36. Anthony Robinson, "Bank Predicts Deep Downturn in E. Europe," *The Financial Times* 19 December 1990: p. 2.

37. William Dullforce, "Eastern Europe Seen Heading for Thirties-type Depression," *The Financial Times* 3 December 1991: p. 2.

38. George Lardner, Jr., "CIA Director Warns of Worst Soviet Strife Since the Revolution," *The International Herald Tribune* 11 December 1991: p. 1.

39. John Goshko, "Washington Smiles but Grumbles," *The International Herald Tribune* 10 April 1991: p. 13.

40. Richard E. Smith, "German Sea Change as the Bills Come In," *The International Herald Tribune* 21 October 1991: p.1.

8. *America in the American Mind*

1. Edward N. Luttwak, "For America, Again, the World Is a New Ball Game," *The International Herald Tribune* 23 September 1991: p.8.
2. Lewis H. Lapham, "How and What Is American?" *Harper's* January 1992: p.45.
3. See results of polls conducted for the Council on Competitiveness in "Looking for Leadership: The Public, Competitiveness and Company '92," Council on Competitiveness, Washington, D.C.: 18 November 1991: p.3.
4. See Paul Krugman, *The Age of Diminished Expectations* (Cambridge, MA: MIT Press, 1990); Kevin Phillips, *The Politics of Rich and Poor: Wealth and the American Electorate in the Reagan Aftermath* (New York: Random House, 1990); and Angus Maddison, *The World Economy in the 20th Century* (Paris: OECD, 1989).
5. "U.S. Power in a Changing World," Committee on Foreign Affairs, U.S. House of Representatives, May 1990: p.3.
6. C. Fred Bergsten, address, "Policy Implications of Trade and Currency Zones," Federal Reserve Bank of Kansas City Symposium, Kansas City, 23 August 1991.
7. Peter G. Peterson, with James K. Sebenius, "Rethinking America's Security: The Primacy of the Domestic Agenda," Seventy-ninth American Assembly, Columbia University, New York, 30 May 1991: p.2.
8. George F. Will, "The Frontier and Civil Virtue," *The Washington Post* 3 March 1991: p.C7.
9. E. J. Dionne, Jr., *Why Americans Hate Politics* (New York: Simon & Schuster, 1991) pp.332, 224.
10. Robert Heilbroner, Op-Ed, "Rough Roads to Capitalism," *The New York Times* 15 September 1991, sec.4: p.7.
11. See, for example, Alice M. Rivlin, address, "A New Vision of American Federalism," 1991 National Academy of Public Administration Webb Lecture, 8 November 1991.
12. For a thoughtful and more extensive treatment of these issues, see Leslie H. Gelb, "Fresh Faces," *New York Magazine* 8 November 1991: p.50.
13. Theodore Roosevelt, address, "The Strenuous Life," Hamilton Club, Chicago, IL, 10 April 1899, in Theodore Roosevelt, *The Works of Theodore Roosevelt*, National Ed. (New York: Scribner's, 1926) Vol. 14: pp.322–323, 331.

BIBLIOGRAPHY

Aaron, Henry J., ed. *Setting National Priorities: Policy for the Nineties.* Washington, D.C.: The Brookings Institution, 1990.

Aho, C. Michael, and Levinson, Marc. *After Reagan: Confronting the Changed World Economy.* New York: Council on Foreign Relations, 1988.

The American Prospect, Spring 1990, No. 1, Princeton, NJ: New Prospect, Inc.

The AMEX Bank Review, American Express Bank, Ltd., London, various issues.

Ardagh, John. *Germany and the Germans.* London: Penguin, 1987.

Ash, Timothy Garton. "Germany at the Frontier." *New York Review of Books.* 17 January 1990.

Bailey, George. *Germans: The Biography of an Obsession.* New York: Discus Books, 1974.

Bailyn, Bernard. *Faces of Revolution: Personalities and Themes in the Struggle for American Independence.* New York: Knopf, 1990.

Balassa, Bela, and Noland, Marcus. *Japan in the World Economy.* Washington, D.C.: Institute for International Economics, 1988.

Balfour, Michael. *West Germany: A Contemporary History.* London: Croom Helm, 1982.

The Bank for International Settlements. *Annual Report,* 1991.

Barnet, Richard J. *The Alliance, America-Europe-Japan: Makers of the Postwar World.* New York: Simon and Schuster, 1983.

Beisner, Robert L. *Twelve Against Empire: The Anti-Imperialists 1898–1900.* New York: McGraw-Hill, 1968.

Bellah, Robert. *Tokugawa Religion: The Cultural Roots of Modern Japan 1957.* New York: Free Press, 1985.

Benedict, Ruth. *The Chrysanthemum and the Sword*. Boston: Houghton Mifflin, 1946.

Bergsten, C. Fred. *America in the World Economy: A Strategy of the 1990s*. Washington, D.C.: Institute for International Economics, 1988.

Bergsten, C. Fred. Address. "Policy Implications of Trade and Currency Zones." Federal Reserve Bank of Kansas City Symposium, Kansas City, 23 August 1991.

Bernheim, B. Douglas. *The Vanishing Nest Egg: Reflections on Saving in America*. New York: Twentieth Century Fund, 1991.

Beyond Rhetoric: A New American Agenda for Children and Families. Washington, D.C.: National Commission on Children, 1991.

Blanchflower, David G., and Freeman, Richard B. "Going Different Ways: Unionism in the U.S. and Other Advanced O.E.C.D. Countries, Working Paper No. 3342." Cambridge, MA.: National Bureau of Economic Research, April 1990.

Bluestone, Barry, and Harrison, Bennett. *The Deindustrialization of America*. New York: Basic Books, 1982.

Boorstin, Daniel J. *The Americans: The Democratic Experience*. New York: Random House, 1973.

Borrus, Michael; Bar, Francois; Cogez, Patrick; Thoresen, Anne Bnit; Warde, Ibrahim; and Yoshikaw, Aki. *Telecommunications Development in Comparative Perspective: The New Telecommunications in Europe, Japan and the U.S.* Berkeley: Berkeley Roundtable on the International Economy, University of California, May 1985.

Borrus, Michael, et al., "Information Networks and Competitive Advantage," Berkeley Roundtable on the International Economy, OECD, Vol. 3, October 1989.

Brock, William, and Hormats, Robert. *The Global Economy, America's Role in the Decade Ahead*. New York: Norton, 1990.

Brown, Dee. *The Year of the Century: 1876*. New York: Scribner's, 1966.

Burns, Arthur F. *The United States and Germany*. New York: Council on Foreign Relations, 1986.

Burstein, Daniel. *YEN!: Japan's New Financial Empire and Its Threat to America*. New York: Simon & Schuster, 1988.

Buruma, Ian. *Behind the Mask*. New York: Pantheon, 1984.

Business Week, New York: McGraw-Hill, various issues.

Calder, Kent E. *Japan's Changing Role in Asia: Emerging Co-Prosperity?* New York: Japan Society, 1992.

Calleo, David. *The German Problem Reconsidered: Germany and the World Order, 1870 to the Present*. Cambridge, New York: Cambridge University Press, 1978.

Carr, E. H. *The Twenty Years' Crisis 1919–1939*. London: Macmillan, 1939.

Challenges, Council on Competitiveness, Washington, D.C., various issues.

Churchill, Winston S. *A History of the English Speaking Peoples: The Great Democracies*. New York: Dorset Press, 1958.

Cohen, Stephen S., and Zysman, John. *Manufacturing Matters: The Myth of the Post-Industrial Economy*. New York: Basic Books, 1987.

Coker, Christopher, ed. *Shifting into Neutral? Burden Sharing in the Western Alliance in the 1990s*. London: Brassey's (U.K.), 1990.

Commager, Henry Steele. *The American Mind: An Interpretation of American Thought and Character Since the 1980's*. New Haven: Yale University Press, 1950.

Cooper, Richard N.; Eichengreen, Barry; Henning, C. Randall; Holtham, Gerald; and Putnam, Robert D. *Can Nations Agree? Issues in International Economic Cooperation*. Washington, D.C.: The Brookings Institution, 1989.

Courtis, Kenneth S. Interview. "Strategic Challenge." *The JAMA Forum*. Vol. 9, No. 1. January 1991.

———. Address. "Japan's World Role in the 1990s," Address to the North American Institute, Vancouver, July 14, 1990.

———. Address. "Perspectives on the Japanese Keiretsu." The National Advisory Board on Science and Technology Symposium, Toronto, 1–2 March 1990.

Cunz, Dieter. *They Came from Germany: The Stories of Famous German-Americans*. New York: Dodd, Mead & Co., 1966.

Dahrendorf, Ralf. *Reflections on the Revolution in Europe*. New York: Times Books, 1990.

———. *Society and Democracy in Germany*. New York: Norton, 1967.

Derian, Jean-Claude. *America's Struggle for Leadership in Technology*. Cambridge, MA: MIT Press, 1990.

Dertouzos, Michael L.; Lester, Richard K.; and Solow, Robert M. *Made in America: Regaining the Productive Edge*. Cambridge, MA: MIT Press, 1990.

de Tocqueville, Alexis. *Democracy in America*. New York: Dell, 1956.

Dionne, E. J. Jr. *Why Americans Hate Politics*. New York: Simon & Schuster, 1991.

Discord or Dialogue: The United States and Japan in 1991. Washington, D.C.: The Reischauer Center at the Paul H. Nitze School of Advanced International Studies, Johns Hopkins University, 1991.

Dogan, Mattei, and Palassy, Dominique. *How to Compare Nations: Strategies in Comparative Politics*. Chatham, NJ: Chatham House, 1990.

Dore, Ronald; Bounine-Cabale, Jean; and Tapiola, Kari. *Japan at Work: Markets, Management and Flexibility.* Paris: OECD, 1989.

Dulles, Foster Rhea. *Yankees and Samurai: America's Role in the Emergence of Modern Japan.* New York: Harper & Row, 1965.

Economic Report of the President. Washington, D.C.: U.S. Government Printing Office, 1987, 1988, 1989, 1990, 1991, 1992.

The Economist, London, various issues.

Emerson, John K., and Holland, Harrison M. *The Eagle and the Rising Sun.* Reading, MA: Addison-Wesley, 1988.

Emmerij, Louis. *One World or Several.* Paris: OECD, 1989.

The European, various issues.

European Economy Annual Economic Report 1989–1990. Brussels: Commission of the European Communities, November 1989.

Fallows, James. *More Like Us: Making America Great Again.* Boston: Houghton Mifflin, 1989.

The Far Eastern Economic Review, various issues.

Fardoust, Shahrokh, and Dhareshwar, Ashok. *A Long-Term Outlook for the World Economy.* Washington, D.C.: The World Bank, 1990.

The Federal Republic of Germany: Adjustment in a Surplus Country. Occasional Paper No. 64. Washington, D.C.: The International Monetary Fund, January 1989.

The Financial Times, London, various issues.

FitzGerald, Frances. *Fire in the Lake: The Vietnamese and the Americans in Vietnam.* Boston: Atlantic–Little Brown, 1972.

Fletcher, William Miles III. *The Japanese Business Community and National Trade Policy, 1920–1942.* Chapel Hill, NC: University of North Carolina Press, 1989.

Foley, Thomas S. Address. "After the Persian Gulf War: American Politics and Policies in the 1990s." Ditchley Foundation Lecture, Ditchley, England, 5 July 1991.

Foreign Affairs, Council on Foreign Relations, Inc., New York, various issues.

Foreign Policy, Carnegie Endowment for International Peace, Washington, D.C., various issues.

Gaining New Ground: Technological Priorities for America's Future: Highlights. Washington, D.C.: Council on Competitiveness, 1991.

Gatzke, Hans W. *Germany and the United States: A "Special Relationship?"* Cambridge, MA: Harvard University Press, 1980.

German Brief, Frankfurt Allgemeine Zeitung GMBH Information Services, Frankfurt, various issues.

German Politics and Society, The Center for European Studies, Harvard University, Cambridge, MA, various issues.

Gerschenkron, Alexander. *Bread and Democracy in Germany: 1943*. Ithaca, NY: Cornell University Press, 1989.

Gilpin, Robert. *War and Change in World Politics*. New York: Cambridge University Press, 1981.

Gluck, Carol. *Japan's Modern Myths: Ideology in the Late Meiji Period*. Princeton: Princeton University Press, 1985.

Graham, Edward M., and Krugman, Paul R. *Foreign Direct Investment in the United States*. Washington, D.C.: Institute for International Economics, 1989.

Grew, Joseph C. *Ten Years in Japan*. New York: Simon & Schuster, 1944.

Griswold, A. Whitney. *The Far Eastern Policy of the United States*. New Haven, CT: Yale University Press, 1962.

Guile, Bruce R., and Brooks, Harvey, eds. *Technology and Global Industry, Companies and Nations in the World Economy*. Washington, D.C.: National Academy Press, 1987.

Halberstam, David. *The Next Century*. New York: Morrow, 1991.

———. *The Reckoning*. New York: Times Books, 1986.

Halloran, Richard. *Japan: Images and Realities*. New York: Knopf, 1969.

Harper's, various issues.

Harris, Townsend. *The Complete Journal of Townsend Harris*. New York: Japan Society, 1930.

Harrison, Bennet, and Kelly, Maryellen R. "The New Industrial Culture." *The American Prospect*. Winter 1991.

Hartman, Geoffrey H., ed. *Bitburg in Moral and Political Perspective*. Bloomington, IN: Indiana University Press, 1986.

Hartz, Louis. *The Liberal Tradition in America*. New York: Harcourt Brace Jovanovich, 1955.

Hayes, Peter. *Industry and Ideology: I. G. Farben in the Nazi Era*. New York: Cambridge University Press, 1987.

Head, Simon. "The East German Disaster." *New York Review of Books*. 17 January 1991: pp. 41–44.

Hersey, John. *Into the Valley: A Skirmish of the Marines*. New York: Knopf, 1943.

Hewlett, Sylvia Ann. *When the Bough Breaks: The Cost of Neglecting Our Children*. New York: Basic Books, 1991.

Hirschmeier, Johannes. *The Origins of Entrepreneurship in Meiji Japan*. Cambridge, MA: Harvard University Press, 1964.

Hofstadter, Richard. *Social Darwinism in American Thought*. Boston: Beacon Press, 1955.

Hufbauer, Gary Clyde. "Europe 1992: Opportunities and Challenges." *The Brookings Review*, Summer 1990.

Huntington, Samuel P. *American Politics: The Promise of Disharmony*. Cambridge, MA: Belnap Press, 1981.

Iklé, Frank W. "Japan's Policies towards Germany." *Japan's Foreign Policy, 1868–1941: A Research Guide*. Ed. James William Morley. New York: Columbia University Press, 1974.

IMF Survey, International Monetary Fund, Washington, D.C., various issues.

Informations Dienste, Frankfurter Allgemeine Zeitung GMBH, Frankfurt, Germany, various issues.

The International Herald Tribune, various issues.

Isaacs, Harold R. *Scratches on Our Mind: American Images of China and India*. New York: The John Dey Company, 1958.

Isaacson, Walter, and Thomas, Evan. *The Wise Men: Six Friends and the World They Made*. New York: Simon & Schuster, 1986.

Jackson, John H. *International Competition in Services: A Constitutional Framework*. Washington, D.C.: American Enterprise Institute, 1988.

Jacobs, Michael T. *Short-Term America: The Causes and Cures of Our Business Myopia*. Boston: Harvard Business School Press, 1991.

The JAMA Forum, New York, Japan Automobile Manufacturers Association, various issues.

James, Harold. *A German Identity 1770–1990*. New York: Routledge, 1989.

The Japan Economic Journal, Tokyo, various issues.

Jasinowski, Jerry J. *America's Work Force in the 1990s: Trends Affecting Manufacturers*. Washington, D.C.: National Association of Manufacturers, March 1990.

Johnson, Chalmers. "*MITI and the Japanese Miracle: The Growth of Industrial Policy 1925–1975*. Stanford, CA: Stanford University Press, 1982.

Johnson, Chalmers. "Taking 'Revisionism' about Japan Seriously," Unpublished Memo, 1991.

Johnson, Sheila K. *American Attitudes towards Japan 1941–1975*. Washington, D.C.: American Enterprise Institute, 1975.

———. *The Japanese through American Eyes*. Stanford, CA: Stanford University Press, 1988.

Julius, DeAnne. *Foreign Direct Investment: The Neglected Twin of Trade*. Washington, D.C.: Group of Thirty, 1991.

———. *Global Companies and Public Policies: The Growing Challenge of Foreign Direct Investment*. London: Royal Institute of International Affairs, 1990.

Kashiwagi, Yusuke. Address, Japan Society, New York, 11 July 1991.

Katzenstein, Peter J. *Industry and Politics in West Germany: Toward the Third Republic*. Ithaca, NY: Cornell University Press, 1989.

Katzenstein, Peter J. *Policy and Politics in West Germany: The Growth of a Semisovereign State*. Philadelphia, PA: Temple University Press, 1987.

Kawai, Kazuo. *Japan's American Interlude*. Chicago, IL: University of Chicago Press, 1960.

Kennedy, Ellen. *The Bundesbank*. London: Royal Institute of International Affairs, 1991.

Kennedy, Paul. *Grand Strategies in War and Peace*. New Haven, CT: Yale University Press, 1991.

Kester, W. Carl. *Japanese Takeovers: The Global Contest for Corporate Control*. Boston: Harvard Business School Press, 1991.

Keynes, John Maynard. *The Economic Consequences of the Peace*. New York: Harcourt Brace Jovanovich, 1920.

Kindleberger, Charles P. *The World in Depression*. Berkeley, CA: University of California Press, 1973.

Kissinger, Henry A. *A World Restored: Metternich, Castlereagh and the Problems of Peace 1815–1848*. Boston: Houghton Mifflin, 1957.

Kitamura, Hiroshi; Murata, Ryohei; and Okazaki, Hisahiko. *Between Friends: Japanese Diplomats Look at Japan–U.S. Relations*. New York, Tokyo: Weatherhill, 1985.

Knorr, Klaus, and Trager, Frank N. *Economic Issues and National Security*. Lawrence, KS: Regents Press of Kansas, 1977.

Koch, H. W. *A History of Prussia*. New York: Dorset Press, 1978.

Kohn, Hans. *The Mind of Germany: The Education of a Nation*. New York: Harper & Row, 1960.

Koppes, Clayton R., and Black, Gregory D. *Hollywood Goes to War*. New York: Free Press, 1987.

Kuhn, Thomas S. *The Structure of Scientific Revolutions*. Chicago, IL: University of Chicago Press, 1962.

Kyodo News Service.

Laqueur, Walter, ed. *Fascism: A Reader's Guide*. Berkeley: University of California Press, 1976.

Lincoln, Edward J. *Japan's Unequal Trade*. Washington, D.C.: The Brookings Institution, 1990.

Lipset, Seymour Martin. *Continental Divide: The Values and Institutions of the United States and Canada*. New York: Routledge, 1990.

List, Friedrich. *The National System of Political Economy: 1855*. New York: Augustus M. Kelley, 1966.

Litan, Robert E.; Lawrence, Robert Z; and Schultze, Charles L., eds. *American*

Living Standards: Threats and Challenges. Washington, D.C.: The Brookings Institution, 1988.

Lodge, George C., and Vogel, Ezra F. *Ideology and National Competitiveness.* Boston: Harvard Business School Press, 1987.

Loewenstein, Karl. *Max Weber's Political Ideas in the Perspective of Our Time.* Amherst, MA: University of Massachusetts Press, 1966.

MacNeill, Jim; Winsemius, Peter; and Yakushiji, Taizo. *Beyond Interdependence: The Meshing of the World's Economy and the Earth's Ecology.* Report to the Trilateral Commission, April 1990.

Maddison, Angus. *The World Economy in the 20th Century.* Paris: OECD, 1989.

Makin, John H., and Hellman, Donald C., eds. *Sharing World Leadership: A New Era for America and Japan.* Washington, D.C.: American Enterprise Institute for Public Policy Research, 1989.

Malabre, Alfred L., Jr. *Within Our Means: The Struggle for Economic Recovery After a Reckless Decade.* New York: Random House, 1991.

Manchester, William. *American Caesar.* New York: Dell, 1978.

Mann, Golo. *The History of Germany Since 1789.* Trans. Marian Jackson. New York: Praeger, 1968.

Marsh, David. *The Germans: Rich, Bothered and Divided.* London: Century, 1989.

Marshall, Byron K. *Capitalism and Nationalism in Pre-War Japan: The Ideology of the Business Elite, 1868–1941.* Stanford, CA: Stanford University Press, 1967.

Mayer, J. P. *Max Weber and German Politics.* London: Faber & Faber, 1956.

Mayne, Richard. *The Recovery of Europe: From Devastation to Unity.* New York: Harper & Row, 1971.

McCauley, Robert N., and Zimmer, Steven A. "Explaining International Differences in the Cost of Capital." *Federal Reserve Bank of New York, Quarterly Review,* Vol. 14, No. 2, Summer 1989.

McGraw, Thomas K. *America Versus Japan.* Boston: Harvard Business School Press, 1986.

―――. "Business & Government: The Origins of the Adversary Relationship." *California Management Review.* Vol. 26, No. 2, Winter 1984.

Mead, Walter Russell. "Coming to Terms with the New Germany." *World Policy.* Fall 1990.

Meinecke, Freidrich. *The German Catastrophe.* Boston: Beacon Press, 1950.

Moran, Theodore H. "International Economics and National Security." *Foreign Affairs.* Vol. 69, No. 5 (1990).

Moran, Theodore H., "The Globalization of America's Defense Industries," *International Security,* Vol. 15, No. 1, Summer 1990.

Morse, Edward L. "The Coming Oil Revolution." *Foreign Affairs*. Vol. 69, No. 5 (1990).

Morone, James A. *The Democratic Wish: Popular Participation and the Limits of American Government*. New York: Basic Books, 1990.

The National Education Association Today, various issues.

The National Interest, National Affairs, Inc., Washington, D.C., various issues.

Nau, Henry R. *Domestic Trade Politics and the Uruguay Round*. New York: Columbia University Press, 1989.

Nester, William R. *The Foundation of Japanese Economic Power*. New York: Macmillan, 1990.

Neumann, William L. *America Encounters Japan: From Perry to MacArthur*. Baltimore: Johns Hopkins University Press, 1963.

New York Magazine, New York, various issues.

The New York Times, New York, various issues.

Newsweek, New York, various issues.

The Nikkei Weekly, Tokyo, various issues.

Nye, Joseph S., Jr. *Bound to Lead: The Changing Nature of American Power*. New York: Basic Books, 1990.

OECD, "Agricultural Policies, Markets and Trade," Paris, 1990.

———. "Development Co-operation in the 1990s," Paris, 1989.

———. "Economies in Transition," Paris, 1989.

———. "Economic Outlook," Paris, various issues.

———. "Economic Survey, the United States, Germany, Japan, 1988, 1989, 1990, 1991," Paris.

———. "Labor Market Policies for the 1990s," Paris, 1990.

———. "New Technology in the 1990s, A Socio-Economic Strategy," Paris, 1988.

———. "Science and Technology Outlook," Paris, 1988.

Oka, Yoshitake. *Five Political Leaders of Modern Japan*. Tokyo: University of Tokyo Press, 1986.

Osgood, Robert. *Ideas and Self-Interest in America's Foreign Relations*. Chicago, IL: University of Chicago Press, 1953.

Ostry, Sylvia. *Governments and Corporations in a Shrinking World: Trade and Innovation Policies in the United States, Europe & Japan*. New York: Council on Foreign Relations, 1990.

Packard, George R. *Protest in Tokyo: The Security Treaty Crisis of 1960*. Princeton: Princeton University Press, 1966.

Peacock, Alan, and Illgerodt, Hans W., eds. *German Neo-Liberals and the Social Market Economy*. New York: 1989.

Peacock, Alan, and Illgerodt, Hans W., eds. *Germany's Social Market Economy: Origins and Evolution*. New York: St. Martin's, 1989.

Peterson, Peter G., with Sevenius, James K. "Rethinking America's Security: The Primacy of the Domestic Agenda." Seventy-ninth American Assembly, Columbia University, New York, 30 May 1991.

Pfaff, William. *Barbarian Sentiments: How the American Century Ends*. New York: Hill & Wang, 1989.

Phillips, Kevin. *The Politics of Rich and Poor: Wealth and the American Electorate in the Reagan Aftermath*. New York: Random House, 1990.

Polak, Jacques J. "The Decline of World Savings." *International Economic Insights*. September/October 1990.

Porter, Michael E. *The Competitive Advantage of Nations*. New York: Free Press, 1990.

Prestowitz, Clyde V., Jr. *Trading Places*. New York: Basic Books, 1988.

Pyle, Kenneth B.; Lincoln, Edward J.; and Johnson, Chalmers. "Japan and the World: Considerations for U.S. Policymakers." Analysis. Seattle, WA: The National Bureau of Asian and Soviet Research, November 1991.

Raff, Diether. *A History of Germany from the Medieval Empire to the Present*. Trans. Bruce Litte. New York: Berg, 1988.

Reforming World Agricultural Trade. Washington, D.C.: Institute for International Economics, The Institute for Research on Public Policy, May 1988.

Reich, Robert B. "Does Corporate Nationality Matter?" Testimony before the Joint Economic Committee. U.S. Congress, 5 September 1990.

————. *The Next American Frontier*. New York: Times Books, 1983.

————. *Tales of a New America*. New York: Times Books, 1987.

————. *The Work of Nations*. New York: Knopf, 1991.

Reuters News Service.

Rivlin, Alice M. Address. "A Vision of American Federalism." National Academy of Public Administration Webb Lecture, 8 November 1991.

Rizopoulos, Nicholas X. *Sea-Changes: American Foreign Policy in a World Transformed*. New York: Council on Foreign Relations, 1990.

Robertson, James Oliver. *American Myth, American Reality*. New York: Hill & Wang, 1980.

Rohl, John, and Sombart, Nicolaus, eds. *Kaiser Wilhelm II—New Interpretations: The Corfu Papers*. New York: Cambridge University Press, 1982.

Romberg, Alan D., and Yamanoto, Tadashi. *Same Bed, Different Dreams: America and Japan—Societies in Transition*. New York: Council on Foreign Relations, 1990.

Roosevelt, Theodore. *The Works of Theodore Roosevelt*. National Ed., 20 vols., New York: Scribner's, 1926.

Rosecrance, Richard. *The Rise of the Trading State: Commerce and Conquest in the Modern World*. New York: Basic Books, 1986.

Samuels, Richard J. "Cooperation and Conflict in Science and Technology." *The JAMA Forum.* Vol. 8, No. 2. December 1989.

Sandholtz, Wayne, and Zysman, John. "1992: Recasting the European Bargain." *World Politics.* Vol. 42, No. 1. October 1981.

Sansom, G. B. *The Western World and Japan: A Study in the Interaction of European and Asiatic Cultures.* New York: Knopf, 1951.

Schlesinger, Arthur M., Jr. *The Almanac of American History.* New York: Putnam, 1983.

———. *The Disuniting of America: Reflections on a Multicultural Society.* Knoxville, TN: Whittle Direct Books, 1991.

Schwartz, Thomas Alan. *America's Germany: John J. McCloy and the Federal Republic of Germany.* Cambridge, MA: Harvard University Press, 1991.

The Science and Technology Resources of West Germany: A Comparison with the United States. Special Report N.S.F. 86–310. Washington, D.C., National Science Foundation, 1986.

Shirer, William L. *The Rise and Fall of the Third Reich: A History of Nazi Germany.* New York: Fawcett, 1950.

Shonfield, Andrew. *Modern Capitalism: The Changing Balance of Public and Private Power.* New York: Oxford University Press, 1965.

Shoven, John B. *Government Policy Toward Industry in the United States and Japan.* Cambridge: Cambridge University Press, 1988.

Smyser, W. R. *Restive Partners: Washington and Bonn Diverge.* Boulder, CO: Westview Press, 1990.

Special Report: International Survey of the Taxation of Personal Saving and Savings Rates. Washington, D.C.: American Council for Capital Formation, August 1990.

Stern, Fritz. *Dreams and Delusions: National Socialism in the Drama of the German Past.* New York: Vintage, 1987.

Stern, Susan. *Meet United Germany.* Frankfurt, Germany: *Frankfurter Allgemeine Zeitung.* GMBH Information Services, 1991.

Stokes, Bruce. *The Inevitability of Managed Trade.* New York: The Japan Society, 1990.

Stokes, Bruce. "Send Money." *National Journal.* 9 December 1990.

Takahama, Tatou. Address. "Japanese Policy Making: The Case of the Gulf Crisis." The Japan Society of New York, 6 May 1991.

Technology and Competitiveness: New Frontiers for the United States and Japan. Washington, D.C.: Council on Competitiveness and the Japan Society, 1990.

Thucydides. *The Peloponnesian War.* New York: Random House, 1982.

Time, New York, various issues.

Tsoukalis, Loukas, and White, Maureen. *Japan and Western Europe*. London: Frances Pinter, 1982.

Turner, Frederick Jackson. *The Frontier in American History*. New York: Henry Holt & Company, 1948.

Tuchman, Barbara W. *The March of Folly: From Troy to Vietnam*. New York: Ballantine, 1984.

Tyson, Laura D'Andrea. Testimony presented to Joint Economic Committee, U.S. Congress, 13 September 1990.

Uchino, Tatsuro. *Japan's Postwar Economy: An Insider's View of Its History and Its Future*. Tokyo: Kodansha International Ltd., 1978.

"The United States and Germany." Policy Paper. Washington, D.C., The Atlantic Council, 31 October 1990.

U.S. Congress, *The 1990 Joint Economic Committee Report*. Washington, D.C.: U.S. Government Printing Office, 1990.

U.S. Department of Commerce, "U.S. Telecommunications in a Global Economy," August 1990.

U.S. Department of Commerce, Technology Administration. "Emerging Technologies: A Survey of Technical and Economic Opportunities." 1990.

U.S. Department of Labor, the Secretary's Commission on Achieving Necessary Skills. *What Work Requires of Schools*. Washington, D.C., 1991.

U.S. House of Representatives. Committee on Foreign Affairs. "U.S. Power in a Changing World." Washington, D.C. Congressional Research Service, Library of Congress, May 1990.

U.S. Senate Subcommittee on Foreign Commerce and Tourism. Hearings: "Japanese Space Industry: An American Challenge," 4 October 1989.

van Wolferen, Karel. *The Enigma of Japanese Power*. New York: Knopf, 1989.

Veblen, Thorstein. *Imperial Germany and the Industrial Revolution*. 1915. Westport, CT: Greenwood Press, 1984.

Vogel, David. "Why Businessmen Distrust Their State: The Political Consciousness of American Executives." *British Journal of Political Science*. Vol. 8 (1978).

The Wall Street Journal, New York, various issues.

Wallich, Henry C. *Mainsprings of the German Revival*. Westport, CT: Greenwood Press, 1976.

Walter, Norbert. *West Germany's Economy: Origin, Problems, Perspectives*. Washington, D.C.: American Institute for Contemporary German Studies, Johns Hopkins University Press, 1987.

Waltz, Kenneth N. *Theory of International Politics*. New York: McGraw-Hill, 1979.

The Washington Post, Washington, D.C., various issues.

Wattenberg, Ben J. *The First Universal Nation*. New York: Free Press, 1991.

Web, Adrian. *German Politics and the Green Challenge*. London: The Economist Intelligence Unit Briefing, Special Report No. 2032, March 1990.

Will, George F. *Suddenly: The American Idea Abroad and at Home, 1986–1990*. New York: Free Press, 1990.

Wilson, Graham K. *Business and Politics: A Comparative Introduction*. Chatham, NJ: Chatham House, 1990.

Wilson, James Q. *Bureaucracy: What Government Agencies Do and Why They Do It*. New York: Basic Books, 1989.

Wolfe, Alan. *America at Century's End*. Berkeley, CA: University of California Press, 1991.

Wolfe, Robert, ed. *Americans as Proconsuls: United States Military Government in Germany and Japan, 1944–1952*. Carbondale, IL: Southern Illinois University Press, 1984.

Wood, Gordon S. *The Creation of the American Republic 1776–1787*. New York: Norton, 1969.

World Development Report 1991. Washington D.C.: The World Bank, 1991.

World Economic Outlook, The International Monetary Fund, Washington, D.C., various issues.

The World Economy, The World Peace Institute, New York, various issues.

Yoshida, Shigeru. *The Yoshida Memoirs*. Westport, CT: Greenwood Press, 1961.

INDEX

ABOUT THE AUTHOR

Jeffrey E. Garten teaches economics, finance, and international relations at Columbia University. An investment banker on Wall Street since 1979, he also held senior posts on the White House staff and at the State Department in the Nixon, Ford, and Carter administrations. His articles have appeared in *The New York Times*, *The Wall Street Journal*, *The Washington Post*, the *Los Angeles Times*, and *Foreign Affairs*. He has lived and worked in both Japan and Germany and currently resides with his wife in New York City.